Counseling Gay Men, Adolescents, and Boys

Counseling Gay Men, Adolescents, and Boys: A Strengths-Based Guide for Helping Professionals and Educators provides practitioners and educators with critical information needed to help navigate the therapeutic and educational terrain of working with gay males. While other books address a broad range of issues when working with LGBTQ individuals, this volume devotes its focus to the specific needs of gay boys, adolescents, and men. This book also presents an important perspective about individuals who identify as bisexual and transgender, and examines the intersection between gender and sexual orientation. Readers will find practical resources, tools, and clinical case studies for mental health practitioners, professionals in school settings, educators, administrators, and medical personnel serving gay males.

Michael M. Kocet, PhD, is associate professor and chair in the department of counselor education at Bridgewater State University. He is a licensed mental health counselor, a nationally certified counselor, and the author of numerous journal articles and book chapters on ethics and LGBT issues. Dr. Kocet is past president of the Association for Lesbian, Gay, Bisexual, and Transgender Issues in Counseling and has presented at local, state, and national conferences in counseling and student affairs. He is sought as a national speaker and consultant on LGBT issues and counseling ethics.

The Routledge Series on Counseling and Psychotherapy with Boys and Men

VOLUMES IN THIS SERIES

Volume 1: *Counseling Troubled Boys: A Guidebook for Professionals*
Mark S. Kiselica, Matt Englar-Carlson, and Arthur M. Horne, editors

Volume 2: *BAM! Boys Advocacy and Mentoring: A Leader's Guide to Facilitating Strengths-Based Groups for Boys—Helping Boys Make Better Contact by Making Better Contact with Them*
Peter Motorola, Howard Hiton, and Stephen Grant

Volume 3: *Counseling Fathers*
Chen Z. Oren and Dora Chase Oren, editors

Volume 4: *Counseling Boys and Men with ADHD*
George Kapalka

Volume 5: *Culturally Responsive Counseling with Asian American Men*
William M. Liu, Derek Kenji Iwamoto, and Mark H. Chae, editors

Volume 6: *Therapy with Young Men: 16–24 Year Olds in Treatment*
David A. Verhaagen

Volume 7: *An International Psychology of Men: Theoretical Advances, Case Studies, and Clinical Innovations*
Chris Blazina and David S. Shen Miller, editors

Volume 8: *Psychotherapy with Older Men*
Tammi Vacha-Haase, Stephen R. Wester, and Heidi Fowell Christianson

Volume 9: *Engaging Boys in Treatment: Creative Approaches to Formulating, Initiating, and Sustaining the Therapy Process*
Craig Haen, editor

Volume 10: *Dying to be Men: Psychological, Social, and Behavioral Directions in Promoting Men's Health*
William Courtenay

Volume 11: *Engaging Men in Couples Therapy*
David S. Shepard and Michelle Harway, editors

Volume 12: *Gender in the Therapy Hour: Voices of Female Clinicians Working with Men*
Holly Barlow Sweet, editor

Volume 13: *Tough Guys and True Believers: Managing Authoritarian Men in the Psychotherapy Room*
John M. Robertson

Volume 14: *Men, Addiction, and Intimacy: Strengthening Recovery by Fostering the Emotional Development of Boys and Men*
Mark S. Woodford

Volume 15: *Breaking Barriers in Counseling Men: Insights and Innovations*
Aaron Rochlen and Fredric E. Rabinowitz, editors

Volume 16: *Counseling Widowers*
Jason Troyer

Volume 17: *Counseling Gay Men, Adolescents, and Boys: A Strengths-Based Guide for Helping Professionals and Educators*
Michael M. Kocet, editor

Counseling Gay Men, Adolescents, and Boys

A Strengths-Based Guide for Helping Professionals and Educators

Edited by
Michael M. Kocet

Routledge
Taylor & Francis Group
NEW YORK AND LONDON

First published 2014
by Routledge
711 Third Avenue, New York, NY 10017

and by Routledge
2 Park Square, Milton Park, Abingdon, Oxon, OX14 4RN

Routledge is an imprint of the Taylor & Francis Group, an informa business

Library of Congress Cataloging-in-Publication Data
Counseling gay men, adolescents, and boys : a strengths-based guide for practitioners and educators / [edited] by Michael M. Kocet.
pages cm. — (The Routledge series on counseling and psychotherapy with boys and men)
Includes bibliographical references and index.
1. Gay men—Counseling of. 2. Gay men—Mental health. 3. Gay men—Psychology. 4. Gay teenagers—Counseling of. 5. Gay teenagers—Mental health. 6. Gay teenagers—Psychology. I. Kocet, Michael M.
RC451.4.G39C679 2014
616.890086'642—dc23
2013047282

ISBN: 978-0-415-50940-4 (hbk)
ISBN: 978-0-415-50941-1 (pbk)
ISBN: 978-0-203-12490-1 (ebk)

Typeset in Minion
by Apex CoVantage, LLC

To Andy Elliott, who was, is, and always will be a special gift in my life and in memory of my Dad, Michael M. Kocet

Contents

About the Editor and Contributors

Michael M. Kocet, PhD, LMHC, NCC, is associate professor and department chair of the department of counselor education at Bridgewater State University. He also serves in the role of student affairs program director for his department. Additionally, Dr. Kocet has held faculty appointments at the University of Massachusetts, Boston, Lesley University, and Suffolk University. Dr. Kocet earned his PhD in counselor education from the University of Arkansas and Master's degree in Counseling from Bowling Green State University. He completed a graduate certificate in dispute resolution at the University of Massachusetts, Boston. He is a licensed mental health counselor and National Certified Counselor. His professional areas of interest include: ethical issues in counseling and student affairs; counseling gay, lesbian, bisexual, and transgender clients; and grief counseling. He is author of numerous journal articles and book chapters on ethics and diversity issues. Dr. Kocet served as member of the American Counseling Association Ethics Committee (2001–2007) and chaired the ACA Ethics Code Revision Taskforce (2002–2005). He is past president of the Association for Lesbian, Gay, Bisexual, and Transgender Issues in Counseling (ALGBTIC) (2009–2010) and also served as past board member of the association. He is a current board member for the Association for Spiritual, Ethical, and Religious Values in Counseling (ASERVIC) and co-chair of the ACPA (College Student Educators International) Ethics Committee. Additionally, he serves on the National Board of Certified Counselors Minority Fellows Program Advisory Council. He has presented at local, state, and national conferences in counseling and student affairs and is sought out as a national speaker and consultant on LBGT issues, grief counseling, as well as ethical issues in counseling. Dr. Kocet is an active volunteer in his community. He provides pro-bono therapy and clinical supervision for the *GLBTQ Domestic Violence Program* in Boston and volunteers as a grief therapist for Comfort Zone Camp, the nation's largest bereavement camp for children ages 7–17. Dr. Kocet resides in South Boston, Massachusetts.

Paul Battle, PhD, completed his doctoral degree at Oakland University. His research focused on lesbian, gay, and bisexual identity management in the workplace. He has worked in the student service and counseling field for over 10 years. He also teaches as an adjunct for Oakland University in the department of counseling.

Michael Brubaker, PhD, LICDC-CS, NCC, is an assistant professor and program coordinator of the Substance Abuse Counseling Program at the University of Cincinnati.

Dr. Brubaker's research, clinical, and advocacy interests have focused on underserved and socially marginalized populations including the homeless, individuals identifying as LGBTQQI, and ethnic minorities. Dr. Brubaker is a prior board trustee for the Association for Lesbian, Gay, Bisexual and Transgender Issues in Counseling, and is currently an editorial board member of the *Journal of LGBT Issues in Counseling,* the *Journal of Counselor Leadership and Advocacy,* and the *Journal of Mental Health Counseling.*

Larry D. Burlew, EdD, NCC, is a professor of counselor education at Montclair State University in New Jersey. He has published extensively and is a past president of the Association for Adult Development and Aging and a former American Counseling Association governing council representative. His research interests include career development, gay men, adult development, and counselor education pedagogy.

Michael P. Chaney, PhD, is an associate professor and coordinator of the addictions specialization in the department of counseling at Oakland University in Rochester, MI. He is a licensed professional counselor, national certified counselor, and approved clinical supervisor, as well as past president of the Association of LGBT Issues in Counseling. Dr. Chaney serves as an editorial board member for both *The Journal of Addictions and Offender Counseling* and the *Journal of LGBT Issues in Counseling.* He has numerous publications in prestigious professional journals in the areas of addictive disorders, sexual compulsivity, sexual orientation/gender-identity development, and social justice and advocacy in counseling.

Joel M. Filmore, EdD, LPC, is an assistant professor at Northern State University in South Dakota in the counselor education program. His areas of specialization include multiculturalism, with a special emphasis on LGBTQ issues, substance abuse, and addiction, as well as sex offender counseling. When he is not teaching in his university program he provides sex offender evaluation and counseling for the state of South Dakota.

Dennis A. Frank, II, PhD, LPC, is an associate professor and clinical mental health coordinator in the counseling & human services program at Roosevelt University in Chicago and is the past president of the Illinois Association of Lesbian, Gay, Bisexual, and Transgender Issues in Counseling. Dr. Frank also has several publications on providing counseling services to LGBT clients, including a monograph titled *Counseling Lesbian, Gay, Bisexual, and Transgender Clients.*

Andrew S. Garland-Forshee, PhD, HS-BCP, is a professor in the department of early education & family studies at Portland Community College in Portland, Oregon, and a contributing faculty member for the school of social work & human services at Walden University. His primary areas of expertise include human services, family studies, human development, sexuality and gender studies. He has published and presented to a variety of professional audiences on diverse topics in human services, family studies, and LGBTQI issues.

Jane Goodman, PhD, is professor, emerita, of counseling, at Oakland University in Michigan. She was 2001–2002 president of the American Counseling Association. She is a past president and Eminent Career Awardee of the National Career Development Association, fellow of ACA and NCDA, and the author of several books, many articles, and book chapters, mostly in the area of transitions and career development. She is the mother or stepmother of seven and has nine grandchildren on whom she dotes.

Kristopher M. Goodrich, PhD, is an assistant professor of counselor education at the University of New Mexico. He is a nationally certified counselor, approved clinical supervisor, and licensed mental health counselor in New Mexico. Dr. Goodrich is a member of the American Counseling Association, Association for Lesbian, Gay, Bisexual, Transgender Issues in Counseling, Association for Specialists in Group Work, and the Association for Counselor Educators and Supervisors. In addition, he is the co-chair for the LGBTQQIA Affirmative Counseling and Social Justice Committee of ALGBTIC and a current board trustee.

Kathleen L. Grant is a PhD student at Montclair State University in the counselor education program. In addition, she is a practicing school counselor at a public high school in New Jersey. She received her master's in counseling from the College of New Jersey. Her research interests include spirituality and meaning making in adolescent population, as well as issues pertaining to LGBT youth.

James E. Leone, PhD, MS, ATC, CSCS, *D, CHES is an associate professor in health studies at Bridgewater State University. He has published extensively in well-known medical and health journals in addition to delivering well over 100 academic presentations. Dr. Leone's academic interests include a heavy emphasis on men's health issues, especially testicular cancer, body image and mental health, substance abuse, and health promotion programs. He has written several chapters for various textbooks in addition to his own book on male health, titled, *Concepts in Male Health: Perspectives Across the Lifespan* (2012, John Wiley & Sons). He also serves as a reviewer and associate editor for various academic journals.

Jeff Lubsen is a nationally certified counselor, a licensed professional counselor candidate in Colorado, and a PhD doctoral candidate in clinical mental health counseling education and supervision. Jeff is a member of Golden Key and Chi Sigma Iota graduate honors societies, and is a two-time graduate scholarship recipient with over 4,000 hours of mental-health based community service. He is the organizer of the Healthcare Guild (healthcareguild.com), a grass-roots organization dedicated to helping sexual and gender minorities find affirming and culturally competent healthcare.

Melissa M. Luke, PhD, is an associate professor, interim chair, and coordinator of the school counseling program at Syracuse University. Her research interests include school counselor preparation and professional identity development. She has served on the editorial board for *Journal of Counseling and Development, Professional School Counseling,* and *The Clinical Supervisor* among others. Dr. Luke is currently the president-elect of the North Atlantic Region of Counselor Educators and Supervisors, the Research Committee Chair for the Association of Specialists in Group Work, and is co-chair of the Safe Schools task force for the Association of Gay, Lesbian, Bisexual and Transgender Issues in Counseling.

Joseph J. Manera, PsyD, completed his doctoral degree at the Wright Institute in Berkeley, CA. His areas of clinical interest include bereavement, trauma, identity concerns, and counseling gay, lesbian, bisexual, and transgender clients. He has worked as the training director at Fordham University and currently provides psychotherapy for geriatrics through CHE Psychological Services in addition to private practice.

Shan Mohammed, MD, MPH, FAAFP, is a clinical associate professor of health sciences at Northeastern University, Boston, MA. He is the founding director of the master of public health program in urban health in the Bouvé College of Health Sciences. He received his MD degree from Case Western Reserve University School of Medicine in Cleveland, OH and completed his residency and fellowship training at University Hospitals of Cleveland. Dr. Mohammed is a board certified family physician and fellow of the American Academy of Family Physicians. His current academic interests include innovation in interprofessional education in order to improve health outcomes for at-risk individuals and vulnerable communities.

Elizabeth M. Mullin, PhD, is an assistant professor of research and statistics in the physical education and health education department at Springfield College. Mullin received her bachelor of arts in psychology, magna cum laude with a high honors thesis, from Mount Holyoke College. She completed her master's degree and PhD in sport and exercise psychology at Springfield College. Her research focuses on the heterosexism in collegiate athletics and its intersection with psycho-social variables and performance. Dr. Mullin is a certified applied sport psychology consultant from the Association for Applied Sport Psychology and certified strength and conditioning specialist from the National Strength and Conditioning Association. She resides in Holyoke, MA, with her wife, Lauren, her son, Will, and their three adopted pets.

Derrick A. Paladino, PhD, LMHC, NCC, is an associate professor in the department of graduate studies in counseling at Rollins College in Winter Park Florida. His clinical and research interests fall in the areas of multiracial/multiple heritage identity and college student development. He is the co-author of the book, *Counseling Multiple Heritage Individuals, Couples, and Families*, published by the American Counseling Association.

Jason Patton, PhD, LPC-S, is a researcher, clinician, and counselor-educator located in Austin, Texas. His primary areas of interest and expertise include: qualitative research methodologies, counselor training and competencies, same-sex parenting, trauma, gay bear sub-culture, and relational-cultural theory. He may be reached by email at drjasonpatton@gmail.com

Nicole Pacheco Pulliam is an assistant director and career advisor at Ramapo College of New Jersey and an adjunct instructor at Montclair State University, where she is completing her PhD in counselor education. Nicole's background includes work in clinical mental health, college counseling, and academic and career advisement. Nicole has been highly committed to enhancing the profession, as evidenced by her active participation in state, regional, and national conferences, where she has presented on some of her research interests, ranging from the intersectionality of race, gender, and sexual identity, campus bullying, secondary to post-secondary education partnerships, and career counseling and development.

Stacee Reicherzer, PhD, LPC, has served the transgender community for more than 10 years in her work as a clinician, researcher, and gender educator. She has written and presented extensively on a variety of transgender topics that include race, ethnicity, and global culture; sexual identity; therapy experiences; and work in the entertainment industry. Her website is www.drstacee.com

Samuel Sanabria, PhD, is a counselor educator at Rollins College clinical mental health counseling program. He is a Licensed Mental Health Counselor and a Nationally Certified Counselor. Dr. Sanabria has extensive experience counseling couples, families, adults, and adolescents regarding sexual and gender identity concerns. His research interests include ethical practices in counseling, the development of prejudicial attitudes and beliefs, human sexuality, and Latino concerns. Dr. Sanabria currently teaches graduate courses in human asexuality and multicultural and social justice counseling.

Joffrey S. Suprina, PhD, LMHC, is the college chair and associate professor of counselor education at Argosy University, Sarasota. As a professor, practitioner, supervisor, and researcher, Dr. Suprina's areas of expertise are holistic wellness, addictions, multiculturalism, and LGBT individuals. As a SafeZone trainer, co-developer of the SACRED model, and director of music ministry at Trinity Metropolitan Community Church, he has a unique perspective for integrating spirituality into counseling with LGBT individuals.

Richmond D. Wynn, PhD, is an assistant professor and clinical director in the clinical mental health counseling program at the University of North Florida. He earned a PhD in counselor education specializing in mental health counseling from the University of Florida. He is a licensed mental health counselor and a certified addiction professional. His research focuses on intersectionality of identity and traumatic stress with an emphasis on marginalized social identity groups. He is specifically interested in the ways in which culturally diverse lesbian, gay, bisexual, and transgender (LGBT) people negotiate their identities.

Series Editor's Foreword

Changing social norms have contributed to a greater societal acceptance of gay boys and men. For centuries, homosexuality was a taboo subject, and gay men were viewed as being sinners, sexual deviants, and suffering from a mental disorder (Herek, 2013). However, since the 1960s, as people became more aware of the fact that a person's sexuality is an orientation, not a deviant lifestyle choice, there has been a gradual shift in attitudes about gay boys and men, as well as changes in pertinent professional and public policies. A gay orientation is no longer considered a mental illness, and several professional organizations, such as the American Psychological Association (2013) and the American Counseling Association (1989), have taken official stands calling on their members to affirm people with lesbian, gay, and bisexual orientations and to work to eradicate prejudices against these populations. Gay marriage now exists in 16 states (ProCon.org, 2013), a recent U.S. Supreme Court ruling has removed restrictions that prevented federal employees in same-sex marriage from receiving federal benefits (LaGrone, 2013), and military policy now allows gays to serve openly in the military with protections from harassment and discrimination based on sexual orientation (Schulman, 2010). Growing numbers of gay boys and men, including many prominent politicians—such as Congressmen Barney Frank of Massachusetts, Jarid Polic of Colorado, and David Cicilline of Rhode Island (It's Conceivable, 2011)—and well-known professional athletes—such as Olympic diving champion, Greg Louganis, NBA player, Jason Collins, and boxer, Orlando Cruz (CBS News, 2013)—have come out of the closet, publicly revealing their sexual orientation. Gay characters have been featured in television shows, such as *Glee, True Blood,* and *Modern Family.* In short, the gay community has become a visible and supported part of the American landscape.

In spite of these positive changes, gay boys and men continue to be the targets of pejorative prejudices, harassment, intimidation, and violence. Two of the most well-known and tragic cases of the maltreatment of gay men involved Matthew Shepard and Tyler Clementi. In 1998, Matthew Shepard, a gay college student, died after being kidnapped, robbed, pistol-whipped, and left tied to a fence for 18 hours in freezing temperatures (*New York Times,* 2013). Tyler Clementi, a closeted 18-year-old college freshman, committed suicide "in September 2010 after discovering that his roommate had secretly used a webcam to stream Mr. Clementi's romantic interlude with another man over the Internet" (*New York Times,* 2012, paragraph 1). Their horrifying deaths illustrate that extreme hatred toward gays still exists, and there is considerable evidence demonstrating that less intense but still hostile attitudes and behaviors toward gays is common:

> Severe antigay prejudice is reflected in the high rate of harassment and violence directed toward lesbian, gay and bisexual individuals in American society. Numerous surveys indicate that verbal harassment and abuse are nearly universal experiences among lesbian, gay and bisexual people. Also, discrimination against lesbian, gay and bisexual people in employment and housing appears to remain widespread. The HIV/AIDS pandemic is another area in which prejudice and discrimination against lesbian, gay and bisexual people have had negative effects. Early in the pandemic, the assumption that HIV/AIDS was a "gay disease" contributed to the delay in addressing the massive social upheaval that AIDS would generate. Gay and bisexual men have been disproportionately affected by this disease. The association of HIV/AIDS with gay and bisexual men and the inaccurate belief that some people held that all gay and bisexual men were infected served to further stigmatize lesbian, gay and bisexual people.
>
> (American Psychological Association, 2013, paragraph 9)

These disturbing expressions of homophobia have contributed to a wide range of psychological and social adjustment difficulties among gay boys and men. Gay males are greatly overrepresented among populations that drop out of school (GLSEN-CO, 2000), run away from home (Savin-Williams, 1994), become infected with a sexually transmitted disease (GLSEN-CO, 2000), abuse drugs (Ryan & Hunter, 2003), are the victim of physical, verbal, and sexual abuse (GLSEN-CO, 2000), experience social isolation and homelessness (GLSEN-CO, 2000), and attempt and complete suicide (Macgillivray, 2004; Stone, 2003).

In summary, although in some ways life has become easier and more open for gay boys and men, their lives also tend to be wrought with significant hardships that warrant the compassionate understanding and assistance of the helping professions. Because this is the case, I realized in my role as series editor that *The Routledge Series on Counseling and Psychotherapy with Boys and Men* must include a book on helping gay boys and men. So, I reached out to Dr. Michael Kocet, associate professor and chair of the Department of Counselor Education at Bridgewater State University and a highly respected, national authority on the ethical treatment of gay boys and men, and asked him if he would produce a book on the topic. Dr. Kocet accepted this invitation, and recruited a team of other authorities on the subject to produce *Counseling Gay Men, Adolescents, and Boys: A Strengths-Based Guide for Helping Professionals and Educators,* which is a proud addition to *The Routledge Series.*

Dr. Kocet and his colleagues have done a masterful job integrating the literature on gay identity development, societal treatment of gay boys and men, the gay community, the adjustment difficulties of gay boys and men, the resiliency and strengths of gay males, cultural and spiritual considerations, and best practices in counseling and psychotherapy to provide a comprehensive and sensitive portrayal of gay boys and men and how to assist them in a gay-affirming manner. In addition, this wonderfully informative book includes chapters on bisexual males and transgender children, women, and men. Thus, it is an invaluable resource for practitioners who want to enhance their work with boys and men who identify as sexual minority males.

I applaud Dr. Kocet and his colleagues for their fine work, and I am honored to have their book as a volume in this series.

Mark S. Kiselica, Series Editor
The Routledge Series on Counseling and Psychotherapy with Boys and Men
The College of New Jersey
December 1, 2013

References

American Counseling Association (1989). *Compilation of resolutions adopted by the association: 1991–2000.* Retrieved November 27, 2013 at www.counseling.org/docs/resolutions/resolutions-1991–2000.pdf?sfvrsn=2

American Psychological Association. (2013). *Sexual orientation and homosexuality.* Retrieved November 27, 2013 www.apa.org/helpcenter/sexual-orientation.aspx

CBS News (2013). *Gay characters on TV.* Retrieved November 27, 2013 at www.cbsnews.com/pictures/gay-characters-on-tv/4/

CBS News (2013). *Openly gay athletes.* Retrieved November 27, 2013 at www.cbsnews.com/pictures/openly-gay-athletes/

GLSEN-CO (2000). *Just the facts: A summary of important statistics about gay and lesbian youth.* Retrieved March 21, 2007 from www.glsenco.org/Educators/Administrators/just_the_facts.htm

Herek, G. (2013). *Facts about homosexuality and mental health.* Retrieved November 27, 2013 from http://psychology.ucdavis.edu/rainbow/html/facts_mental_health.html

It's Conceivable (2011). *Famous gay politicians: A list inspired by Tammy Baldwin's Senate bid.* Retrieved November 27, 2013 from http://itsconceivablenow.com/2011/09/11/famous-gay-politicians-list-inspired-tammy-baldwins-senate-bid/

LaGrone, S. (2013). Updated: History of U.S. policy and law on gays in the military. *USNI News,* June 26, 2013. Retrieved November 27, 2013 from http://news.usni.org/2013/06/26/a-history-of-gays-in-the-military

Macgillivray, I. K. (2004). Gay rights and school policy: A case study in community factors that facilitate or impede educational change. *International Journal of Qualitative Studies in Education, 17*(3), 347–370.

New York Times (2013). *Matthew Shepard.* Retrieved November 27, 2013 from http://topics.nytimes.com/top/reference/timestopics/people/s/matthew_shepard/index.html?8qa

New York Times (2012, March 16). *Tyler Clementi.* Retrieved November 27, 2013 from www.nytimes.com/top/reference/timestopics/people/c/tyler_clementi/index.html

ProCon.org (2013). Gay marriage. Retrieved November 27, 2013 from http://gaymarriage.procon.org/view.resource.php?resourceID=004857

Ryan, C., & Hunter, J. (2003). Clinical issues with youth. *A provider's introduction to substance abuse treatment for Lesbian, Gay, Bisexual, and Transgender individuals* (DHH Publication No. BKD392, pp. 99–103). Washington, DC: Substance Abuse and Mental Health Services Administration.

Savin-Williams, R. C. (1994). Verbal and physical abuse as stressors in the lives of lesbian, gay male, and bisexual youths: Associations with school problems, running away, substance abuse, prostitution, and suicide. *Journal of Consulting and Clinical Psychology, 62*(2), 261–269.

Schulman, K. (2010). The president on the Don't Ask, Don't Tell Repeal Act of 2010: "An historic step." December 18, 2010. Retrieved on November 27, 2013 from www.whitehouse.gov/blog/2010/12/18/president-dont-ask-dont-tell-repeal-act-2010-historic-step

Stone, C. B. (2003). Counselors as advocates for gay, lesbian, and bisexual youth: A call for equity and action. *Journal of Multicultural Counseling and Development, 31,* 143–155.

Preface

From Struggle to Resiliency—Supporting and Strengthening Gay Males

When I was originally approached to edit a book on counseling gay males, I asked myself if it was really still necessary to have a book devoted specifically to men, adolescents, and boys who identify as sexual/affectional minorities. Clearly, society has made such significant progress and cultural advances that a book like this would not be needed; or so I thought. But then I thought about Asher Brown (age 13), Tyler Clementi (age 18), Seth Walsh (age 13), and Zach Harrington (age 19). These young boys are just a few examples of the hundreds of young boys and men who have committed suicide in recent years because they were gay and bullied. An online article in *Psychology Today* reported that between 2011 and 2012 an 11 percent increase in anti-LGBT attacks in New York City was reported. While society has made progress through the ban of the military's "Don't Ask, Don't Tell" policy, the removal of the Defense of Marriage Act, and, as of this writing, while it should be celebrated that 16 states have legalized same-sex marriage, more progress is still needed. I came to the realization that helping professionals and educators still need a resource devoted to curbing the prejudice and violence inflicted on gay males of all ages.

The professional literature in the field of counseling and mental health has devoted significant scholarship to issues with gay, lesbian, bisexual, and transgender individuals in clinical settings (Bieschke, Perez, & DeBord, 2007; Chernin & Johnson, 2003), colleges and universities (Dilley, 2002; Wall & Evans, 2000), and with multicultural populations (Crawford, Allison, Zamboni, & Soto, 2002). Books have even been written on very specific subjects of interest such as romantic relationships for gay men (Wheaton, 2008) and unprotected sexual behavior between men (Shernoff, 2006; Weiss, 2005); however, there have been limited resources on working specifically with sexual minority men, adolescents, and boys (Baker, 2002; D'Augelli, 2002).

While some books have devoted a chapter or two addressing the counseling needs of gay boys, adolescents, and men (Kiselica, Englar-Carson, & Horne, 2008; Pollack, 1999), no work to date has devoted its focus on gay men, adolescents, and boys exclusively. More work has been written about ways to provide better counseling interventions to heterosexual young boys and adolescents, but there is still a lack of attention devoted to the experiences of sexual minority men, adolescents, and boys, particularly those under the age of 15. Most counseling and mental health-related books provide a resource with a wide-ranging scope covering a smattering of chapters on gay, lesbian, bisexual, and transgender issues (Hardin, 2008). A challenge with those types of books is that, while the reader may be exposed to a wider breadth of issues in the LGBT community, such a volume does not provide the reader with a deeper examination of issues critical to any part of the LGBT community. This book, *Counseling Gay Men, Adolescents, and Boys: A Strengths-Based Guide for Helping Professionals and Educators,* seeks to fill that much needed void and to provide a more holistic examination of the challenges of working with men, adolescents, and boys who identify as non-heterosexual. While it is critical to have scholarly and clinical writings that address the wider ranging LGBT community, this volume is intentionally focusing on the sexual identity of men and boys and how this is negotiated in the twenty-first century construct of what it means to be masculine today.

While there has been limited research on counseling boys who identify as questioning, bisexual, or gay, there has been an explosion of stories and experiences (both fiction and non-fiction) devoted to gay boys, adolescents, and adult men. These stories range from tales of coming out and growing up gay (Gideonse & Williams, 2006), dealing with bullying and harassment in schools (Hartinger, 2003; Levithan, 2013; Sanchez, 2001; Sanchez, 2006; Summer, 2004), and trying to synthesize a gay identity into one's cultural and religious traditions (Dahl & Gallaher, 2010; Farizan, 2013; Sanchez, 2007; Sulayman X, 2005). Even mainstream political magazines are publishing stories about the lived experiences of gay teenagers. A cover story of the October 10, 2005, edition of *TIME* magazine, "The Battle Over Gay Teens," cites that gay teens and young boys are coming out earlier and earlier compared with previous generations. This development challenges those who provide services to gay males to examine the types of interventions and programs that are needed to support sexual minority men, adolescents, and boys.

There is a variety of issues affecting the mental, emotional, and physical health of gay men, adolescents, and boys. Increase in substance abuse, higher risk for suicide (Kitts, 2005), engagement in risky sexual behavior (Hamilton & Mihalik, 2009), higher instances of bullying, and physical altercations due to sexual orientation are just some of the types of issues facing this population (Chernin & Johnson, 2003; D'Augelli, 2002; Garofalo et al., 1998; Shernoff, 2006). Anderson (1998) recommends that practitioners take a strengths-based approach when working with gay adolescents, particularly noting the sense of resiliency that exists in gay boys. This resiliency is due in part to dealing with the lack of support from family and friends while attempting to synthesize a healthy gay identity and to rely on one's own internal sense of strength and self-reliance. It is important for us to examine how gay boys, adolescents, and men cope with the stigma that still persists regarding masculinity and sexual orientation (David & Knight, 2008).

Savin-Williams (2005) states that the developmental theories that currently exist lack the focus and attention on gay boys and adolescents. Many of the developmental theories in the literature were created decades ago and do not speak to the current experiences of sexual minority youth and adults. While society at large appears to be more positively embracing gay and lesbian issues, there are still many hindrances to ensuring that gay boys and men are working, studying, playing, and living in safe environments that demonstrate civility and respect. The fields of medicine, mental health, and education need to examine "best practices" and improve the type of services that boys, adolescents, and men who are gay, bisexual, or transgender receive (Hamilton & Mihalik, 2009; Riley, 2010).

Currently, there are significant gaps in the literature regarding the needs of gay boys, adolescents, and men. For example, there are very few societal role models for gay boys and adolescents regarding the development of healthy dating and relationship norms. With the explosion of gay chat, instant messaging (IM), and other technological advances, gay boys and adolescents are meeting and chatting with others online and lack the guidance necessary to assess if these types of social connections are safe and healthy. Simple dating rituals, norms, and challenges when creating same-sex marriages are complex and lack societal acceptance for gay, bisexual, and transgender boys, adolescents, and men (Pennington, 2009). Also, there are few resources that can be used by professionals who work with sexual minority youth and men in a variety of settings.

In order to address this gap in the literature, this book is designed to serve as a guide for counselors, social workers, psychologists, psychiatrists, medical personnel, physicians, ministers/clergy, educators, administrators, and parents of gay boys, adolescents, and young men. The aim of this book is to provide a holistic reference tool to provide comprehensive treatment to sexual minority males. Specifically, this book is designed to be a practical manual on how to respond to the developmental and special issues facing this population of boys and men.

The goal of this volume is to serve as a handy reference for practitioners working with gay boys, adolescents, and men who need additional guidance on how to do an effective assessment that will optimize treatment and services to improve the quality of life for gay males. This book is especially geared toward professionals who seek further training and understanding of this population. This volume is also designed to provide guidance for parents and family members who want to better understand the complex issues of their loved ones who are gay. I hope readers find this a user-friendly reference that will support their work for years to come.

Michael M. Kocet, PhD
Editor

References

Anderson, A. (1998). Strengths of a gay male youth: An untold story. *Child and Adolescent Social Work Journal, 15*, 55–71.

Association for Lesbian, Gay, Bisexual, and Transgender Issues in Counseling. (n.d.). *LGBT competencies.* American Counseling Association. Alexandria, VA: Author.

Baker, J. M. (2002). *How homophobia hurts children: Nurturing diversity at home, at school, and in the community.* New York: Harrington Park Press.

Barret, B., & Logan, C. (2002). *Counseling gay men and lesbians: A practice primer.* Pacific Grove, CA: Thomson Learning Brooks/Cole.

Bieschke, K., Perez, R., & DeBord, K. (2007). *Handbook of counseling and psychotherapy with lesbian, gay, bisexual, and transgender clients* (2nd ed.). Washington DC: American Psychological Association.

Chernin, J. (2006). *Get closer: A gay men's guide to intimacy and relationships.* New York: Allyson.

Chernin, J., & Johnson, M. (2003). *Affirmative psychotherapy and counseling for lesbians and gay men.* Thousand Oaks, CA: Sage.

Cloud, J. (2005, October 10). *The battle over gay teens. TIME* magazine.

Crawford, I., Allison, K., Zamboni, B., & Soto, T. (2002). The influence of dual-identity development on the psychosocial functioning of African-American gay and bisexual men. *The Journal of Sex Research, 39*, 179–189.

Dahl, A., & Gallaher, R. (2010). LGBQQ young adult experiences of religious and sexual identity integration. *Journal of LGBT issues in counseling, 3,* 92–112.

D'Augelli, A. (2002). Mental health problems among lesbian, gay, and bisexual youths ages 14–21. *Clinical Child Psychology and Psychiatry, 7,* 433–455.

David, S., & Knight, B. (2008). Stress and coping among gay men: Age and ethnic difference. *Psychology and Aging, 23,* 62–69.

Dilley, P. (2002). *Queer man on campus: A history of non-heterosexual college men, 1945–2000.* New York: Routledge.

Downs, A. (2006). *The velvet rage: Overcoming the pain of growing up gay in a straight man's world.* Cambridge, MA: Perseus.

Farizan, S. (2013). *If you could be mine.* New York: Algonquin.

Garofalo, R., Wolf, R., & Kessel, S. et al. (1998). The association between health-risk behaviors and sexual orientation among a school-based sample of adolescents. *Pediatrics, 101,* 895–902.

Gideonse, T., & Williams, R. (2006). *From boys to men: Gay men write about growing up.* New York: Carroll & Graf.

Hamilton, C., & Mihalik, J. (2009). Minority stress, masculinity, and social norms predicting gay men's health risk behaviors. *Journal of Counseling Psychology, 56,* 132–141.

Hardin, K. (2008). *Loving ourselves: The gay and lesbian guide to self-esteem.* New York: Alyson.

Hartinger, B. (2003). *Geography club.* New York: HarperTempest.

Kiselica, M., Englar-Carson, M, & Horne, A. (Eds.). (2008). *Counseling troubled boys.* New York: Routledge.

Kitts, R. (2005). Gay adolescents and suicide: Understanding the association. *Adolescence, 40,* 621–628.

Levithan, D. (2013). *Two boys kissing.* New York: Knopf.

Logan, C., & Barret, B. (2005). Counseling competencies for sexual minority clients. *Journal of LGBT Issues in Counseling, 1,* 3–22.

Marcus, E. (1999). *The male couple's guide: Finding a man, making a home, building a life* (3rd ed.). New York: Harper Collins.

Mustanski, B. (2013, June 12). Are violent hate crimes against LGBT people on the rise? *PsychologyToday.com.* Available from www.psychologytoday.com/blog/the-sexual-continuum/201306/are-violent-hate-crimes-against-lgbt-people-the-rise (accessed October 30, 2013).

Pennington, s. (2009). Bisexuals "doing gender" in romantic relationships. *Journal of bisexuality, 9,* 33–69.

Pollack, W. (1999). *Real boys: Rescuing our sons from the myths of boyhood.* New York: Henry Holt.

Riley, B. (2010). GLB adolescent's "coming out." *Journal of child and adolescent psychiatric nursing, 23,* 3–10.

Sanchez, A. (2007). *The God box.* New York: Simon Pulse.

Sanchez, A. (2006). *Getting it.* New York: Simon Pulse.

Sanchez, A. (2001). *Rainbow boys.* New York: Simon Pulse.

Savin-Williams, R. (2005). *The new gay teenager.* Cambridge, MA: Harvard University Press.

Shernoff, M. (2006). *Without condoms: Unprotected sex, gay men, and bare backing.* New York: Routledge.

Sulayman X. (2005). *Bilal's bread.* Los Angeles, CA: Alyson.

Summer, J. (2004). *Not the only one: Lesbian & gay fiction for teens.* Los Angeles, CA: Alyson.

Wall, V., & Evans, N. (2000). *Toward acceptance: Sexual orientation issues on campus.* Lanham, MD: University Press of America.

Weiss, R. (2005). Cruise *control: Understanding sex addiction in gay men.* Los Angeles, CA: Alyson.

Wheaton, G. (2008). *The 7-day dating and relationship plan for gay men.* New York: Alyson.

Acknowledgments

The process of editing and writing a book is a significant task and one, at first, I wasn't sure I was ready to tackle. I remember the moment when Mark Kiselica, series editor of the *Routledge Series on Counseling and Psychotherapy with Boys and Men* first approached me about editing this book. He talked about how important it was for him to have a book devoted to gay males as part of his series with boys and men. To say that I was humbled by the invitation is an understatement. In my years of knowing Mark, I have found him to be a man of principle, integrity, and compassion—*with a passion* for advocacy and counseling males. Even through the bumps and challenges that came with the process of putting this book together, Mark was a consummate professional and encouraged this project to move forward from its early days as a seedling to the full-grown book you now hold in your hands.

Dana Bliss, former editor at Routledge (and now with Oxford University Press), was a staunch supporter of this book in its early days of development. While he left Routledge before this book was completed, I am eternally grateful for his professional expertise, but, more importantly, for the budding friendship that grew from this process (not to mention our shared love of cooking and culinary therapy). Thank you, Dana. I also thank Anna Moore, editor at Routledge for her dogged and persistent nudging to see this book come to press.

I am eternally grateful to the wonderful group of colleagues who make up the contributors for this volume. Some are new colleagues and others are professionals I have served with on committees and known through professional associations for many years. Each of them has shared in this volume their wealth of knowledge and expertise regarding counseling sexual and gender minorities. Their work and diligence makes this book possible. To my colleagues and friends in the American Counseling Association and, in particular, in the Association for Lesbian, Gay, Bisexual, Transgender Issues in Counseling. Working with all of you has been a rewarding opportunity and I am thankful for the deep and abiding connections I have made over these many years. I am also grateful to the staff at the Boston Public Library and their wonderful facility where much of the work for this book took place.

I want to thank the students, faculty, and staff in the Department of Counselor Education at Bridgewater State University who have supported my work throughout the years. I am mindful of our university motto, "*Not to Be Ministered Unto, But to Minister*" and how relevant that motto is to the work we do as counselors. You have taught me many important life lessons that I continue to carry with me.

I am appreciative of the opportunity to give back to my community in two significant ways. I thank the staff and volunteers at the *GLBTQ Domestic Violence Project* in Boston. I am deeply touched by their boundless confidence in me. I also thank the staff and volunteers of *Comfort Zone Camp.* Working with grieving children and their families has been one of the most gratifying experiences of my life and I am humbled each time I spend time walking with a child on his or her grief journey.

An important part of life is having a strong friendship network and I am so very grateful for the friendship and love of good friends and colleagues who supported and encouraged me during the process of working on this book: David Balardini, Cecil Blanton, Amanda Brace, Matthew Branfield, Belinda Cavazos, Bill Cervenik, Mike Chaney, Makeba L. Clay, Viki Cvitkovic, Sean Daughtry, LICSW, Harrison Davis, Domenic Di Francesco, Greg Dodge, Chandra Johnson, Denise Lenares, Andy Kovacic, Manny Lim, Lisa Manera, Ariel Margolis, Eric Martin, Chris Miller, Tom Moeggenberg, Rochelle Moss, Joey Murzynski, Audrey Negri, Abdu Nessralla, Barb Novak, Monica Osburn, Derrick Paladino, Chuck Roach, Sam Sanabria, Cary Sherman, Kathy Sherman, Daniel Steger, Timothy B. Toudouze, Dave Vaughn, Brooke Vimtrup, Matt Wagner, Aaron Welch, Erin Yeckley, and all my friends who have played such a special role in my life. I am also especially grateful to Ashley Grillo, Michael McDonald, and Mary Moore for watching Malley all those many hours while I was away doing research and editing the book.

I am blessed to have a wonderful family who constantly show their love to me in so many ways. I am grateful to my mother Barbara, my sister Michelle, brother-in-law Gregg, niece Olivia, and my aunts, uncles, and cousins who have been with me at each step of my professional career.

Finally, I thank each and every one of my clients and students I have had the privilege of counseling over the years, especially my gay male clients. Doing this work is a tremendous privilege and one that I never take for granted. Thank you for your trust in me.

Part I

Understanding the Developmental Needs of Gay Men, Adolescents, and Boys

1 Coming Out and Identity Development Needs in Gay Men, Adolescents, and Boys

Joseph J. Manera & Dennis A. Frank, II

"Coming out" or "coming out of the closet" refers to the developmental process that gay boys, adolescents, and men go through as they accept and then reveal their sexual orientation to other people (Schubotz & McNamee, 2009). The phrase "coming out of the closet" is a metaphor that has been used since the 1970s to symbolize the sense of relief that gay and lesbian people feel after coming to terms with being gay and then telling other people, as well as openly associating with other gay people.

Coming out is not a singular action or a one-time event; it is an on-going process that spans many months or years, and for some people "coming out" is a life-long process. Unlike ethnic and racial minorities who often visibly identity with their cultural identity, gay men are not visibly identifiable and, therefore, must identify by self-report. In other words, gay men are only considered to be gay if they define themselves as such (Greene, 1994). Gay boys typically grow up in families and communities that are outside of the gay community and the transition from a presumed heterosexual identity to a gay identity is a complex and often solitary journey (Frank & Cannon, 2010).

The heterosexist assumption that individuals are straight until and unless they disclose being gay led to the development of idealized linear stage models that describe common experiences of gay identity formation and integration that are part of the coming out process. These models focused on the resolution of internal conflict related to identification as gay, and inform what is commonly termed the coming out process (e.g., Cass, 1979; Coleman, 1982; D'Augelli, 1994; Savin-Williams, 1988; Troiden, 1988). There is general agreement between the different theories that coming out is a developmental process and, while there is less agreement on the number of stages and the necessary associated tasks, they do share common characteristics. According to Gonsiorek (1995), these models typically begin with a stage in which individuals use numerous defense strategies to block or minimize the recognition of personal same-gender feelings. The process of expending energy to deny or minimize these feelings may have negative consequences for overall mental health. Yet, for many individuals, a gradual recognition and cautious acceptance of same-gender feelings emerge as they come to accept their feelings.

Identity Development in Gay Men and Boys

Much has been written about the process of identity development in human beings. This chapter will focus on identity development in gay men, adolescents, and boys, an oft-marginalized group that has unique considerations that need to be taken into account when exploring issues of selfhood. The goals of this chapter are to summarize the most significant models of identity development, address issues that pertain to specific age groups of gay boys, adolescents, and men, and discuss concerns that relate to specific cultural groups.

Definitions

Berger and Luckman (1966) posited that theories about identity are, at their cores, rooted in theories about reality. Cass (1984) describes reality as all that "reflects our past experiences, present social and psychological functioning, and future aspirations" (p. 109). Identity theories can be likened to broad canvasses depicting various permutations of self along the lifespan.

According to Cass, the term *identity* incorporates all of the self-perceptions an individual maintains, the affects associated with them, and the self-perceptions of an individual's ideal future self. An individual's identity encompasses a blend of his view of himself and his beliefs on how others perceive him. An identity is successfully developed only when self-perceptions and perceptions of others' views of self align.

In reviewing the work of various identity theorists, Cass identified several commonalities. Significantly, most major identity theorists considered identity in both individual and social terms. Cass (1984) noted that theorists refer to "a personal aspect of individual functioning conceived of as self-representations and self-perceptions" (p. 110). This is generally referred to as *personal identity* or *self-concept.* Theorists also refer to "a social aspect of identity that is the representation of the personal aspect to others in a relatively consistent way" (p. 110). This is generally termed *public identity* or *social identity.*

So what, then, should an effective identity development model aim to achieve and explain? Cass (1984) suggests that solid theories should meet the following criteria: they

> (1) offer a clear definition of what "identity" means and of its relationship to self-concept, (2) outline the structural components of identity, (3) trace the changes that occur as identity develops, and (4) describe both internal and external factors influencing such changes.
>
> (p. 118)

Furthermore, detailing the cognitive, behavioral, and emotional changes an individual encounters through each stage of development is crucial in any theory (Cass, 1984). These are the pieces that imbue a model with meaning and grant it its heartbeat.

Models of identity development should also address the milestones that gay men potentially achieve during their lifetimes. Troiden (1989) described the criteria for adopting a homosexual self-identification. He explained that, before gay men can identify themselves in terms of a particular category, they must learn that such a category incorporating their activities or feelings (i.e., same-sex attractions) actually exists. They must then learn that others are members of this social category; that gay men constitute an actual group. Most gay men subsequently realize that their own needs are more similar to those that occupy this newly discovered social category (other gay men) than they are dissimilar. At this point, gay men generally begin to identify with individuals in this social category, and they ascertain if they meet the criteria for membership in this group based on their emotions and behaviors in a variety of contexts.

Gay men may choose to label themselves in terms of the social category of "gay men" in relevant situations. Troiden posits that prior to self-identifying as a gay, a man will experience "generalized feelings of marginality, and perceptions of being different from same-sex peers" (p. 50). Self-designation as homosexual, particularly in conjunction with meaningful contact with other gay men, allows opportunities to learn about being gay and potentially increases feelings of belongingness with a group while reducing feelings of alienation. After labeling himself as gay, a man might then "incorporate and absorb these situationally-linked identities into [his] self-concept over time" (p. 49).

Models of Identity Development

Most of the models for identity development in gay men follow a similar progression. Most identity development models adhere to what might be referred to as an Essentialist perspective. They describe a trajectory from first same-sex attractions, through a range of potentially challenging experiences, to some kind of resolution.

Vivienne Cass

One of the first models of homosexual identity development was proposed by Vivienne Cass (1979). Cass's model, developed during several years of clinical work with men who identified as gay, describes how individuals come to contemplate and then adopt homosexual identities as pertinent dimensions of self. Cass's six-stage model encompasses both private and public aspects of personality and is informed by interpersonal congruency theory. Interpersonal congruency theory posits that "stability and change in human behavior are dependent on the congruency or incongruency that exists within an individual's interpersonal environment" (p. 220). Cass hypothesized that the incongruency between a person's homosexual feelings, thoughts, and behaviors, and his environment spurs movement from one stage of the model to another. Homosexual identity formation is viewed as a process in which one moves from defining oneself as non-homosexual to defining oneself as homosexual.

Case Study: "Ben"

"Ben" is in his mid-20s, born and raised in a suburban neighborhood. Growing up, Ben's supportive but conservative family instilled the idea that his future would involve a wife, children, and a charming house with happy sunflowers in the window boxes. Bright and quiet, Ben felt different from other boys for as long as he could remember, but he did not begin to suspect he may be gay until age 13. Ben struggled with feelings of guilt and shame, and he often felt disconnected from his peers, whom he worried would ostracize him if they knew "the real Ben." Ben was active in school with sports, activities, and academics, but he felt he was "always on the periphery, never inside the circle."

Stage 1 of Cass's model is Identity Confusion. In this stage, an individual labels his own behavior as potentially homosexual. This realization begins the identity formation process and presents an incongruency, as the individual's feelings and behaviors clash with his perception of himself as heterosexual. As a result, he experiences distress and alienation. He links homosexual feelings and behaviors with the possibility of being homosexual. Ben entered this stage around age 13, when he began to masturbate, which heightened his awareness that his sexual fantasies involved men. Ben had previously managed to convince himself that his attractions to men were not sexual, but it became increasingly difficult for him to do so. This awoke within Ben feelings of anxiety, confusion, and fear. He began to imagine that he might actually be gay, and found it difficult to reconcile a possible homosexual identity with his (and his family's) visions for his future.

According to Cass, individuals resolve their conflict in the Identity Confusion stage in one of three ways. The first response is to attribute meaning to homosexual behaviors and feelings, and to view a potential homosexual identity as correct and acceptable. In these scenarios, incongruency is intensified—for example, a man may think of himself as heterosexual but finds himself sexually and emotionally attracted to a male friend. This necessitates passage into the second stage of identity development.

The second potential response is for the individual to perceive his behaviors and feelings as accurate, but undesirable. This closely aligns with Ben's emotional reaction to the possibility of being gay. Ben felt he could "pass" as straight by associating himself with stereotypically "masculine" activities. He joined the football team, although he would have secretly preferred to spend his after-school hours taking a dance class or joining the school chorus. According to Cass, a man inclined toward this second response might inhibit any behaviors that could be perceived as gay, restrict any information he might receive relating to homosexuality, or deny that such information pertains to him. The ability to withdraw from potentially provocative situations and employ defense mechanisms such as denial are key in inhibiting homosexual behaviors. Unsuccessful attempts herald the beginning of what could become a self-hating identity.

The third potential response is for the individual to determine the meaning of his behavior as incorrect and undesirable. In this case, an individual re-frames his behavior as non-homosexual. For example, he might redefine physical intimacy with another man as "an experiment," "being taken advantage of," or "a favor for a friend." He might choose to define passionate kissing and showing emotion as homosexual, but rationalize that genital sex only constitutes "fooling around." At any stage in the developmental process, identity foreclosure occurs when an individual chooses not to develop further.

If identity foreclosure has not occurred at the end of Stage 1, the individual moves toward Stage 2, Identity Comparison. In this stage, an individual begins to realize that adopting a homosexual identity means that all of the guidelines for behavior, ideals, and plans for the future that accompany heterosexual identity no longer apply to him and are replaced. The task in Stage 2 is to manage the resulting social isolation that arises. Individuals might respond to this task by enjoying being different, accepting the homosexual meaning of one's behavior but finding a homosexual self-image undesirable, accepting oneself as homosexual but not accepting homosexual behaviors, or accepting neither homosexual self-image or behaviors. Individuals in the latter category, who are unsuccessful in denouncing homosexuality and viewing themselves as heterosexual, are at risk for suicide. Marszalek, Cashwell, Dunn, and Heard Jones (2004) noted that individuals in Stage 2 of Cass's identity development model are increasingly able to express same-sex feelings but that acceptance of those feelings would require more abstract thinking.

Ben spent his high school and early college years suppressing his homosexual identity, but a number of factors softened his stance. Especially meaningful to him were the friendships he established with a supportive group of classmates and increasingly positive media presence of out gay men. Seeing positive examples of homosexuals shifted Ben's perspectives on what it might mean to be gay, and he began to allow himself to more fully embrace the fact that he is, in fact, gay, and that this might not actually be a bad thing. Ben eventually came out to select friends and family.

Stage 3 of Cass's model is Identity Tolerance. The greater level of commitment to a homosexual identity that marks the end of Stage 2 creates additional dissonance between the way the person sees himself and the way others view him. In this stage, the individual often feels isolated and begins to seek out others of the same persuasion. Cass (1979) asserted that superficial contact with other gay men is insufficient for meeting the person's social needs: "Although making contact with other homosexuals is important at this stage, a more critical factor is the emotional quality of that contact" (p. 230). Individuals may respond to the same situations differently based on personality, preference, and temperament: "One person, for example, may find a bar or nightclub exciting . . . whereas another may find it depressing" (p. 230). Several variables might contribute to negative experiences—timidity, fear of being exposed, feelings of inadequacy, or poor interpersonal skills.

After initiating the coming out process, Ben began to dip his toe into the local gay scene, feeling a range of emotional experiences: nervousness at the possibility of being "seen" at a gay bar, excitement at being able to act on his fantasies, and a certain melancholy that he had "missed out" on experiences during his teenage years. According to Cass, Stage 3 can be a thrilling time for a gay man. While there are various risks and stressors, there are also opportunities to meet romantic partners, learn ways of managing identity, create a social network of gay friends, seek out role models, and feel more at ease with one's identity. According to Marszalek et al. (2004), individuals in this stage use "causal, if-then logic to reason that if they have same-sex feelings, thoughts, or actions, then they are *probably* gay" (p. 110).

By the time an individual reaches Stage 4, Identity Acceptance, he begins to identify a preference for spending time with other homosexual individuals. He increases his social contacts with other gay people and develops friendships. The stage is marked by embracing rather than simply tolerating a homosexual self-image. After the initial awkward flirtation with gay culture, Ben found himself wanting to spend more time with other gay men, and actively sought out clubs, organizations, and activities that were specifically geared toward gay men.

Haldeman (2007) asserts that community plays a crucial function in gay men's development:

> For the gay man coming out in a heterocentric culture, community serves essential corrective and replacement functions . . . some heterosocial patterns of relating that many gay men have attempted to master will have no place in their lives as out gay men. (p. 80)

Meaningful social contacts allow gay men to identify with those that are similar to themselves. This identification can reduce feelings of guilt and shame that LGBT individuals often feel. Ben described the experience of finding a community as allowing him to "become more [himself]." He began to expand his horizons, pursuing his musical interests without shame, and enjoying more substantial friendships.

More complicated, perhaps, was Ben's relationship with his family during this time. How does an individual manage relationships with persons from different realms of his life in Stage 4? According to Cass, by the time a man reaches this juncture, "passing has become a routine strategy for compartmentalizing a homosexual way of life and reducing the likelihood of being confronted with the reactions of heterosexuals" (p. 322). Around this time, Ben limited his contact with certain family members and made arrangements to avoid potentially awkward situations, such as scenarios where someone might ask him if he has a girlfriend. During Stage 4, a man might disclose his sexual orientation to specific heterosexual contacts, who serve to keep his secret. If these strategies are carried out successfully and the individual is satisfied with this arrangement, identity foreclosure occurs. According to Marszalek et al. (2004), individuals in this stage are "using abstract logic to make the connection that if they have homosexual feelings and behaviors, they are gay" (p. 110).

For some individuals, disclosure to select persons feels limiting. For these men, using strategies to devalue heterosexuals and evaluate homosexual contacts more positively may become a coping strategy. A sense of group identity and belonging develops. The individual in this stage, Stage 5, Identity Pride, immerses himself in gay culture. He not only accepts his homosexual identity—he finds it preferable to a heterosexual one. He rejects values (such as sex-role structures) that Cass (1979) believes work to "promote the concept of homosexual inferiority" (p. 233). In his daily life, however, he may be confronted with situations that heighten the inconsistency between heterosexual and homosexual values. Additionally, he may abandon strategies he has used to conceal his homosexual identity and use sexual orientation disclosure as a means of coping. Ben referred to this as a "pre-emptive strike—staving off feeling rejected by coming out to people before they really knew [him]."

Disclosing sexual orientation as a coping skill has two positive effects: it lends support to a gay man's view of himself as homosexual and closes the gap between his public and private selves. If others respond negatively to the disclosure, it is as the individual feared, and identity foreclosure may occur. A positive response, however, is inconsistent with the individual's expectations, which pushes him into the final stage of identity formation. Marszalek et al. (2004) stated that individuals in Stage 5 are able to "reflect on the patterns in their lives and realize how their experiences, thoughts, and feelings in the past have connected to their gay identities" (p. 110).

In Stage 6, Identity Synthesis, the individual acknowledges that there are others who accept his homosexual identity in the same manner that he does. The individual still feels a sense of pride, but the split between homosexual and heterosexual worlds is reduced. He is able to integrate his homosexual identity with other aspects of himself, such as racial identity, religious/spiritual affiliation, and life roles such as son/brother/friend. His sexual orientation, rather than being his defining feature, is now considered just one aspect of his identity. According to Marszalek et al. (2004), individuals at Stage

6 may also contemplate existential concerns. For Ben, it was important to feel that he "didn't need to live in a gay bubble," noting an increased sense of comfort with himself regardless of where he was and with whom he was keeping company.

Fassinger and Miller

Cass (1979) acknowledged that, over time, changes in societal attitudes and expectations would necessitate changes in her model. Fassinger and Miller (1996) posited that previous models of identity development such as Cass's tended to conflate individual and group identity development, with a focus on public and politicized identity as an indicator of emotional maturity. Lack of disclosure in Cass's and other models is equated with developmental stagnation. Fassinger and Miller's model hypothesizes two separate but reciprocal processes of individual sexual identity development and group membership identity development.

Fassinger and Miller's model allows for greater range of expression, since it teases out one's individual sense of self from the extent to which he decides to participate in gay culture. In this model, the same four stages are relevant for both individual and group identity: Awareness, Exploration, Deepening/Commitment, and Internalization/Synthesis.

Phase 1 in individual development, Awareness, involves feeling conscious of being different from the heterosexual norm. Gay men in this stage are likely to experience fear, uncertainty, and disorientation. The Exploration stage involves exploring strong feelings, usually sexual, about others of the same sex, or perhaps just one individual of the same sex. Individuals in this stage often experience longing, excitement, and wonder, "as hitherto unknown aspects of one's sexuality are discovered" (p. 56).

After an individual embarks on the journey of Exploration, he enters into a stage in which Deepening/Commitment to a gay identity occurs. This stage "involves a deepening of sexual and emotional self-knowledge, crystallization of choices about sexuality (e.g., deciding to relate exclusively to same-sex partners), and the recognition that preferred forms of intimacy imply certain things about identity" (p. 56). This stage is likely to be accompanied by feelings of sadness and anger, as the context in which this sharpened insight develops is likely a heterosexist culture. Along with these feelings comes an increase in self-acceptance and confidence. In the Internalization/Synthesis stage, a man embraces same-sex affection and desire as part of his identity. He is unwilling to change his values and experiences a greater sense of pride and satisfaction.

Fassinger and Miller differentiate themselves from Cass's model by emphasizing that some reconceptualization of public identity needs to take place during the coming out process, and that this reformulation will involve different meanings and consequences depending on the individual and the culture. They stress that "it is the process of resolving these questions that creates a mature identity, not the content of their resolution" (p. 58), and that group membership identification is greatly influenced by preexisting beliefs about homosexual sexual orientations. These beliefs differ across cultures, time frames, and other contexts. The Fassinger/Miller model "assumes flexibility in disclosure behaviors as the lesbian or gay individual develops an internally coherent sense of self, without the political tyranny of viewing public disclosure as the main route to achieving a healthy, mature identity" (pp. 73–74).

The Awareness stage in Group Membership Identity is marked by a new awareness of alternatives regarding sexual orientation. This realization coincides with an acknowledgment of the existence of sexual prejudice, resulting in confusion. Sexual prejudice, according to Herek (1999), refers to "all negative attitudes based on sexual orientation, whether the target is homosexual, bisexual, or heterosexual" (p. 2). Herek asserts that due to the "current social organization of sexuality" (p. 20), prejudice is almost always aimed at individuals who identify as gay or participate in homosexual behavior.

In the next stage of Fassinger and Miller's model, Exploration, the individual explores his views of the LGBT community as a group and considers the possibility of joining this group. The Exploration stage involves an even more heightened awareness of sexual prejudice, which arouses feelings of anxiety and anger. Simultaneously, the individual feels a sense of excitement and curiosity, as he is exploring social opportunities with other LGBT persons.

The Deepening/Commitment phase involves a greater dedication to involvement in the LGBT community. Individuals in this stage experience a greater understanding of the consequences of committing to a homosexual identity. They are likely to feel a combination of pride, excitement, and anger. Many will respond by identifying more intensely with the LGBT community and rejecting heterosexual society. In the final stage, Internalization/Synthesis, gay men completely internalize their identities as members of a marginalized group. They incorporate this membership into their self-concept and experience greater feelings of security and contentment. A gay man in this stage has a greater ability to maintain his sense of himself as gay across a variety of contexts.

Eli Coleman

Coleman (1982) offered a perspective on the developmental stages of the coming out process that "does not assume that every individual follows each stage and naturally evolves through all. Some become locked into one stage or another and never experience identity integration. Some individuals will begin tasks at higher levels of development before focusing on the task of an earlier stage" (p. 32). Coleman's model details a series of stages and extends advice to men who are in the coming out process. Coleman's first stage is the Pre-Coming Out stage. In this stage, both parent and child know that the child's sexual orientation is different:

> the child learns about the ethical values of the family and society and incorporates external rules into a personal structure.... A major crisis is created for the individual, the family, and ultimately society when a child appears to break these expectations. (pp. 32–33)

A gay boy is likely to feel alone and alienated. Individuals at this stage are not consciously aware of homosexual feelings. Therefore, "they can only communicate their conflict through behavioral problems, psychosomatic illnesses, suicide attempts, or various other symptoms" (p. 33). Individuals in this stage might hide their feelings and suffer from low self-esteem, commit suicide, or face the conflict and acknowledge same-sex feelings.

Coming out is the next phase. Coleman links disclosure of one's sexuality to others to self-acceptance. Coleman (1982) notes that, once an individual gains acceptance from a few individuals and feels some support and connection, it is easier to cope with rejection. He also notes that the "perceived status" (p. 35) of the person an individual comes out to is relevant. For example, it is more meaningful to gain acceptance from a beloved friend than from a stranger. Coleman (1982) notes that often individuals look for support solely from other men and women who identify as gay, which he believes is limiting: "Since an individual's original conceptions of homosexuality are mostly negative, the perceived status of other homosexual people is usually not very high, and acceptance from them can have limited impact or value" (p. 35). Coleman (1982) also advises disclosing to family members only after one has received enough support from important others in his life.

The next stage in Coleman's model is Exploration. It involves the first major experiences of erotic and social activity with others. During this period, a gay man might not have the skills to develop a relationship with another man, as he has been socialized as heterosexual. Coleman (1982) sees three main developmental tasks. First, the individual should develop social skills in order to meet other men with a similar sexual persuasion. Second, he needs to develop "a sense of personal attractiveness and sexual competence" (p. 36). Third, he must realize that his self-worth is not entirely predicated around sexual exploits. Coleman (1982) notes: "Many individuals lose sight of their goals while in this adolescent adventure. Adolescents are known to act out, rebel, and act in a self-destructive manner; adolescents whose self-esteem is low have a greater tendency to engage in self-destructive behavior" (p. 37). Even gay men who come out at a later stage in life may experience an adolescent-like period of development regarding their emotions, thoughts, and behaviors.

First relationships are the next stage. Coleman (1982) characterizes first relationships by "intensity, possessiveness, and lack of trust" (p. 38) and sees them as unlikely to succeed. The person has expectations about relationships that are grounded in fantasy, and he lacks relationship experience. As anyone who has ever been in any kind of relationship knows, it is usually impossible to live up to another person's ideals. Attempts at asserting independence within the relationship might be viewed as a lack of interest in the other. Loss of sexual interest can be perceived as evidence of falling out of love.

Integration is the final stage in Coleman's identity model. Similar to Cass, new relationships and self-concepts emerge in this stage. The person's private and public selves merge. At this point in their lives, men are better prepared to be in relationships, and to weather their endings.

D'Augelli Identity Model

Anthony R. D'Augelli, a psychologist and professor of human development, believed that the stage models of gay male identity formation focused too greatly on internal process of personal development. In contrast, he offered an alternative to the stage models of homosexual identity development. His life-span model of sexual orientation development accounts for social influences that were not addressed in the earlier stage models.

According to this model, the development of a gay identity in society takes place through a series of non-linear phases of development, each stage reflecting a deeper level of personal understanding and a new relationship with the surrounding community. These six phases—exiting heterosexual identity, developing a personal gay identity status, developing a gay social identity, becoming a gay offspring, developing a gay intimacy status, and entering a gay community—represent a fluid process that changes over time depending on the development and experiences of each individual (D'Augelli, 1994).

D'Augelli's model theorized that the individual is able to show development in more than one area simultaneously or may develop in one process area more than others (Bilodeau & Renn, 2005). Additionally, he believed that people transition in of and out of the phases multiple times depending on their needs and life circumstances rather than definitively completing it and moving on like the stage models seem to imply (Cooper, 2008).

D'Augelli's model addresses leaving the socially constructed heterosexual identity (Exiting Heterosexuality), in which an individual realizes they are no longer a part of the dominant construct and proceed to develop a gay male identity. In order for an individual to begin this process, the person must first realize that their sexual orientation conflicts with the societal norm and then reject their heterosexual identity and culture. Part of exiting from a heterosexual orientation deals with the individual's struggle to form an identity status in relation to their environment. This new identity formation is contingent upon the gay person coming out and disclosing their sexual identity to other people in order to separate himself from society's heteronormative standards.

Developing a Personal Gay Identity Status is the next phase discussed in D'Augelli's model. Individuals gain a certain amount of definition through their interactions with others who share a similar identity. Developing a gay identity within a social construct, an important part of the formation process, allows for the dispelling of myths designed to oppress or reduce gay individuals to caricatures (e.g., all gay men get AIDS). In this phase, social interaction provides a means for which individuals who are new to their gay identity can safely ask questions and hear positive stories. This effectively allows the individual to amend preconceived beliefs and assumptions about being gay while gaining an understanding of their gay identity.

The next phase, Developing a Gay Social Identity, is the construction of a gay social status. The creation of social status allows gay individuals to form a social network that is affirmative of their identity. This task requires the individual to come out to their social network and, when necessary, build a new social network that is affirming. D'Augelli (1994) places a large emphasis on the difference between tolerance and acceptance. Tolerance tends to reinforce social invisibility and is detrimental to the developmental process. Societal acceptance tends to reinforce social visibility and is beneficial to the developmental process.

Becoming a gay offspring is next. In this phase, gay individuals are faced with coming out to their family, specifically their parents. After the family has been made aware of the new identity of a gay family member, the initial reaction is often mixed, with elements of tolerance rather than affirmation.

The disclosure to parents is typically followed by one of four reactions. The first of these is called loving open, which is a positive reaction with limited denial by the parents. The parents are willing to tell some friends and extended family members about their son's sexual orientation. The second reaction is called loving denial. In this instance, parents react positively but are unwilling to disclose the information outside of the immediate family. They accept their son, but require a set of boundaries as a condition of their acceptance.

The third reaction is called resentful denial, which can be described as the parents' refusal to accept their child's same-gender orientation. The fourth reaction is hostile recognition in which parents respond with verbal and/or physical aggression (D'Augelli, 1994).

As part of the processes of accepting their gay child, parents often deal with a number of common themes following the coming out. They may feel that they lack a script on how to react and therefore need time to recover from a feeling of loss; they may gain an interest in emphasizing their child's heteronormative behaviors. In other words, they attempt to separate the child from gay stereotypes (D'Augelli, 1994).

Developing a gay intimacy status is the next part of the identity development process. Dating, let alone forming significant, intimate relationships, is a challenging concept. Same-sex couples are not a dominant part of society and the lack of visible role models increases the complexity of developing intimate relationships as gay men. Fortunately, since the early 2000s, same-gender couples have become much more visible and same-sex marriage has seen unprecedented public support.

The final part of D'Augelli's model deals with entering the gay community and becoming a constructive and active member of this community. The final piece of D'Augelli's model deals with becoming a socially visible and politically active member of the gay community. However, due to the same social constructs that reinforce heterosexism, this commitment to action may come with personal risk and could be detrimental to their family life, career, or social relationships. This risk is compounded due to the fact that the basis of a gay male identity is in direct opposition to societal norms, not by choice, but because identity is a social construct. This risk becomes compounded due to the fact that gay men set the basis for their identity in direct opposition to the norms, not by choice, but because identity is a social construction.

Becoming empowered as a gay person involves awareness of the structure of heterosexism, the nature of relevant laws and policies, and the limits to freedom and exploration. To be gay in the fullest sense—to have a meaningful identity—leads to a consciousness of the history of one's own oppression. It also, generally, leads to an appreciation of how the oppression continues, and a commitment to resisting it (D'Augelli, 1994, p. 328).

Criticism of the Models

Both the linear and non-linear identity models have continued to receive criticism. The first critique focuses on the models that seem to only be relevant for gay men who came out during the period of time between the Stonewall Revolution and the end of the twentieth century; essentially from 1970 to 2000. Contemporary young people do not follow the stages described in the literature; instead they are more likely to experience an abridged coming out process. These youth experience a more rapid identity development than has been seen in previous generations, coming out to others while still in their teens (Savin-Williams, 2005).

Another significant criticism is that the general premises of these models are based upon ethnocentric assumptions, and they ignore the socio-cultural factors in an individual's developmental process. These models (e.g., Cass, 1979; Coleman, 1982; Troiden, 1988) have relied upon retrospective accounts from predominately White men, creating an illusion of uniformity. Additionally, many of these models hold rigid perspectives of what happens when, but do not explain how or why it happens when it does (Cooper, 2008). They do not account for the individual's personal story or life experiences. Racial and ethnic minority youth are strongly impacted by specific socio-economic, cultural, and historical contexts in which they live; however these models ignore these personal aspects of development.

Several new coming out process models have been developed that do attempt to address some of the criticisms the stage models have generated. The Integrative Empowerment Model (Matthews & Salazar, 2012) builds upon and goes beyond the premise of the stage models. The authors believe that gay men must successfully navigate and integrate these various stages in order to have a healthier life and to minimize future problems.

Integrative Empowerment Model

Matthews and Salazar (2012) proposed the Integrative Empowerment Model (IEM) to assist counselors in helping lesbian, gay, and bisexual youth negotiate the coming out process; however the focus of this overview is specifically relevant to the coming out process for boys and adolescents. The IEM is a holistic approach that assists the counselor in viewing the entire environment in which the gay youth lives.

The model begins with an exploration of the Internal and External Factors that the client brings to counseling with him (Client Inputs). Depending upon the client inputs, the model provides the counselor with Strategies and Interventions that may be relevant. This leads the actual coming out process, which may take place over a short or long period of time depending on a multitude of factors, including the number and severity of the client inputs, which then ideally leads to positive client outputs. Counselors can work collaboratively with clients to identify and explore each salient factor, which guides treatment strategies and interventions. Feedback from the outputs of counseling treatment helps determine areas of focus for continued support inside and outside the counseling environment.

Client inputs are factors that influence the coming out process, and are divided into internal and external factors. Internal and external factors are not distinctly separate or mutually exclusive; instead they interact and affect each other. There are four key internal factors that affect the coming out process: (a) stage of sexual identity formation; (b) internalized feelings of homoprejudice; (c) self-esteem and self-acceptance issues; and (d) mental health behaviors. Additionally, there are six key external factors that impact the coming out process: (a) family environment; (b) school/peer environment; (c) access to a gay support network; (d) race/culture; (e) religion; and (f) previous counseling experience.

Each client will present with combinations of different internal and external factors that are either negatively or positively impacting the coming out process. Counselors working from an empowerment and advocacy stance have many strategies and interventions available to help the client understand and move forward in their sexual identity development, including (a) helping gay youth connect with others to combat isolation; (b) exploration of fears, anxieties, and self-perceptions; (c) issues of coming out; (d) pros and cons of coming out; (e) resiliency; and (f) helping them realize the coming out process may span weeks, months, or even years.

RAC Model

Cooper (2008) proposed a comprehensive framework: the RAC Model, composed of Realization, Activation, and Consolidation. While this model is applicable to both gay men and women, the focus of this overview is on the aspects of gay identity development for boys, adolescents, and men.

Realization is the first phase, which begins with feelings of being different, though initially there is little understanding of this difference. These feelings of being different may lead to self-alienation and isolation from peers due to fear of having this difference discovered by others. Eventually the individual receives information that allows them to assign the label of gay to these feelings of difference. It should be noted that, while the individual is able to label this difference now, it does not imply that they have accepted themselves as being gay (Cooper, 2008).

Activation occurs when the individual acknowledges their same-gender feelings, whether it is a thought, feeling, or fantasy. It is at this point that the person first begins to disclose to other people and allows himself to become sexual with members of his own gender. This phase is fraught with awkwardness and intensity that is beyond the normal scope of adolescence (Cooper, 2008).

Consolidation symbolizes the union of the private identity ("I'm gay") with the public identity ("I'm gay and don't want other people knowing it"). This results in a cohesive, healthy self-image ("I'm gay and I don't mind [some] people knowing it"). The effect of this self-definition as a gay man is a need for intimacy and relationships, which leads the individual to seek out romantic relationships. The ability for these relationships to become stable, committed relationships is no different from those in heterosexual partnerships (Cooper, 2008).

The priority in this framework is coming out or disclosing one's gay identity to self and others since it represents a shift in the person's core identity. The model recognizes that coming out is a lifelong task that gay men face. The number of times that the individual needs to come out and the emotional turmoil involved will decrease as the individual becomes more comfortable with their gay identity. Representing coming out in this manner addresses the criticism that previous models did not reflect upon the lived reality of the individual.

Differential Developmental Trajectories

According to Savin-Williams (2005), the one big mistake that sexual identity development theorists made was to create "universal" stage models to represent the lives of gay youth. He believes that these researchers have failed to capture the diversity and complexity of the contemporary "gay" youth. He continues by saying that

> the new gay teenager is in many respects the non-gay teenager. For these young people, being labeled as gay or even being gay matters little. They have same-sex desires and attractions but, unlike earlier generations, new gay teens have much less interest in naming these feeling or behaviors as gay.
>
> (p. 1)

The differential developmental trajectories (DDT) is a framework of sexual identity development that accounts for the lived lives of same-gender attracted youth, and includes milestones, transitional incidents, fluidity, and positive development. A basic premise of the DDT is that sexuality is a valid developmental issue for all adolescents regardless of sexual orientation (Savin-Williams, 2005). In order to bring this framework to fruition, the model discards three antiquated assumptions of the previous models: (1) life progresses in sequential, ordered stages; (2) the developmental process is so complex and diverse it need not be addressed; and (3) the lives of gay youth can be understood based upon research conducted on adolescents who openly identify as gay.

In place of these assumptions, Savin-Williams (2005) proposed four basic tenants of the DDT framework. The first can be described using "adolescents are adolescents." Or, in other words, gay adolescents are first and foremost adolescents and therefore are developmentally similar to all other adolescents. Most adolescents share most basic developmental tasks and process—focusing entirely on the consequences of being gay in a heteronormative society may misattribute typical adolescent experiences to difficulties with their sexual orientation.

The next tenet of the DDT framework is that gay teens are dissimilar from heterosexual teens in their developmental trajectory. This may possibly be due to the pervasive heterocentrism, often manifested in disapproval of sex-atypical activities, disposition, and interests, that is found in modern society. A second factor in this tenet proposed as being different is the impact of socialization. Growing up in a heteronormative society that presumes and prescribes heterosexuality impacts the personal development of gay youth differently from how it does with heterosexual youth.

The third tenet is that the developmental trajectory of same-sex attracted youth varies from child to child. The interaction of sexuality with ethnicity, geography, socio-economic status, and cohort results in individualized and distinctive paths. It is incorrect to view same-sex desire, behavior, and identity as a singularity with similar patterns and outcomes.

The final proposed tenet in the DDT framework is that the developmental path of one person is not similar to the path of any other person who has ever lived. Due to the significant innate diversity in individual lives, there is little benefit to applying general descriptions of group-mean differences and similarities to one specific person.

Critiques of Models and New Ideas

Despite the noted criticisms, these models should not be considered irrelevant because the different stages do represent issues with which many gay men struggle as they figure out who they really are. These models provide insight into some of the unique challenges related to developing a positive gay identity. When viewed as broad patterns rather than as normative developmental progressions, these models provide the counselor with a point of entry in which to engage in the client. However, it is necessary to look for how the stage models fit the client rather than attempting to fit the client into a specific model.

McDonald (1982) questioned the stage-sequential nature of most models of gay sexual identity development, noting that it "overlooks individual differences from the prescribed pattern" (p. 48). He set out to discover the average ages of milestone events in the coming out process. His results indicated that, overall, coming out developed in an orderly fashion: "Respondents progressed from an awareness of same-sex attractions through homosexual behavior to eventual self-labeling, self disclosures, and the final stabilization of a positive gay identity" (p. 52).

McDonald's (1982) research revealed the following: awareness of same-sex sexual attractions occurred at an average age of 13; first sexual experiences and understanding of the word "homosexual" occurred at age 15; disclosure of sexual orientation to a non-gay other took place at an average age of 23; and viewing oneself as having a positive gay identity took place at an average age of 24. What he learned, however, was that despite the averages there was great disparity in terms of the length of time between stages. For example, "the time elapsed between awareness of same-sex feelings and self-labeling ranged from 1 to 33 years" (p. 52). Also, "notable differences existed across studies in reference to the time lapses occurring between milestone events—especially those in adulthood" (p. 54). McDonald (1982) notes that social context is crucial to understanding milestone achievements in the coming out process. He also argues that rigid adherence to a sequential stage model, the prototype for heterosexual identity development models, ignores the influence of cultural factors such as society's views on homosexuality during a particular time frame on gay men's emerging senses of self.

Alderson (2003) is also a critic of the stage models, arguing that they do not take social factors into consideration in a satisfying manner. He proposed an Ecological Model of Gay Male Identity that incorporates both psychological and social influences. He divides his model into timeframes—Before Coming Out, During Coming Out, and Beyond Coming Out. Alderson believes that gay men have internal struggles between catalysts that indicate they might be gay and hindrances that encourage them to suppress feelings. A catalyst might be an erotic dream or falling in love with another man. A good example of a hindrance would be deeply internalized homophobia. When there is enough cognitive dissonance to propel the catalysts beyond the hindrances, a gay man is able to come out.

During the Coming Out timeframe, the individual is grappling with internalized homophobia, assuming a gay identity, and managing conflicting emotions. The degree of intensity depends on the balance of catalysts and hindrances: "If his environment is tolerant or accepting at every level (societal, parental/familial, cultural/spiritual, peer influence), he will have a much easier time self-identifying as a gay man than someone raised within an intolerant environment at any or all levels" (p. 78). The Beyond Coming Out phase refers to an individual's "own unique way to integrate connections to self, connections to the gay world, and reconnections to the straight world" (p. 80). Alderson's (2003) model is noteworthy for honoring external and internal influences that lead to gay identification and for incorporating both stages and processes in describing identity development. It also acknowledges that gay men will never "arrive at the same destination" (p. 82), thereby honoring everyone's identity.

Gay Teens

What narratives of identity development relate to gay youth? As cultural acceptance of the LGBTQ community increases, several of the classic models of identity development might feel dated. Citing Savin-Williams (2005), Cohler and Hammack (2007) note that "a new generation of youth, with the support of a new cultural discourse on sexual identity diversity, appears to enjoy same-sex relationships without recourse to concern that their same-sex desire makes them 'abnormal'" (p. 48). Cohler and Hammack (2007) criticize theories that insist on one way of developing: "We suggest that divergence in conceptual accounts of gay adolescent development emerges from a failure to fully acknowledge the salience of context—in understanding the relationship between identity and lived experience" (p. 48). Social changes, such as the Internet, social media, and the emergence of openly gay figures in the media, have altered the way gay adolescents live their lives and perceive their options.

As Cohler and Hammack (2007) explain, there are two competing narratives to describe adolescent sexual identity development:

> The first narrative, which we term the narrative of struggle and success, depicts gay youth as the victims of harassment and internalized homophobia, accompanied by serious mental health problems such as anxiety, depression, and suicidal ideation. But this narrative also suggests success in spite of struggle.
>
> (p. 49)

They describe another, different model:

> The second narrative, the narrative of emancipation, reveals the increasing fluidity in self-labeling among youth with same-sex desire, de-pathologizes the experience of sexual identity development among these youth, emphasizes the manner in which sexual minority youth cope with issues of minority stress (so significant as a factor accounting for personal distress among these youth), and extends the concept of normalcy.
>
> (p. 49)

Each narrative reflects a particular historical context, and each continues to be championed within certain circles.

According to Cohler and Hammock (2007),

> For many youth, a narrative of struggle and success continues to provide the best discursive frame for their own life stories. In this way, we argue that the narrative of emancipation has not *supplanted* but rather *supplemented* the narrative of struggle and success, creating greater heterogeneity in the developmental trajectories of youth with same-sex desire.
>
> (p. 54)

While the narrative of emancipation offers a more hopeful portrait—"they need not be promiscuous, get AIDS, and live in a ghetto" (p. 54)—it does not account for the experiences of youths who may want to hold on to the uniqueness of their sexual orientation. The model emboldens youth to dismiss their differences from the mainstream culture.

Hetrick and Martin (1987) noted that gay teens may use a number of coping strategies to manage social stigmatization. In particular, "the most important coping strategy for the homosexually oriented adolescent is learning to hide" (p. 35). One who is trying to hide is constantly monitoring his appearance, behaviors, and responses to others.

Over-monitoring of one's behavior can lead to neglecting or distorting others' responses and can reinforce one's belief in their inferiority.

Wright and Perry (2006) discussed the need for social support for gay youth, which is echoed by virtually all other models. Developing a sense of community is enormously important in terms of identity development. According to Wright and Perry, "the types of relationships a young person establishes during this period will shape the types of socialization opportunities they have" (p. 105). Wright and Perry's (2006) findings indicate that being out to one's social network is associated with experiencing lower levels of sexual identity distress. They posit that "the early effect of sexual identity distress is specific to people in the early phases of coming out and may have different effects at different ages or in later phases of psychosocial sexual development" (p. 106).

Providing affirmative services to gay youth often presents a challenge to counselors who hold traditional, conservative values, or have had little exposure to gay people. Even those who intellectually accept homosexuality may emotionally reject same-sex relationships or individuals who do not conform to established gender norms. Unless the counselor becomes aware of their faulty assumptions and homoprejudice, they may project their misconceptions and fears onto their clients. Counselors must confront their personal prejudice, myths, fears, and stereotypes regarding sexual orientation as part of the process of expanding their self-awareness about gay people in general and the meaning of gay identity to particular individuals. The first thing to remember is that it is impossible to help someone who is struggling with coming out if they do not perceive you as being open to, comfortable with, and supportive of this type of conversation.

Midlife

According to Kimmel and Sang (2003), there are three complementary views on identity development during midlife. The first is that "adult development is a relatively continuous process of maturation or unfolding of personality themes that were laid down early in life" (p. 604). The second is that adult development consists of a "series of predictable stages or periods when significant change or crisis may occur" (p. 604). The third is that "social age norms, historical effects, and idiosyncratic transitions combine to provide the pattern of adult lives" (p. 604). Alas, research on adult development has been almost exclusively heterosexual in focus. "One implication of this omission is that gays and lesbians have had few developmental models for conceptualizing their own life course or interpreting normative crises they may experience" (p. 604).

Kimmel and Sang (2003) note that, in the absence of models for development, one can at least identify certain themes that may be unique to gay men at midlife. They noted that one crucial factor that influences midlife is timing of coming out.

> For example, men who do not come out as gay until midlife experience these years as a prolonged search for identity, especially in terms of sexuality. Guilt, secrecy, heterosexual marriage, conflicted relationships with both women and men, and tentative forays into gay social life often characterize this struggle. The result can be delayed social development, traumatic family crises, and a dramatic change in life when one comes out.
>
> (pp. 614–615)

A marked contrast is "the gay man who recognizes that he is gay early in life and takes advantage of the benefits this identity offers, such as an opportunity to cross social boundaries of race, class, and age" (p. 615).

Several studies (Kimmel & Sang, 2003) assert that a variety of factors contribute to gay men potentially experiencing intensified midlife crises. Among these factors are "concerns about issues of mortality and a search for meaning and wholeness in life within a heterosexist society" (p. 620), fears of loss of virility, attractiveness, and physical health; and, possibly, family and occupational stressors, such as caring for sick relatives or missing out on a promotion. Kimmel and Sang reference the unpublished work of Kooden in discussing some of the developmental challenges for gay men at midlife, namely "confronting the fact that one's physical persona has changed so that one cannot be loved for physical attributes alone, taking responsibility for the choices one has made so far, and finding one's own voice." The importance of finding one's voice in midlife is pertinent given that many gay men "often hide part of themselves from others" (p. 621) for at least some stretches of their lives. Midlife can be an important time for gay men to more confidently direct themselves toward what they want in life, and to reflect on the families and connections they have established.

Kimmel and Sang also forward a strengths-based attitude about gay men at midlife, noting that many gay men deal with crises regarding their identities from earlier ages and may be particularly well-equipped to deal with new developmental challenges. Gay men who have successfully managed crises in their lives may be in a plum position to "take advantage of a creative stance towards midlife that yields high levels of developmental potential" (p. 621).

Aging

Baltes and Baltes (1993) posited that psychological, biological, and social variability increases as individuals get older. Many assume that older gay men are lonely and miserable, but much has been done to dispel these myths. According to Reid (1995), new models have argued that "the unusual challenges experienced by older bisexuals, lesbians, and gay men place them at an advantage and, hence, promote successful aging" (p. 215). Whereas in recent history homosexuals were ignored by social scientists, today the increased demand for civil rights by the gay community have focused attention on older gay men.

Like Kimmel and Sang, Reid credits Francher and Henkin (1973; cited in Reid, 1995) for suggesting that successful adaptation to the loneliness and pain associated with living in a homophobic culture could translate into learning valuable coping skills that will aid a gay man later in life. Reid (1995) cites Featherman, Smith, and Peterson's (1990) concept of "adaptive competence" (p. 220), which is described as the skill needed to weather the inevitable changes and challenges associated with aging. According to Reid (1995), the

> individualized nature of development in late life draws our attention to individual differences in adaptation to varying developmental conditions, events, and outcomes. Such concepts of variability and plasticity are crucial components in our understanding of successes and difficulties in the lives of older lesbians, gay men, and bisexuals. (pp. 220–221)

Reid (1995) cites Baltes and Baltes (1993), who posit their model of successful aging—selective optimization with compensation: Optimal aging states that people select behaviors and experiences that will optimize their personal control, life goals, the activities they choose to engage in, and their interests. Optimization reflects adjustment to the reality of those relationships and behaviors that are fulfilling to the individual. Friend's model addresses adaptability and resilience and how these qualities benefit the LGBTQ community in the aging process.

Friend imagines two outcomes in terms of identity formation. As described by Reid (1995), the first and more preferable is to reject homophobic ideas and "reconstruct a new meaning for the feelings and experiences associated with being lesbian or gay (p. 222). These seniors are referred to as "affirmative." The other alternative is to incorporate homophobic ideas into beliefs and feelings about the self. The individual might internalize homophobia, keep his identity a secret, and be filled with self-loathing. Alternately, he might focus on "passing." There are unique challenges gay men may face as seniors that might make hiding one's identity a self-protective strategy. Many gay men do not have adult children to care for them in their older age; if medical conditions dictate, a gay man might need to transfer to an assisted living or nursing home facility. If dealing with homophobic staff, a gay man may feel the need to re-enter the closet to cope, which could bring up feelings of sadness, loneliness, and anger.

According to Reid (1995), positive adjustment to a gay identity is linked with higher self-esteem and self-acceptance. He credited the work of Kimmel (1978) in noting that, as men age, their sexual experiences change in meaning and amount, with older men reporting that they put "less accent on genitals and more on the total person" (Reid, 1995, p. 223).

Besides those already mentioned, there are a number of other unique concerns related to aging in gay men. These include "discriminatory social practices; rules, laws, and attitudes; absence of children to provide emotional support, physical security, and emotional assistance; being prevented from visiting or being visited by life partners in hospitals and nursing homes; and legal discrimination in terms of being prevented from inheriting a life partner's properties and assets" (p. 224). Ageism adds another layer of difficulty to the lives of older gay men. Gay male culture in particular is youth-oriented; privilege is granted to the young and hard-bodied. The concept of accelerated aging applies here. Studies have been conducted in which gay men were asked at which age middle age begins and at what age one becomes old. Gay men tended to believe they entered middle and older age sooner than straight men.

Writing on gay men at midlife emphasizes how the timing of coming out impacts a gay man's experience of middle age, and how various factors can create an intensified midlife crisis for gay men. Establishing one's voice is an important theme in midlife, and gay men who have successfully adapted to previous struggles may be in a strong position to handle the transitions of middle age. Similarly, gay seniors may have experiences managing conflict, turmoil, and change that can ease the transition to older age.

In thinking about sexual identity development for gay men, it is crucial to consider other identities an individual possesses. Garnets (2002) wrote about the challenges gay men of color have in terms of integrating multiple identities that each have the potential to result in social oppression. Current research focuses on how members of ethnic minorities negotiate establishing a dual identity as a sexual minority and as a person of color. Additionally, accepting a homosexual identity may have different meaning for different groups.

References

Alderson, K. G. (2003). The ecological model of gay male identity. *The Canadian Journal of Human Sexuality, 12,* 75–85.

Allport, G. (1955). *Becoming: Basic considerations for a psychology of personality.* New Haven: Yale University Press.

Baltes, P., & Baltes, M. (1993). *Successful aging: Perspectives from the behavioral sciences.* New York: Cambridge University Press.

Berger, P. L., & Luckman, T. (1966). *The social construction of reality.* New York: Doubleday.

Bilodeau, B. L., & Renn, K. A. (2005). Analysis of LGBT identity development models and implications for practice. In R. L. Sanlo (Ed.), *Sexual orientation and gender identity: Research, policy, and personal perspectives: New directions for student services, number 111.* San Franciso, CA: Jossey-Bass.

Cass, V. C. (1979). Homosexual identity formation: A theoretical model. *Journal of Homosexuality, 4*(3), 219–233.

Cass, V. C. (1984). Homosexual identity: A concept in need of definition. *Journal of Homosexuality, 9*(2/3), 105–126.

Cohler, B. J., & Hammack, P. L. (2007). The psychological world of the gay teenager: Social change, narrative, and "normality." *Journal of Youth and Adolescence, 36,* 47–59.

Coleman, E. (1982). Developmental stages of the coming out process. *Journal of Homosexuality, 7,* 31–43.

Cooper, L. (2008). On the other side: Supporting sexual minority students. *British Journal of Guidance & Counseling, 36*(4), 425–440. doi: 10.1080/03069880802364577

D'Augelli, A. R. (1994). Lesbian and gay male development: Steps toward an analysis of lesbians' and gay men's lives. In B. Greene and G. Herek (Eds.), *Contemporary perspectives in gay and lesbian psychology,* Vol. 1, (pp. 118–132). Newbury Park, CA: Sage.

Davies, D. (1996). Towards a model of gay affirmative therapy. In D. Davies and C. Neal (Eds.), *Pink therapy: A guide for counselors working with lesbian, gay and bisexual clients.* Buckingham, UK: Open University Press.

Dube, E. M., & Savin-Williams, R. C. (1999). Sexual identity development among ethnic sexual-minority male youths. *Developmental Psychology, 35*(6), 1389–1398.

Fassinger, R. E. (1991). The hidden minority: Issues and challenges in working with lesbians and gay men. *Counseling Psychologist, 19,* 157–176.

Fassinger, R. E. (1996). Notes from the margins: Integrating lesbian experience into the vocational psychology of women. *Journal of Vocational Behavior, 48,* 160–175.

Fassinger, R. E., & Miller, B. A. (1996). Validation of an inclusive model of sexual minority identification on a sample of gay men. *Journal of Homosexuality, 32*(2), 53–78.

Frank, D. A., II, & Cannon, E. P. (2010). Queer theory as pedagogy in counselor education: A framework for diversity training. *Journal of LGBT Issues in Counseling, 4*(1), 18–31.

Garnets, L. D. (2002). Sexual orientations in perspective. *Cultural Diversity and Ethnic Minority Psychology, 8*(2), 115–129.

Gonsiorek, J. C. (1995). Gay male identities: Concepts and issues. In A. R. D'Augelli and C. Patterson (Eds.), *Lesbian, gay, and bisexual identities over the lifespan: Psychological perspectives.* New York: Oxford University Press.

Greene, B. (1994). Lesbian and gay sexual orientations: Implications for clinical training, practice, and research. In B. Greene and G. M. Herek (Eds.). *Lesbian and gay psychotherapy: Theory, research, and clinical applications.* Thousand Oaks. CA: Sage.

Grossman, A., & Kerner, M. (1998). Support networks of gay male and lesbian youth. *International Journal of Sexuality and Gender Studies, 3,* 27–46.

Haldeman, D.C. (2007). The village people: Identity and development in the gay male community. In K. J. Bieschke, R. M. Perez, and K. A. DeBord (Eds.), *Handbook of counseling and psychotherapy with lesbian, gay, bisexual, and transgender clients.* Washington, DC: American Psychological Association.

Herek, G. M. (1999). The psychology of sexual prejudice. *Current Directions in Psychological Science, 9*(1), 19–22.

Hetrick, E. S., & Martin, A.D. (1987). Developmental issues and their resolution for gay and lesbian adolescents. *Journal of Homosexuality, 14,* 25–43.

Kimmel, D.C., & Sang, B. E. (2003). Lesbians and gay men in midlife. In L. Garnets and D.C. Kimmel (Eds.), *Psychological perspectives on gay, lesbian, and bisexual experiences.* New York: Columbia University Press.

Marszalek, J. F. III, Cashwell, C. S., Dunn, M. S., & Heard Jones, K. (2004). Comparing gay identity development theory to cognitive development: An empirical study. *Journal of Homosexuality, 48*(1), 103–122.

Matthews, C., & Salazar, C. F. (2012). An integrative, empowerment model for helping lesbian, gay, and bisexual youth negotiate the coming-out process. *Journal of LGBT Issues in Counseling, 6,* 96–117.

McDonald, G. J. (1982). Individual differences in the coming out process for gay men: Implications for theoretical models. *Journal of Homosexuality, 8*(1), 47–60.

Reid, J. D. (1995). Development in late life: Older lesbian and gay lives. In A. R. D'Augelli and C. Patterson (Eds.), *Lesbian, gay, and bisexual identities over the lifespan: Psychological perspectives.* New York: Oxford University Press.

Savin-Williams, R. C. (1988). Theoretical perspectives accounting for adolescent homosexuality. *Journal of Adolescent Health, 9*(6), 95–104.

Savin-Williams, R. C. (2005). *The new gay teenager.* Cambridge, MA: Harvard University Press.

Schubotz, D., & McNamee, H. (2009). "I knew I wasn't like anybody else": Young men's accounts of coming out and being gay in Northern Ireland. *Child Care in Practice, 19,* 193–208.

Troiden, R. R. (1988). *Gay and lesbian identity: A sociological analysis.* New York: General Hall.

Troiden, R. R. (1989). The formation of homosexual identities. *Journal of Homosexuality, 17*(1/2), 43–73.

Wright, E. R., & Perry, B. L. (2006). Sexual identity distress, social support, and the health of gay, lesbian, and bisexual youth. *Journal of Homosexuality, 51*(1), 81–110.

2 The Role of Friendships in the Lives of Gay Men, Adolescents, and Boys

Michael M. Kocet

Gay men are often forced to internalize identities that conform to traditional hegemonic conceptualizations of how society believes masculinity should be portrayed (Fassinger, 1991; Price, 1999). Consequently, gay men are presented with many challenges that prevent them from seeking out their true identities or finding their true selves. For some, identifying as a gay man is not a clear or easy decision. These men have not yet reconciled the possibility of sharing their identity with family and friends. Instead, they live in a state of dissonance. This dissonance exists because disclosing one's sexual orientation can sometimes bring with it fear of rejection by significant others, as well as other risks, such as job loss or subtle or blatant forms of harassment (Eichberg, 1990). There are multiple issues that can prevent gay men from creating and maintaining healthy gay identities. Indeed, personal support systems may serve to empower gay men in helping to reduce the risks related to substance abuse, depression, anxiety, and other mental health issues. One such form of personal support systems is through friendships. This chapter will explore how friendships between gay males impacts the coming out process, as well as creating a self-affirming positive gay identity. This chapter will also address how counselors, educators, and other helping professionals working with gay boys, adolescents, and men can help these males form healthy and meaningful friendships with other gay men and boys in order to foster a strong support system.

The Role of Gay Friendships

Gay friendships, according to Nardi (1999), not only offer social support, but also influence identity formation and assist in creating a personal sense of what it means to be gay. Nardi states that "friendship among gay men is a means toward learning more about one's gay identity and a source of freedom from the limitations imposed by the culture on being able to live a gay life" (p. 167).

While there are certain types of relationships that have clear societal, familial, and even legal definitions, such as wife and husband, son or daughter, aunt or uncle, the literature on friendship offers no conclusive or generally accepted definition. However, Fehr (1996) defines friendship as an intimate, personal, interdependent relationship between two persons; a relationship that is mutual, reciprocal, and involves varying degrees of companionship, intimacy, affection, trust, mutual sharing, and self-disclosure. It is a voluntary relationship in which the participants respond to one another personally and have some sort of social closeness to one another. Further, friendship involves an interdependence that helps facilitate the social-emotional goals of the participants and may involve varying types of companionship, intimacy, affection, and mutual assistance (Deci, LaGuardia, Moller, Scheiner, & Ryan, 2006). The relationship lasts over a significant period of time.

The literature on friendship delves into why these kinds of relationships are significant and why certain friendships are more important than others and often play more of a key role than others (Allan, 1979). The literature covers a variety of friendships, from early childhood (Duck, 1983; Elman & Kennedy-Moore, 2003; Selman & Schultz, 1990) to adult (Flora, 2013) and even more specifically to friendships between women (Bonior, 2011; Levine, 2009), boys' friendships (Way, 2011), friendships between straight and gay men (Price, 1999), male friendships (Brooks, 2006), and friendships between gay men (Gottlieb, 2008; Kocet, 2001; Nardi, 1999). By engaging in friendships with other gay men, men who have not openly disclosed their sexual orientation can share these "private understandings"—the daily struggles of managing and accepting a gay identity. Due to the burden of having to manage multiple identities, gay men often feel alone and disengaged from their primary network of family, friends, and co-workers. Duck (1983) underscores the critical role that friendships between gay men and boys play in creating psychologically healthy "safe zones." These safe zones can help create a place where gay men can speak honestly about their fears, desires, and interests. Further, it allows them to question what it means to be a gay man in today's world in a context that is unconditionally supportive and understanding.

A continuum of friendships appear to exist in the literature, beginning with more casual friendships, often referred to as acquaintances, and progressing to more significant friendships, sometimes classified as close or best friends (Fehr, 1996; Kocet, 2001; Nardi, 1992). In his study on gay men's friendships, Kocet (2001) reported that study participants spoke of having volley ball friends, dinner friends, and bar friends and that gay men often categorize their gay friends as either casual, serious, or close. The friendship literature attests to the fact that all types of friendships have value and meaning. Casual relationships help serve as a reinforcement of social norms or affirmation of being a part of a shared culture of gay men. Casual friends also provide gay men with ways to view other expressions of gay identity that can be tested and applied by boys, adolescents, or men just coming out. Having closer friends provides opportunities for deeper intimacy and caring. This can result in more significant kinds of sharing of one's life and a stronger awareness of self.

Gay friendships can serve as a buffer against dealing with traumatizing or difficult experiences. Fear of physical or emotional harm from strangers, or even family and friends is a daily concern for many gay boys, adolescents, and men. On a basic level, if gay men and boys select to socialize with other gay males, they reduce the risk of being exposed to harassment or serious emotional or physical injury by others who have negative views about homosexuality. By limiting their socialization to primarily gay men, they can eliminate much of the fear or distrust of confiding in heterosexual individuals who may not understand or support their sexual orientation. However, a disadvantage of limiting contact to just gay men leaves out the possibility of developing strong connections with lesbians, as well as heterosexual individuals who may share their personal hobbies, interests, and insights (Price, 1999).

Woolwine (2000) conducted an extensive study to investigate the concept of "gay community," if it truly exists, and how it is experienced by gay men. Through his research Woolwine identified three ways that gay men experience "gay community": one way to be considered a part of the gay community is to have a gay identity, including gay friendships, also, an additional way is to be involved in gay political organizations, or live in a gay neighborhood. Another way to create a gay community is through membership in gay organizations or groups where gay men can meet others like themselves. Finally, gay community can be achieved through face-to-face interactions, through friendship networks.

Friendship Theories

There are various types of friendship theories that have evolved within the literature (Adams & Blieszner, 1989, 1994; Cole & Bradac, 1996; Conville, 1991; Duck, 1977, 1998; Fehr, 1996). These theories have guided the examination of friendship networks. One theory is the Reinforcement Theory. This theory grew out of behavioral psychology and maintains the notion that we are friends with individuals who give us rewards. A second theory is the Reinforcement-Affect Model, which stresses that others' agreement with us reinforces positive responses from us. This theory also believes that we like others who espouse values/attitudes similar to our own and choose to be friends with those who think and hold beliefs similar to our own. A third theory of friendship is the social exchange and equity theory. This theory believes that the process of assessing satisfaction involves comparisons with the outcomes other people are receiving in the relationship as well as comparisons with our own past relationships. A basic assumption of equity theory is that we have to try to maximize our outcomes in relationships. Actual equity exists when there is a legitimate and real balance within a friendship or relationship, whereas psychology equity exists where one partner in the relationship creates an illusion that equity (or reciprocity) exists within a relationship, when, in fact, it does not. Friendship models change over the lifespan and individuals' expectations or needs in a friendship change over time.

Challenges in Men's Friendships

The literature addresses the difficulty that many men have in forming mutually satisfying and life-enhancing friendship. As Cohen (2001) points out, male friendship remain activity-based. Men share feelings of liking one another and being liked by their friendships through what Swain (2001) terms "covert intimacy." This covert intimacy is a sharing of sports, doing favors for their male friends, and teasing. Men do express intimacy with one another, just not in words. Men's friendships can sometimes be in a state of dissonance; men desperately seek a connection with other men, but often times feel a disconnection and do not have the skills necessary to facilitate open and direct communication. They also have difficulty expressing a wider range of affect in their male-to-male interactions. Men sometimes have difficulty self-closing personal information, but will share through physical gesturing, as well as by maintaining a joking behavior to communicate closeness (Nardi, 1992; Price, 1999; Swain, 2001). This can be said of gay friends. Humor and teasing are often found to be an integral part of friendships between gay men (Kocet, 2001).

Many gay men report that they feel closer to other gay men than to other individuals, regardless of other status characteristics of the gay men, such as age or race. This closeness is due in part to their shared identity and a set of values that develop in a culture that has routinely marginalized and oppressed them. Gay men consistently talk about their friends in terms of: having a shared belief system; sharing of feelings and emotions; having a sense of belonging to a larger community of gay men and having men to do things with; and tangible aid in terms of doing favors and providing assistance to other gay men. Participation in the gay communities' institutions contributes to gay identity achievement and gay identity leads to the creation and maintenance of gay communities, which provide a context for reproducing identity in a new generation of people searching for meaning and friendship.

Gay men need social support for personal and professional need fulfillment and to allow social cohesion to occur. Gay men create social networks as a way to empower each other and to create an identity that enhances self-awareness. Gay men just beginning the self-exploration process regarding their sexual identity often learn about themselves and who they are through their interactions with gay men who are out of the closet. These gay networks of friends and acquaintances, manifested through the institutions and organizations, assist people in making the transition into a gay identity, into gay neighborhoods, and into gay political and social communities (Gottlieb, 2008; Nardi, 1999; Wood, 2000).

Gay Men's Social Networks

Nardi (1999) purports that gay men's friendships are "a unique combination of normative 'male' topics, such as work and politics, and normative 'female' topics, such as personal relationships, friendships, sexual behavior, health concerns, and thoughts about the future" (pp. 144–145). Gluth and Kiselica (1994) state that

> through the process of coming out to others, the gay client comes to understand the consequences (both good and bad) of his or her actions. If the client develops strong social networks, he or she is better able to risk rejection. By finding homosexual friends, the client is not only getting practice in coming out to more risky people but forming a strong support network as well.
>
> (p. 167)

Nardi and Sherrod (1994) address the unique role that gay men sometimes serve within each other's lives—that of family member. Oftentimes, this role is referred to within the gay community as "families of choice" (Penn, 1997). Nardi (1999) notes that friendships among gay men often replicate a family-life role, especially when a gay man's family-of-origin or biological family is either emotionally or geographically distant.

Gay Social Proxemics

Proxemics is defined as the study of the individual's use and perception of social and personal space. Proxemics also involves how people control their use of space to enhance their life. Space and social distance is facilitated and controlled by people in order to foster certain types of social interaction and development of the self (Frey & Carlock, 1989).

Kocet (2001) coined a term, "gay social proxemics," to better explain gay men's friendships. Gay social proxemics is defined as

> the closeness among gay male friends as demonstrated through social distance, usually in the form of touch and spatial distance, as well as through emotional and physical closeness. Gay social proxemics involves the normative greeting patterns among gay male friends
>
> (pp. 107–108)

For example, gay male friends frequently greet one another with some type of physical contact, such as a hug, a kiss, or a combination of the two. Gay social proxemics involves touching that is often indicative of comfortability, affirmation, and connection among gay men. It appears that proxemics in gay men strongly builds social networks and is a demonstration of the commonality and shared life with other gay men, adolescents, and boys. Whether kissing, hugging, or sitting on each other's laps, gay men and boys will often stretch the boundaries of gender conformity and will break traditional social distance assumed by heterosexual men and boys when it comes to their friendships with other gay males.

Gay Social Network Facilitators

Gay social network facilitators are those activities, places, icons, and institutions that foster a sense of identity in gay men, both individually and collectively as a member of the gay community. Gay social network facilitators help normalize the coming out process and help build a sense of commonality with other gay individuals (Kocet, 2001). Examples of gay social network facilitators can be gay newspapers, gay magazines, gay blogs, LGBT places of worship, gay movies, gay-themed television programs, and gay organizations and clubs. Another facilitator that helps many gay men find support and resources about the gay community is through technology, particular the Internet, smart phones, and social media.

Through chat rooms, gay dating/friendship websites, and gay social smart phone applications, gay men can learn about various sources of information about gay culture, health information, ways to come out to family, friends, and co-workers, meet potential romantic partners, and establish and maintain friendships with other gay males. Gay bars and dance clubs can also serve as a facilitator of gay social networks and provide a safe haven for gay men to socialize with one another. Going to a gay establishment is often one of the first steps for gay men to begin the coming out process. However, it is important to note that for gay males who are in recovery from drugs or alcohol, seeking gay friendship and support in a bar environment may not be conducive to maintaining sobriety. Likewise, gay boys and adolescents not able to populate gay clubs need healthy and age-appropriate alternatives. Many gay boys and young adults seek out such friendship support through Gay-Straight Alliances in middle school, high school, and colleges/universities. As Nardi (1999) points out,

> maintenance of friendship depends on a combination of factors that include proximity, interaction, and communication (either face-to-face, email, phone calls,

> or contact through social media), similarity on a variety of characteristics, self-disclosure, openness, assurances that the friendship is important, social support, communal rewards (concern with the others' well-being), allowing friends to be themselves, following social conventions and rules about friendship maintenance, engaging in constructive discussions about disagreements, making the effort to keep in touch, and finding time to interact.
>
> (pp. 152–153)

Social Network Activities with Gay Friends

Social network activities are those mostly pleasurable events or activities that gay men, adolescents, and boys participate in as friends. These social activities can be either spontaneous or planned in advance, depending on the group or pair of individuals involved in the activity. Woolwine (2000) contends that active membership in a gay organization is

> a means of achieving supportive and nurturing relationships for oneself and because they activate, and develop, that part of oneself which one believes to need support and nurturing. Involvement in expressive or primary groups represents calculated attempts to bring about a certain type of self or to develop a specific part of the self.
>
> (pp. 21–22)

For example, many gay men are active members in formal gay sports organizations, such as gay softball or gay volleyball leagues. Participation in these organizations can be extremely important and can serve two primary purposes: 1) to engage in healthy competition with other men, but without the fierce de-masculinization that often occurs in traditional male sports; 2) but it also provides a safe environment to ask other gay men questions about their experiences. Gay sports, gay book clubs, or other gay organizations can provide a healthy alternative to gay bars and clubs to help gay men fulfill the need to socialize and seek out support.

Gay organizations can also serve as a model for positive coping for gay males. Through a meshing of traditional masculine interaction (more action-oriented, activity based) coupled with a traditional feminine model of social interaction (focus more on emotions, connections, and expression of feelings), gay organizations take the strengths from both masculine and feminine socialization models and create a social network that is strong and cohesive. This model accentuates resiliency in the gay community and constructive communal action to collectively resolve difficulties and challenges from a society that typically discriminates against gay men. Through these gay organizations, gay men can face these challenges together and identify areas for personal growth that sustains psychological wellbeing (Kocet, 2001).

Gay social organizations and gatherings do not have to be established through formal means. For example, small, intimate gatherings of gay men, such as Saturday morning "breakfast clubs" consisting of groups of gay male friends who gather weekly for food and fellowship can also provide the necessary support system to help gay men face work, social, and familial challenges. These informal groups provide a stable and on-going support network and allow new members to join on a more fluid and flexible basis.

While adult gay men often have these formal sports, political, and social organizations, younger gay adolescents and boys often lack such formal opportunities to bond. Adult gay men are encouraged to help younger gay men form similar sports, music, and other types of social clubs and groups, that pay special attention to the needs of being gay males that cannot be achieved through mainstream groups.

Friendships as Therapeutic Interventions

As Rubin (1985) and Fehr (1996) have indicated, friendships are without formal societal recognition and lack social rituals. Because the meanings of friendship are deeply embedded in the lives of gay boys and men, they may not be consciously aware of the significance that these lasting friends play in helping facilitate movement within the gay identity process. When gay males have supportive friendships from other gay men and boys, there appears to be less confliction in the authoring of one's identity.

Social networks play a central role in helping men and youths in the early phases of the coming out process feel safe and comfortable while testing, exploring, and developing a new understanding of self. As Nardi points out: "Friendship among gay men is a means toward learning more about one's gay identity and a source of freedom from the limitations imposed by the culture on being able to live a gay life" (1999, p. 166). Gay friends also assist those just coming out by helping facilitate entry into the socialization process of the gay community. Gay social networks serve multiple purposes, including a source of companionship, a surrogate family, and a shared common experience, as well as providing the ability to discuss the coming out process with others in similar experiences, and ways to manage homophobia and discrimination from the outside world. The tendency for gay men to socialize primarily within gay social circles comes out of the need to feel safe and secure. While during the past few decades we have seen a more positive shift in societal attitudes and beliefs about gay people, there is still negative sentiment that exists regarding sexual orientation.

By becoming familiar with friendship interventions, counselors and helping professionals can assist gay men in connecting with community programs and service providers to help reduce social isolation, offer emotional support, improve communication, and to provide them with the primary services they need to foster personal growth and awareness (Blieszner & Adams, 1992). Adams and Blieszner (1994) state that the friendship literature has failed to develop a significant understanding of the effects of friendship on both social structural position and psychological disposition. Kocet's (2001) study on gay men's friendships found a positive psychological impact of friendships between gay men on reducing social isolation, anxiety and depression, and increasing self-esteem, social cohesion, and support. Friendship networks can facilitate acclimation into the gay community despite these underlying struggles.

Therapists need to be comfortable discussing issues of sexuality, the coming out process, and the creating and maintaining of gay romantic relationships, and must create safe environments to share. Counselors are also encouraged to bring a sense of creativity and spontaneity to the therapeutic relationship. Counselors and helping professionals working with gay men, adolescents, and boys need to be familiar with the cultural importance of friendships within the gay community. Counselors need to create therapeutic structures to ensure that gay men and boys who are just coming out are creating gay social networks that help in the transition phase of adopting a healthy gay identity.

One of the goals of providing treatment for gay male clients is to help these men create unencumbered lives that assist them in fashioning gay identities that are based on personal strengths and the utilization of community and school resources. When working with gay clients, it is important for counselors and helping professionals to develop a comprehensive treatment plan that meets the goals of the therapeutic relationship. Counselors need to engage in a "friendship assessment" with gay male clients to assess the quality of their clients' friendships with other gay men and boys and to work through any social challenges, difficulties, or inability to access community resources where gay males can meet one another through shared interests, hobbies, or common pursuits. Therapists should help clients identify what may be preventing them from engaging in mutually satisfying and growth filled friendships with other gay males.

Alexander (1998) encourages therapists working with gay clients to reflect on how they will deal with issues such as: self-disclosure to clients if the therapist is also gay, explaining the purpose of therapy, and establishment of trust and assurance of safety. Gay clients will often be apprehensive about seeking treatment for fear that the counselor may not be accepting of gay issues and may not have the training or ability to deal with clients who are sexual minorities.

A main consideration when working with gay boys, adolescents, and men just beginning the coming out process is the establishment of a friendship network. Goals of the sessions need to be created in collaboration with the client and should empower the client to work at creating friendships based on mutuality, sharing, and connection with other gay males. Therapists, educators, and other service providers working with gay men can utilize an understanding of gay friendship networks to better facilitate the coming out process, which will ultimately help gay males achieve psychological well-being. Counselors need to encourage clients to create friendships that are healthy and affirming. By having positive friendships, gay men and boys can work on reducing their feelings of isolation, despair, and anxiety, and provide alternatives to self-harming and abusive behavior. Friendship networks can facilitate acclimation into the gay community despite these underlying struggles.

Another area for counselors to consider, when working with gay males, is geographic location. This is especially true for gay boys and men who live in rural or remote areas that lack formal gay organization and support systems. In cases like these, counselors may need to help gay males facilitate connections through gay social chat rooms, blogs, and apps designed for gay men to form friendships or romantic relationships, or through social media, such as Facebook and Twitter. However, counselors must caution clients' use of the Internet and other social media and use proper judgment when creating virtual connections. This is especially true for younger gay boys and adolescents who may need appropriate supervision when attempting to forge "cyber-relationships" with other gay kids online. Further study needs to investigate the role that technology and social media play in the formation and fostering of gay friendships online. Counselors need to work with clients and explore alternative forms of support and community. Counselors and service providers must caution clients that these alternative online communities may be laden with inaccurate or altered identities and that men and boys who participate in these virtual communities may not be who they appear. Technology however may serve as a primary vehicle of fostering gay friendships for men who feel socially isolated or who live far away from any type of openly gay community.

Two questions can be posed to gay males that may aid professionals in their work with gay boys and men: How can counselors create interventions that assist gay men and boys in creating friendship networks that contribute to an increase in self-acceptance, emotional and psychological wellbeing, self-efficacy and empowerment, goal achievement, and overall quality of life for gay men and boys? And, what types of friendship interventions are most effective for counselors to utilize with gay boys, adolescents, and men to reduce mental health and medical crises and provide strengths-based services?

Counselors can utilize various techniques to build the interpersonal skills of clients in order to prepare them to create healthy social networks with other gay boys, teens, and men. For example, counselors may give clients homework assignments that help reduce the fear or apprehension of socializing in gay establishments or clubs. Counselors may assign a client to go to a gay dance club, join a gay book club, play on a gay sports team, or attend a GSA meeting. For clients who are at further stages of development, encouraging them to become active in leadership positions within political or religious organizations that are gay affirming might help increase self-worth and universality with others in their communities.

By assisting gay boys and men find and become active participants in organizations within the gay community, gay males can reduce feelings of isolation, depression, suicidality, and a proclivity to engage in unhealthy or high-risk behavior. Gay males who have strong friendship networks with other gay men may have a stronger propensity for higher self-esteem and sense of purpose.

Suggestions for Future Research

One area that is sorely lacking in the professional literature is the impact that gay friendships have, especially on gay men and boys of color. Most of the studies and literature in the field focus on Eurocentric perspectives, leaving out racial, ethnic, and other cultural considerations.

As Woolwine (2000, p. 21) states:

> One identifies emotionally with certain particular other gay men, one feels a "kinship," and through this one experiences the community. It is here primarily that one learns how to be "in the life," and it is here that one comes to identify as gay by identifying emotionally with particular other gay men.

Further study also needs to be done to compare gay friendship networks between boys and men in large metropolitan areas and in small cities or rural areas, including the similarities and differences between the two.

Coming to terms with one's sexual identity is not an easy process. Some gay men and boys are not able to achieve psychological wellbeing and, instead, get caught in a cycle of addiction (either sexual, drug, or alcohol related, or a combination of all three) or engage in other unhealthy behavior. While friendships with other gay men, adolescents, and boys cannot alone prevent psychological distress, gay social networks and friendships certainly can alleviate the burden of managing a sexual identity alone. As the research on gay men suggests, friendship networks can be instrumental in maintaining psychological wellbeing and can assist in creating satisfying and enriching lives as gay boys, adolescents, and men.

References

Adams, R., & Blieszner, R. (1989). *Older adult friendships.* Newbury Park, CA: Sage.

Adams, R., & Blieszner, R. (1994). An integrative conceptual framework for friendship research. *Journal of Social and Personal Relationships, 11*(2), 163–184.

Alexander, C. (1998). Treatment planning for gay and lesbian clients. *Journal of Gay and Lesbian Social Services, 8*(4), 95–106.

Allan, G. (1979). *A sociology of friendship and kinship.* Boston, MA: George Allen & Unwin.

Blieszner, R., & Adams, R. (1992). *Adult friendship.* Newbury Park, CA: Sage.

Bonior, A. (2011). *The friendship fix.* New York: Thomas Dunne Books.

Brooks, M. (2006). Man-to-man: A body talk between male friends. *Qualitative Inquiry, 12*(1), 185–207.

Cohen, T. (2001). Men and masculinity: A text reader. Belmont, CA: Wadsworth Thompson Learning.

Cole, T., & Bradac, J. (1996). A lay theory of relational satisfaction with best friends. *Journal of Social and Personal Relationships, 13*(1), 57–83.

Conville, R. (1991). *Relational transitions: The evolution of personal relationships.* New York: Praeger.

Deci, E., LaGuardia, J., Moller, A., Scheiner, M., & Ryan, R. (2006). On the benefits of giving as well as receiving autonomy support: Mutuality in close friends. *Personality and Social Psychology Bulletin, 32*(3), 313–327.

Duck, S. (1977). *The study of acquaintance.* Westmead, UK: Saxon House.

Duck, S. (1983). *Friends for life: The psychology of close relationships.* New York: St. Martin's Press.

Duck, S. (1998). *Human relationships.* Thousand Oaks, CA: Sage.

Eichberg, R. (1990). *Coming out: An act of love.* New York: Plume.

Elman, N., & Kennedy-Moore, E. (2003). *The unwritten rules of friendship: Simple strategies to help your child make friends.* Boston, MA: Little Brown & Company

Fassinger, R. E. (1991). The hidden minority: Issues and challenges in working with lesbians and gay men. *Counseling Psychologist, 19,* 157–176.

Fehr, B. (1996). *Friendship processes.* Thousand Oaks, CA: Sage.

Fehr, B. (2000). The life cycle of friendship. In C. Hendrick and S. Hendrick (Eds.). *Close relationships: A sourcebook.* Thousand Oaks, CA: Sage.

Flora, C. (2013). *Friendfluence: The surprising ways friends make us who we are.* New York: Doubleday.

Frey, D., & Carlock, J. (1989). *Enhancing self esteem* (2nd ed.). Muncie, IN: Accelerated Development.

Gluth, D., & Kiselica, M. (1994). Coming out quickly: A brief counseling approach to deaing with gay and lesbian adjustment issues. *Journal of Mental Health Counseling, 16*(2), 163–173.

Gottlieb, A. (2008). *On the meaning of friendship between gay men.* New York: Routledge.

Kocet, M. M. (2001). *An examination of friendship between gay men and its impact on psychological well-being and identity disclosure: A case study.* Unpublished doctoral dissertation. University of Arkansas.

Levine, I. (2009). *Best friends forever: Surviving a breakup with your best friend.* New York: Overook Press.

Madon, S. (1997). What do people believe about gay males?: A study of stereotype content and strength. *Sex Roles, 37*(9/10), 663–685.

Nardi, P. (1992). *Men's friendships: Research on men and masculinities.* Newbury Park: Sage.
Nardi, P. (1999). *Gay men's friendships: Invincible communities.* Chicago, IL: University of Chicago Press.
Nardi, P. (2000). *Gay masculinities.* Thousand Oaks, CA: Sage.
Nardi, P., & Sherrod, D. (1994). Friendships in the lives of gay men and lesbians. *Journal of Social and Personal Relationships, 11,* 185–199.
Penn, R. E. (1997). *The gay men's wellness guide: The national lesbian and gay health association's complete book of physical, emotional, and mental health and well-being for every gay male.* New York: Henry Holt and Company.
Price, J. (1999). *Navigating differences: Friendships between gay and straight men.* New York: Hayworth.
Rubin, L. (1985). *Just friends: The role of friendships in our lives.* New York: Harper & Row.
Selman, R. L., & Schultz, L. H. (1990). *Making a friend in youth: Developmental theory and pair therapy.* Chicago, IL: University of Chicago Press.
Swain, S. (2001). Covert intimacy: Closeness in men's friendships. In T. Cohen (Ed.), *Men and masculinity: A text reader.* Belmont, CA: Wadsworth Thompson Learning.
Way, N. (2011). *Deep secrets: Boys' friendships and the crisis of connection.* Cambridge, MA: Harvard University Press.
Wood, J. (2000). *Relational communication: Continuity and change in personal relationships.* Belmont, CA: Wadsworth.
Woolwine, D. (2000). Community in gay male experience and moral discourse. *Journal of Homosexuality, 38*(4), 5–37.

Part II

Cultural Issues with Sexual Minority Men, Adolescents, and Boys

3 Cultural Considerations

Helping Gay Men, Teens, and Boys Integrate a Racial and Sexual Identity

Richmond D. Wynn, Joel M. Filmore, & Derrick A. Paladino

Many gay males of color—boys, adolescents, and men—are challenged in their efforts to integrate their racial, ethnic, and sexual orientation identities (David & Knight, 2008; Hatzenbuehler, Nolen-Hoeksema, & Erickson, 2008; Zamboni & Crawford, 2007). These challenges are in large part due to the homophobia they face in society, the lack of acceptance from their families (Carpineto, Kubicek, Weiss, Iverson, & Kipke, 2008; Wise, 2001), the discrimination by religious institutions (Griffin, 2006; Miller, 2007), as well as their experiences of marginalization in the predominantly White, gay community (Greene, 2001; Parks, 2001). Identity development of gay males of color is further complicated by: a) their internalization of mainstream pejorative views that inhibit expression of identity; and b) prevailing and systemic heterosexist and racist attitudes in society that create ecosystemic obstacles to identity integration (Greene, 2001).

Managing multiple identities is a task that is faced by many culturally diverse gay people, including those of various ethnic groups (Fukuyama & Ferguson, 2000; Garrett & Barret, 2003), multiple heritage persons (Henriksen & Paladino, 2009b), women (Brown, 1995), the elderly (Reid, 1995), and those persons with different abilities (Whitney, 2006). Members of these groups are often forced to develop ways of negotiating their identities that exist outside the mainstream. The intersection of multiple identities is complex; salience of identity often shifts depending on an individual's current social environment and stage of psychosocial development (Greene, 2001).

Past attempts to explain identity development among gay males of color have illuminated the complexities of negotiating their racial, ethnic, and sexual orientation identities (Crawford, Allison, Zamboni, & Soto, 2002; Parks, Hughes, & Matthews, 2004; Rosario, Schrimshaw, & Hunter, 2004; Salazar & Abrams, 2005; Wise, 2001). This attention to multiple identities is warranted, especially given what is known about the identity development of many gay males regardless of race or ethnicity.

For males of color, coming out may create additional stress and further complicate the identity development process. Although these identity development challenges are profound and can cause great distress among gay males, many emerge from this dilemma unscathed. The discussion of resilience highlights other aspects of the lives of gay boys, adolescents, and men.

Resiliency Factors

Although challenged by the experience of marginalization and oppression, many gay males demonstrate resilience that insulates them from the effects of discrimination and supports their positive identity development (Saewyc, 2011). It is believed that gay males and others who identify as sexual minorities are self-aware at an early age; they become aware of the world around them, and develop resilient adaptations to a generally hostile environment (Sanders & Kroll, 2000). A similar process has been observed in people of color in general in response to the long history of marginalization and oppression that they have faced.

Jenkins (2005) describes dialectical thinking, or the tendency of human thought to consider alternative possibilities, even in the presence of unpleasant realities as one of the resilience factors people of color have drawn on to survive. He asserts that a key feature of this dialectic capacity is the imaginative power available to human mentality that can provide perspectives leading to new and liberating behavior or at the very least to an alternative vision that sustains one's sense of humanity. For the often-marginalized gay community, this skill would prove invaluable to their survival. In a study of culture and resilience with a sample of African Americans, Utsey, Bolden, Lanier, and Williams (2007) found that spiritual and collective coping significantly predicted quality of life. This finding is significant for gay males of color as, in some racial communities, religion and spirituality often have a high priority; however, the homophobia that many experience in mainstream religious organizations has led them to abandon their spiritual selves altogether. "Queering" religion and spirituality, making it accessible to all, allows gay males of color to develop this resource as a part of their resiliency repertoire. Other protective factors such as intentionality and redefinition also help to insulate gay males of color from the obstacles they face in synthesizing their multiple identities.

Oswald (2002) describes intentionality and redefinition as gay-specific resiliency factors. Intentionality involves choosing kin by embracing friends as family and bringing people that are gay-affirming closer together while creating distance from those who are more hostile. In addition, building community by participating in supportive community resources enables gay males of color to experience an extended family network. Ritualizing is another aspect of intentionality where drawing upon culturally normative symbols while subverting their meaning to be inclusive of gay identity and introducing new symbolism gives gay males of color access to norms and values associated with their familial and cultural roots that many have been denied or abandoned. Finally, legalizing or using creative strategies to legalize relationships such as filing power of attorney and purchase of joint property, and in some places getting legally married, minimizes the sense of vulnerability and supports confidence and empowerment.

Meaning-making, which Oswald (2002) describes as redefinition, affirms the existence of gay males of color in their relationships. It involves politicizing or understanding the socio-political aspects of gay life and naming, attaching familial meanings to otherwise unmarked identities, events, and relationships that acknowledge and legitimize their existence. Attending to the intersectionality of their identities provides a framework for understanding their lived experience that is more effective than an "either/or" orientation that requires choosing to align exclusively with their cultural orientation or their sexual orientation. These protective factors mitigate the strong cultural influences that gay males of color experience in their communities and in the larger society that could inhibit their growth. At the same time, they allow gay males of color to cultivate aspects of their racial and sexual orientation identities that support the evolution of an integrated self. Additional protective factors for gay boys and adolescents include a nurturing family, supportive friends, connection to caring adults such as teachers, coaches, and mentors, and feeling safe at school. In addition, involvement in gay–straight alliances (GSAs) as well as community-based gay youth organizations helps to build confidence and reinforce positive coping skills.

Sexual Identity Development

Several researchers have developed theoretical models that describe identity formation among sexual minorities (Cass, 1979; Minton & McDonald, 1984; Troiden, 1979). In general, these models lay out stages that lead to an eventual positive gay identity. They are marked by a general sense of feeling different, an awareness of same-sex attraction, individual realization that his or her attraction can be labeled as gay, and an eventual acceptance of a gay identity that is punctuated by "coming out" (disclosure of one's sexual identity) to significant others. Although these models receive criticism for overlooking the influence of race, ethnicity, and other identities on sexual orientation development, they are helpful in understanding the challenges that sexual minorities experience in a culture that is generally hostile and oppressive toward them.

Racial Identity Development

Racism and systemic oppression have had a significant negative impact on the racial and ethnic identity of people of color (Carter, 2007). Racial identity development models purported by Cross (1971, 1991, 1995) and Helms (1995) describe psychological and emotional stages that people of color move through toward acceptance of their racial and ethnic identity. This process involves first denying their racial and ethnic identity and aligning with Whites, confronting that denial, embracing an ethnocentric worldview, displaying a greater sense of acceptance of self and others, and, finally, using their personal identities as agents for change. Ethnic identity development models, developed primarily with Hispanic clients, describe similar stages and go further to describe contributing factors to ethnic identity conflict, address language, and incorporate counseling interventions (Ruiz, 1990).

According to Phinney (1991), racial and ethnic identity achievement is associated with self-esteem and adjustment. Among people of color, achievement of positive racial and ethnic identity is often supported by intergenerational family units that provide emotional, psychological, social, and financial resources that aid them in coping with systemic oppression (Nobles, 1997; Sudarkasa, 1997). Achievement of a positive racial and ethnic identity also incorporates a state of mental health that is free of psychological ailments and supports an individual's growth and ability to reach their full potential (Parham, White, & Ajamu, 2000).

Identity development models are useful in understanding certain developmental tasks that individuals may encounter. Racial, ethnic, and sexual identity development models receive criticism for suggesting that growth is linear and bound by well-defined categories that are uncharacteristic of human development (Martinez & Sullivan, 1998). Racial and ethnic identity development models fail to acknowledge the role of sexual orientation and homophobia in identity formation. Gay identity development models overlook the influence of race and racism in the evolving gay identity and they only recognize one's positive gay identity after acknowledgment of one's sexual orientation to significant others (Martinez & Sullivan, 1998). Fukuyama and Ferguson (2000) point out that a primary limitation of exclusively recognizing single identities is that individuals who embrace multiple identities are often invisible members within specific social reference groups. Furthermore, one's salience of identity, the identity that emerges into one's awareness, often depends on one's social, familial, and community context. Theories that do not acknowledge multiple cultural identities obscure the complexity of identity integration. In response to increasing criticism of these identity development models, scholars called for consideration of multiple identities among gay people of color (Fukuyama & Ferguson; Icard, 1996; Israel & Selvidge, 2003; Savin-Williams, 2001).

The Multiple Heritage Connection

Living with multiple identities can be a complex experience with many challenges, both personal and ecological. When considering the intersection of race and sexual identity, the multiple heritage population offers a unique way to examine and understand this connection. In general, a multiple heritage person is identified as an individual that may "possess multiple aspects of heritage, including, race, ethnicity, religion, language, gender, and national origin (Henriksen & Paladino, 2009a, p. xiii). Evolution to the term *multiple heritage* (subsequent to biracial, multiracial, and mixed race) was created in order to allow individuals to express and honor multiple dimensions of one's background. Henriksen and Paladino (2009a, p. xiii) believe this is a necessary shift because "people are more than race, especially as race is a social construction and does not truly describe the individual". This scope allows individuals to identify through multiple lenses including sexual orientation.

The multiple heritage individual may have to navigate not only his racial identity and environments, but additional intersections of culture and identity. One of the earliest descriptions of individuals living with multiple identities is found in Everett Stonequist's 1937 text, *Marginal Man*. Stonequist described the marginal man as "one whom fate has condemned to live in two societies and in two but not merely different but antagonistic cultures" (Stonequist, 1937, p. xv). He continues, describing the marginal man as "living in two social worlds, between which there is antagonism and prejudice, he experiences in himself the same conflict (p. 25), thus provoking feelings of isolation, personal conflict, and suffering while trying to navigate society. Though much has changed since Stonequist's days, individuals from marginalized singular and multiple identity groups still experience discrimination and hostility. It is their current environment that impacts how much of their racial identity and sexual orientation they feel comfortable sharing and even acknowledging.

Exploring identity is paramount in understanding the experiences and development of multiple heritage individuals living with both racial and sexual orientation identities.

This development's impact can begin in childhood as children can sense they are different. Characteristics such as phenotype and cultural traditions can illuminate differences among family members and peers. Most likely, a multiple heritage individual will look and identify differently from his parents. For example, multiple heritage children may have monoracial and/or straight parents. It is when this difference is noted that children start reflecting on identity. Rice and Nakamura (2009) suggest that "many lesbian, gay, and bisexual (LGB) people reflect that they always knew that they were different, even when they were young children" (p. 167). In addition, LGB multiple heritage individuals may also "attribute this difference to something else, such as their unique racial heritage" (p. 167), further demonstrating the complexity in identity formation. With multiple identities individuals may feel pressured to choose one identity at the expense of the other or rank them based on their perception of loyalty or safety (Rice and Nakamura, 2009). These choices can be attributed to environmental, cultural, or familial pressures regarding their racial and/or sexual orientation identity.

The multiple heritage individual experiences a unique journey where identity development can be quite complex (Carter, 1995; Henricksen, Jr. & Paladino 2009; Jacobs, 1977, 1992; Kerwin & Ponterotto, 1995; Kich, 1992; Phinney, 1993; Phinney & Alipura, 1990; Poston, 1990; Root, 1990, 1999).

Several models describe the identity development experience of multiple heritage individuals (e.g., Henriksen & Paladino, 2009b; Kich, 1992; Choi-Misailidis 2004; Poston, 1990; Root, 1990, 1999). Two that are of note are Root's (1999) Ecological Model of Racial Identity Development and Henriksen and Paladino's (2009b) Multiple Heritage Identity Development (MHID) Model.

Root's Ecological Model of Racial Identity Development Model (IDM) (later revised in 2002) was created due to an absence of contextual issues in prior IDMs. This model introduced specific considerations such as geographic history, family socialization, community attitudes, and phenotype. More specifically, Root's multiracial IDM frames identity development through four contexts: regional and generational history of race and ethnic relations; sexual orientation; gender; and class. Root's (1999) ecological framework allows for numerous possibilities regarding racial identity outcome; it acknowledges that racial construction is dynamic despite its historic roots, and it recognizes that individuals with multiple heritage identities live with secondary statuses that influence overall identity construction and development. Root's model was groundbreaking in that it exposed the flaws in linear IDMs. Acknowledging the ecological impact on identity development allows for a greater understanding of the individual and reduces the level of generalizations postulated about the multiple heritage population.

Henriksen and Paladino's (2009b) Multiple Heritage Identity Development Model (MHID) offers a non-linear approach to understanding the identity development process of multiple heritage individuals and provides a foundation for appropriate development of clinical interventions. In the MHID model a multiple heritage individual is defined as a person who is exploring different heritages and combination of identities. These identities include ethnicity, gender, sexual orientation, national origin, religion/spirituality, indigenous heritage, and language. Since the MHID periods are not distinct and linear they can be applied to individuals of any age. In addition, periods can be experienced at the same time and revisited as an individual moves through their identity experience. The MHID involves six periods: Neutrality, Acceptance, Awareness, Experimentation, Transition, and Recognition.

The Neutrality period occurs before an individual gains awareness of their racial or ethnic differences. At this point, with no awareness it is difficult for the individual to understand how race and ethnicity affect their ecological world. In the Acceptance period a multiple heritage individual has some initial recognition and acceptance of a basic racial identity. At this point they perceive themselves as racially and ethnically different but do not see it as an issue or understand the impact. In addition, Henriksen and Paladino (2009b) suggest that families have a large influence during this period. They state that "the acceptance period could be the first time multiple heritage people encounter negative attitudes from others as well as the first time they recognize that they have been categorized by someone other than a family member" (p. 39). The Awareness period introduces an understanding regarding what it means to be racially and ethnically different. This difference can be found in the majority population, family, peers, and environment. Individuals in this period may experience interactions that expose their lack of belonging to an identified group. As a result, they may begin experiencing feelings of alienation and isolation.

In the Experimentation period the multiple heritage individual attempts to experience one part of his racial or ethnic identity. This immersion is an attempt to experience connection with others who understand their identity. In addition,

> the experimentation period is not just a time of trying to fit into one part of the individual's race or ethnicity, it is also a time when some individuals seem to be more actively involved in moving toward determining their own racial or ethnic group identity as well as their sexual identity, their religious identity, and other aspects of their identity.
>
> (Henriksen & Paladino, 2009b, p. 39)

Individuals in the Transition period realize that they may not be able to identify as a member of any one group. In this period "some people move toward a sense of racial self-recognition, fueled by inner turmoil and a search for a racial identity or racial group with which to identify" (Henriksen & Paladino, 2009b, p. 39). Lastly, in the Recognition period, individuals begin to accept their heritage and identity. This includes their racial, ethnic, sexual, and religious identity. In this period, individuals may demonstrate a sense of pride in themselves and have a solid awareness of how they wish to identify. A multiple heritage individual will also be able to verbalize their identity along with meaning. As this is not a linear model, there is potential for a multiple heritage individual to return to several other periods as they encounter new life experiences and environments.

With the application of a multiple heritage outlook, the journey of gay men and boys of color is illuminated. This not only presents assistance to the clinician in their work, but also the client as he navigates the sometimes tricky nature of living in multiple worlds. Both Root's (1999) and Henriksen and Paladino's (2009b) identity development models offer acknowledgment and voice to the significant roles both sexual orientation and race play within identity development. In addition, the ecological effects of a society that historically and currently holds discrimination and bias toward minority races and sexual identity is accounted for. This, of course, highlights micro as well as macro ecological influences. As gay men and boys of color move through their identity development, the intersection of race and sexual identity can be simultaneously explored regardless of the client's age and life circumstances.

The social construct of modern masculinity owes its existence, in part, to the effects of discrimination and oppression. In Western society, the dominant culture defines what it means to "be a man," yet black masculinity is said to be fragmented due to the denial of traditional opportunities of affirmation such as education, employment, and property ownership; this has been attributed to institutional and personal racism (Malebranche, 2003). Within minority communities gay identity is often seen as a deviance that has infiltrated their community from the White community (Harris, 2010).

Due to the history of slavery and subjugation, some blacks may take a negative view of "all things White." It is not uncommon for an African American who speaks proper English, or who pursues higher education, to be deemed as "trying to act White" by others in their own community; the implication here is that "acting White" is bad. The images of minority men are too often reflected through hyper-heterosexual athletes, and "thugs," while images of "gays" are often seen as effeminate with hypersexual displays of affectionate, colorful parades and other cultural norms that have been manufactured by the White gay community (Malebranche, Errol, Bryant &, Harper, 2009).

Because of this, gay males of color are often victims of stigma within their own communities as this contradicts the images and expectations of how males of color are socialized from an early age; this is counterintuitive to what it means to be a man (Davis, 1999). This misalignment between perceived White versions of being gay and normative minority masculinity suggests that there is potent influential factor in masculine socialization that impacts the disclosure patterns and behaviors of gay males of color (Malebranche et al., 2009). Within the minority communities the concept of "cool pose" is prolific; this is a ritualized, exaggerated form of masculinity and sexual prowess that has specific behaviors, scripts, posturing, emotional/impression management and performances that serve a single purpose, to send a message of pride, strength and control (Malebranche, 2003).

Intersectionality of Identity

Multiple intersections make up the lived experiences of gay males of color. However, family, community, and religious/spiritual identities are salient to many (Christian, 2005; Brown, 2005). Many gay males of color experience their racial and ethnic communities as homophobic (Bridges, Selvidge, & Matthews, 2003; Greene, 2001; Parks, 2001). Some seek validation in the predominantly white, gay community where they face the possibility of experiencing racism. If their sexual orientation becomes known or is openly discussed, if they "come out" they may lose the solidarity that would ordinarily be available to them in communities of color. They may also be ostracized from their families once the code of silence about their gay identity is broken (Carpineto et al., 2008; Wise, 2001).

Methods of coping with this dilemma involve: (i) prioritizing one's racial and ethnic identity over gay identity; (ii) embracing the Down Low (DL) or secretive gay life that is often enhanced by a hyper-masculine appearance or persona; and (iii) differentiating sexual preference (simply being attracted to other males) and the gay lifestyle (alluding to the effeminate, flamboyant stereotype) (Christian, 2005). Gay males of color have also reported that being overtly homophobic helps them to separate their sexual identity from their male identity, enabling them to be accepted and maintain a high ranking in the hierarchy of men (Brown, 2005). Negotiating these identities is further complicated by the difficulties that some gay males of color experience with religion and spirituality; considered by many in communities of color as a primary resource for resolving intrapersonal conflicts.

Gay males of color often experience exclusion from the mainstream LGBT culture and from their ethnic and familial communities, leaving them at risk for isolation, estrangement, and increased psychological vulnerability (Martinez & Sullivan, 1998). The loss of the expected communal support and fictive kinship (Chatters, Taylor, & Joyakody, 1994), which are central to communities of color, has a profound impact on their wellbeing and their identity development (Bridges et al., 2003; Greene, 2001; Parks, 2001; Wise, 2001). In addition, coming out as gay is often viewed as an assault on the traditional masculine gender role and therefore considered counterproductive to the success of communities of color (Bridges et al., 2003; Greene, 2001; Parks, 2001; Wise, 2001). Other considerations that further complicate the identity integration trajectory in gay men of color include the fear of violence, the fear of AIDS, and an overall fear of compounding oppressions (Martinez & Sullivan, 1998). While coming out is purported by some theorists to be the pinnacle of gay identity development, for gay males of color it may add yet another oppression to be managed in their lives. Therefore, they may identify as gay and choose not to come out or they may choose not to embrace a gay label at all.

Family Acceptance

Communities of color generally provide a sense of solidarity against racism that may be positively reinforcing for its members. However, gay males of color are less likely to experience that solidarity if their sexual orientation becomes known or is openly discussed; if they "come out." In fact, they may even be ostracized. Although gay males of color have historically been key figures in their families, they often become devalued once the code of silence about their sexual orientation is broken (Carpineto et al., 2008; Icard, 1996; Wise, 2001).

Many in communities of color view gay identity as a lack of masculinity or manhood (Icard, 1996; Wise, 2001). Because of their sexual orientation, gay males of color are depicted as anything but masculine and because of the ridicule from their peers, and the silencing from their families, their masculinity is compromised (Bridges et al., 2003; Greene, 2001; Parks, 2001). Gay men of color have been depicted as having a triple consciousness: being a man of color within the context of white society; being a man within the context of one's racial and ethnic community; and being a man of color who is also a sexual minority (Wise, 2001).

Religion and Spirituality

People of color have a long history of strong connections to religion and spirituality as sources of strength, particularly as a buffer against racism (Bowen-Reid & Harrell, 2002; Greene, 2001; Parks, 2001). However, the traditional, mainstream churches have either ignored or denigrated their gay members leaving them spiritually empty with fewer coping skills and a smaller support network (Greene, 2001; Griffin, 2006; Parks, 2001). In a qualitative study of African American men, AIDS, and the Black church (Miller, 2007), participants described the hostile environment that they experienced in many Christian denominations. Despite the unwelcoming experience, some of the participants in this study revealed that they viewed church as an extension of their families and have remained in these congregations and found ways to integrate their sexual orientation identity with their religious identity, usually by forming unofficial subgroups of other gay men who are also involved in the church. Other participants reported that they eventually left those churches, not because of their demeaning homophobic environments, but due to their church's apathetic response to the AIDS crisis.

Religious guilt, rejection by the church community, and fear of eternal damnation are sources of stress and often motivate gay people to seek a solution (Tozer & Hayes, 2004). Those who maintain this mindset hold their religious or spiritual identity as essentially as their sexual orientation. For some gay males of color, changing their sexual orientation may seem more feasible and less troublesome than trying to let go of their religious beliefs and communities. Many gay males engage in heterosexual relationships or commit to celibacy in order to manage the stress of their conflicting identities, even though studies show that these choices have been, for the most part, unsatisfactory and unsuccessful (Haldeman, 2002).

Counseling Implications

Conceptualizing the concerns of gay males of color in the appropriate cultural context is critical for successful outcomes (Wynn & West-Olatunji, 2008). Effective case conceptualization engenders positive results over the course of the counseling experience from the initial rapport building to the establishment of trust and counselor credibility to successful termination (Pedersen & Ivey, 1993). Conversely, ineffective case conceptualization can further complicate existing problems, contribute to the development of new issues, and may lead to additional psychological stress through acts of microaggression (Sue, 2007).

Effective counseling with gay males of color utilizes a strengths-based approach, which enables them to view their problems as secondary to their assets (Satterly & Dyson, 2005). In addition, culturally competent counselors assist gay males of color in generalizing their coping skills. The strategies that they use in dealing with other forms of oppression such as racism, sexism, and class bias are also effective in confronting oppression based on sexual orientation (Adams, Cahill & Ackerlind, 2005; Kulkin, 2006). Culture-centered approaches are responsive to individual self-expression and honor personal narratives. For example many gay males of color may choose not to embrace a gay label while others may choose a gay label, but decide not to come out (Savin-Williams, 2001). Culturally competent counselors avoid pathologizing these decisions and, instead, seek to understand the interplay of variables that might make such decisions optimal. When the unique experiences of gay males of color are acknowledged and addressed, their developmental difficulties are minimized.

For gay males of color, their own cultural orientations affect the types of coping strategies employed. As such, counseling interventions informed by cultural values can increase effectiveness by adapting to an individual's coping strategies (Pedersen & Ivey, 1993; Wynn & West-Olatunji, 2009). Eurocentric values such as emphasizing individualism in human interactions and development are in contrast with nondominant cultures within U.S. society (Sue & Sue, 2008). In many communities of color, for example, intergenerational family units provide collective economic, social, and emotional resources that have historically aided them in coping with systemic oppression (Nobles, 1997).

Working with clients that intersect racial and sexual identities requires additional awareness, knowledge, and skills. Counselors should be aware of their own biases and values when working with clients holding multiple social locations and racial identities. The authors suggest that counselors become intentional in this exploration and not only reflect on themselves but also their approach. This begins in the first session. Counselors should be aware that clients who identify themselves as holding a racial or sexual identity on their intake form may be entering counseling for different reasons. Individuals of multiple identities have many strengths and it is important not to assume their identity as a source of distress.

Counselor training is vital. Attending workshops on multicultural counseling, and taking advanced human sexuality and multicultural courses can assist clinicians with their sensitivity when working with these populations. In addition, counselors should become familiar with racial and sexual identity models to gain additional understanding and empathy for the potential plight these individuals experience. Multiple heritage models such as Root's (1999) Ecological Model of Racial Identity Development and Henriksen and Paladino's (2009b) Multiple Heritage Identity Development (MHID) Model give a good understanding of what it is like to live with multiple identities. In addition, sexual identity models such as those of Cass (1979) and Coleman (1981/1982) and monoriacial minority identity development models (IDM), such as Cross's (1971) Black racial identity model and Ruiz's (1990) Hispanic/Latino IDM, offer additional insights into specific social locations a client may hold. Since these clients may have encountered negative experiences due to their identity, it is suggested that counselors become knowledgeable of the socio-political history regarding discrimination and racist and homophobic issues that these populations have and currently face. Literature on how these events shape their worldview of counseling is beneficial.

Counselors should also be skilled at facilitation of critical consciousness so that clients become aware of their social positioning and the socio-political context of their concerns. These interventions are critical for increasing agency and, ultimately, resilience. A key component of emotional and psychological health is the ability to advocate on one's own behalf and that of other marginalized individuals. In order for counselors to become facilitators of critical consciousness for their clients, it is important that they also develop the ability to reflect, dialogue, and act in relation to their own lived experiences (Freire, 2000).

When working with identity development as a presenting issue, the Ecomap (Logan, Freeman, & McRoy, 1987) can be very helpful. The Ecomap is a technique similar to the genogram in that it allows an individual to explore his connection to both family and external networks. By allowing the client to explore his ecological world he is able to visually detect significant areas and networks of support. Since living with multiple social locations can be confusing, having a visual depiction of one's world can assist to initiate further exploration of identity. Lastly, a complete Ecomap has the ability to show locations of safety and risk when navigating through life or understanding acceptance.

With young children living with multiple identities, it is important to understand that even though their home life may feel safe, they are still navigating an outside world that can be harmful. With this in mind, it is important to work with families. More specifically, counselors working with children should understand how parents and guardians can influence identity development and/or comfort with identity. Root (1998) discussed constructs that influence one's ability to become a fully integrated multiple heritage individual. These constructs serve as a beneficial assessment when working with children living in multiple social and racial locations. A clinician can explore (with both parents and child) the following areas: languages in the home, parents' identity, home values, extended family identity and values, school environment, community environment, and peer and friends. From exploration, the clinician has a good jumping-off place from where to identify more specific presenting issues and construct a well-defined treatment strategy.

The multiple heritage literature also gives us additional suggestions for working with youth living with multiple identities. Herring (1995) suggests that it is important to create an intentional environment where children can feel safe, self-ventilate, and begin building positive relationships with the clinician. For some children (and even adults), the therapy session may be the first time they have fully opened up about their identity, therefore making the open space in the clinical environment of great importance.

At any age, psychoeducation is of great benefit. With individuals in this population most likely not holding the exact identity of their parents or peers, psychoeducation is a great way to begin exploring and understanding one's identity. This can be done through bibliotherapy and literature (i.e., reading historical and biographical works connected to one's identity), journaling and storytelling, viewing movies depicting individuals of multiple heritage descent and in the gay population, and exploring websites of support.

References

Adams, E. M., Cahill, B. J., & Ackerlind, S. J. (2005). A qualitative study of Latino lesbian and gay youths' experiences with discrimination and the career development process. *Journal of Vocational Behavior, 66,* 199–218.

Bowen-Reid, T. L., & Harrell, J. P. (2002). Racist experiences and health outcomes: An examination of spirituality as a buffer. *Journal of Black Psychology, 28*(1), 18–36. doi: 10.1177/0095798402028001002

Bridges, S. K., Selvidge, M. M. D., & Matthews, C. R. (2003). Lesbian women of color: Therapeutic issues and challenges. *Journal of Multicultural Counseling and Development, 31,* 113–130.

Brown, L. (1995). Not outside the range. In C. Caruth (Ed.), *Trauma: Explorations in memory* (pp. 100–112). Baltimore, MD: Johns Hopkins University Press.

Brown, E., II (2005). We wear the mask: African-American contemporary gay male identities. *Journal of African American Studies, 9*(2), 29–38.

Carpineto, J., Kubicek, K., Weiss, G., Iverson, E., & Kipke, M. D. (2008). Young men's perspectives on family support and disclosure of same-sex attraction. *Journal of LGBT Issues in Counseling, 2*(1), 53–80. doi: 10.1080/15538600802077533

Carter, R. T. (1995). *The influence of race and racial identity in psychotherapy.* New York: Wiley.

Carter, R. T. (2007). Racism and psychological and emotional injury: Recognizing and assessing race-based traumatic stress. *The Counseling Psychologist, 35*(1), 13–105. doi: 10.1177/0011000006292033

Cass, V. C. (1979). Homosexual identity formation: Testing a theoretical model. *Journal of Homosexuality, 4,* 219–235.

Chatters, L. M., Taylor, R. J., & Joyakody, R. (1994). Fictive kinship relations in Black extended families. *Journal of Contemporary Family Studies, 25,* 297–312.

Choi-Misailidis, S. (2004). Multiracial-heritage awareness and personal affiliation: Development and validation of a new measure to assess identity in people of mixed race descent (Doctoral dissertation, Fordham University, 2004). *Dissertation Abstracts International, 64,* 3556.

Christian, T. Y. (2005). Good cake: An ethnographic trilogy of life satisfaction among gay Black men. *Men and Masculinities, 8*(2), 164–174.

Coleman, E. (1981/1982). Developmental stages of the coming out process. *Journal of Homosexuality,* 7(2/3), 31–43.

Crawford, I., Allison, K. W., Zamboni, B. D., & Soto, T. (2002). The influence of dual-identity development on the psychosocial functioning of African American gay and bisexual men. *The Journal of Sex Research, 39*(3), 179–189.

Cross, W. E. (1995). The psychology of nigrescence: Revising the Cross model. In J. Ponterotto, J. Manuel Casas, L. A. Suzuki, and C. M. Alexander (Eds.), *Handbook of multicultural counseling* (pp. 93–122). Thousand Oaks, CA: Sage Publications.

Cross, W. E., Jr. (1971). The Negro-to-black conversion experience. *Black World, 20*(9), 13–27.

Cross, W. E., Jr. (1991). *Shades of black: Diversity in African-American identity.* Philadelphia, PA: Temple University Press.

David, S., & Knight, B. G. (2008). Stress and coping among gay men: Age and ethnic differences. *Psychology and Aging, 23*(1), 62–69. doi: 10.1037/0882-7974.23.1.62

Davis, J. E. (1999). Forbidden fruit: Black males' constructions of transgressive sexualities in middle school. In W. J. S. Letts and J. T. Sears (Eds.), *Queering elementary education: Advancing the dialogue about sexualities and schooling.* Boulder, CO: Rowan & Littlefield.

Freire, P. (2000). *Pedagogy of the oppressed.* New York: Continuum.

Fukuyama, M. A., & Ferguson, A. D. (2000). Lesbian, gay, and bisexual people of color: Understanding cultural complexity and managing multiple oppressions. In R. M. Perez, K. A. DeBord, and K. J. Bieschke (Eds.), *Handbook of counseling and psychotherapy with lesbian, gay, and bisexual clients* (pp. 81–105). Washington, DC: American Psychological Association.

Garrett, M. T., & Barret, B. (2003). Two spirit: Counseling Native American gay, lesbian and bisexual people. *Journal of Multicultural Counseling and Development, 31,* 131–142.

Greene, B. (2001). Heterosexism and racism among African Americans: The connections and considerations for African American lesbian and bisexual women: A clinical psychological perspective. *Rutgers Law Review, 54,* 931–957.

Griffin, H. L. (2006). *Their own receive them not: African American lesbians and gays in Black churches.* Cleveland, OH: The Pilgrim Press.

Haldeman, D. C. (2002). Gay rights, patient rights: The implications of sexual orientation conversion therapy. *Professional Psychology: Research and Practice, 33*(3), 260–264. doi: 10.1037/0735-7028.33.3.260

Harris, A. C. (2010). Sex, stigma, and the Holy Ghost: The Black Church and the construction of AIDS in New York City. Journal of African American Studies, *14,* 21–43.

Hatzenbuehler, M. L., Nolen-Hoeksema, S., & Erickson, S. J. (2008). Minority stress predictors of HIV risk behavior, substance use and depressive symptoms: Results from a prospective study of bereaved gay men. *Health Psychology, 27*(4), 455–462. doi: 10.1037/0278-6133.27.4.455

Helms, J. E. (1995). An update of Helms' White and people of color *racial identity* models. In J. Ponterotto, J. Manuel Casas, L. A. Suzuki, and C. M. Alexander (Eds.), *Handbook of multicultural counseling* (pp. 93–122). Thousand Oaks, CA: Sage.

Henriksen, R. C., & Paladino, D. A. (Eds.) (2009a). *Counseling individuals, couples, and families with multiple heritages.* Alexandria, VA: American Counseling Association.

Henriksen, R. C., & Paladino, D. A. (2009b). Identity development in a multiple heritage world. In R. C. Henriksen and D. A. Paladino (Eds.), *Counseling individuals, couples, and families with multiple heritages.* Alexandria, VA: American Counseling Association.

Herring, R. D. (1995). Developing biracialethnic identity: A review of the increasing dilemma. *Journal of Multicultural Counseling & Development, 23,* 29–38.

Icard, L. D. (1996). Assessing the psychosocial well-being of African American gays: A multidimensional perspective. *Journal of Gay & Lesbian Social Services, 5*(2/3), 25.

Israel, T., & Selvidge, M. M. D. (2003). Contributions of multicultural counseling to counselor competence with lesbian, gay and bisexual clients. *Journal of Multicultural Counseling and Development, 31,* 84–98.

Jacobs, J. H. (1977). Black/White interracial families: Marital process and identity development in young children. *Dissertation Abstracts International, 38*(10-B), 5023.

Jacobs, J. H. (1992). Identity development in biracial children. In M. P. P. Root (Ed.), *Racially mixed people in America* (pp.190–206). Newbury Park, CA: Sage.

Jenkins, A. H. (2005). Creativity and resilience in the African American experience. *The Humanistic Psychologist, 33*(1), 25–32.

Kerwin, C., & Ponterotto, J. G. (1995). Biracial identity development: Theory and research. In J. G. Ponterotto, J. M. Casas, L. A. Suzuki, and C. M. Alexander (Eds.), *Handbook of multicultural counseling* (pp. 199–217). Newbury Park, CA: Sage.

Kich, G. K. (1992). The developmental process of asserting a biracial, bicultural identity. In M. P. P. Root (Ed.), *Racially mixed people in America* (pp. 304–317). Newbury Park, CA: Sage.

Kulkin, H. S. (2006). Factors enhancing adaptive coping and mental health in lesbian youth: A review of the literature. *Journal of Homosexuality, 50,* 97–111.

Logan, S. L., Freeman, E. M., & McRoy, R. G. (1987). Racial identity problems of bi-racial clients: Implications for social work practice. *Journal of Intergroup Relations, 15*(2), 11–24.

Malebranche, D. J. (2003). Black men who have sex with men and the HIV Epidemic: next steps for public health. *American Journal of Public Health, 93,* 862–865.

Malebranche, D. J., Errol, L., Bryant, L. O., & Harper, S. R. (2009). Masculine socialization and sexual risk behaviors among Black men who have sex with men. *Men and Masculinities, 12*(1), 90–112.

Martinez, D. G., & Sullivan, S. C. (1998). African-American gay men and lesbians: Examining the complexity of gay identity development. *Journal of Human Behavior in the Social Environment, 1*(2/3), 243–264.

Miller, R. L. Jr. (2007). Legacy denied: African American gay men, AIDS, and the Black church. *Social Work, 52*(1), 51–61.

Minton, H. L., & McDonald, G. J. (1984). Homosexual identity formation as a developmental process. *Journal of Homosexuality, 9,* 91–104.

Nobles, W. (1997). African American family life: An instrument of culture. In H. P. McAdoo (Ed.), *Black families* (3rd ed.), (pp. 83–93). Thousand Oaks, CA: Sage.

Oswald, R. F. (2002). Resilience within the family networks of lesbians and gay men: Intentionality and redefinition. *Journal of Marriage and Family, 64,* 374–383.

Parham, T. A., White, J. L., & Ajamu, A. (2000). *The psychology of Blacks* (3rd ed.). Upper Saddle River, NJ: Prentice Hall.

Parks, C. W. (2001). African American same-gender-loving youth and families in urban schools. *Journal of Gay and Lesbian Social Services, 13,* 41–56.

Parks, C., Hughes, T., & Matthews, A. (2004). Race/ethnicity and sexual orientation: Intersecting identities. *Cultural Diversity and Ethnic Minority Psychology, 10*(3), 241–254.

Pedersen, P. B., & Ivey, A. (1993). *Culture-centered counseling and interviewing skills: A practical guide.* Westport, CT: Praeger.

Phinney J. (1991). Ethnic identity and self-esteem: A review and integration. *Hispanic Journal of Behavioral Science, 13,* 193–208.

Phinney, J. S. (1993). A three stage model of ethnic identity development in adolescence. In M. E. Bernal and G. P. Knight (Eds.), *Ethnic identity: Formation and transmission among Hispanics and other minorities* (pp. 61–79). Albany, NY: SUNY Press.

Phinney, J. S., & Alipura, L. L. (1990). Ethnic identity in college students from four ethnic groups. *Journal of Adolescence, 13,* 171–183

Poston, W. S. C. (1990). The biracial identity development model: A needed addition. *Journal of Counseling and Development, 69,* 152–255.

Reid, J. D. (1995). Development in late life: Older lesbian and gay lives. In A. R. D'Augelli and C. J. Patterson (Eds.), *Lesbian, gay, and bisexual identities over the lifespan* (pp. 216–240). New York: Oxford University Press.

Rice, T., & Nakamura, N. (2009). Bridging the margins: Exploring sexual orientation and multiple heritage identities. In R. C. Henriksen and D. A. Paladino (Eds.), *Counseling individuals, couples, and families with multiple heritages.* Alexandria, VA: American Counseling Association.

Root, M. P. P. (1990). Resolving "other" status: Identity development of biracial individuals. In L. S. Brown and M. P. P. Root (Eds.), *Diversity and complexity in feminist therapy* (pp.185–205). New York: Haworth.

Root, M. P. P. (1998). Experiences and processes affecting racial identity development: Preliminary results from the biracial sibling project. *Cultural Diversity and Mental Health, 4*(3), 237–247.

Root, M. P. P. (1999). The biracial baby boom: Understanding ecological constructions of racial identity in the 21st century. In. R. H. Sheets, R. Hernandez, and E. R. Hollins (Eds), *Racial and ethnic identity in school practices: Aspects of human development* (pp. 67–89). Mahwah, NJ: Erlbaum.

Rosario, M., Hunter, J., Maguen, S., Gwadz, M., & Smith, R. (2001). The coming-out process and its adaptational and health-related associations among gay, lesbian, and bisexual youths: Stipulation and exploration of a model. *American Journal of Community Psychology, 29*(1), 133–160.

Rosario, M., Schrimshaw, E. W., & Hunter, J. (2004). Ethnic/racial differences in the coming out process of lesbian, gay and bisexual youths: A comparison of sexual identity development over time. *Cultural Diversity and Ethnic Minority Psychology, 10*(3), 215–228.

Ruiz, A. S. (1990). Ethnic identity: Crisis and resolution. *Journal of Multicultural Counseling & Development, 18,* 29–40.

Saewyc, E. M. (2011). Research on adolescent sexual orientation: Development, health disparities, stigma, and resilience. *Journal of Research on Adolescence, 21*(1), 256–272. doi: 10.1111/j.1532-7795.2010.00727.x

Salazar, C., & Abrams, L. (2005). Conceptualizing identity development in members of marginalized groups. *Journal of Professional Counseling: Practice, Theory, & Research, 33,* 47–59.

Sanders, G. L., & Kroll, I. T. (2000). Generating stories of resilience: Helping gay and lesbian youth and their families. *Journal of Marital and Family Therapy, 26*(4), 433–442.

Satterly, B. A., & Dyson, D. A. (2005). Educating all children equitably: A strengths-based approach to advocacy for sexual minority youth in schools. *Contemporary Sexuality, 39*(3), 1–7.

Savin-Williams, R. C. (2001). A critique of research on sexual-minority youths. *Journal of Adolescence, 24,* 5–13.

Stonequist, E. V. (1937). *The marginal man: A study in personality and culture conflict.* New York: Russell & Russell.

Sudarkasa, N. (1997). African American families and family values. In H. P. McAdoo (Ed.), *Black families* (3rd ed.), (pp. 9–40). Thousand Oaks, CA: Sage.

Sue, D. W. (2007). *Racial, gender and sexual orientation micro aggressions.* Paper presented at the University of Florida Provost Diversity Speaker Series, Gainesville, FL, February 21, 2007.

Sue, D. W., & Sue, D. (2008). *Counseling the culturally diverse: Theory and practice* (5th ed.). New York: Wiley & Sons.

Tozer, E. E., & Hayes, J. A. (2004). Why do individuals seek conversion therapy? *The Counseling Psychologist, 32*(5), 716–740. doi: 10.1177/0011000004267563

Troiden, R. R. (1979). Becoming homosexual: A model gay identity acquisition. *Psychiatry: Journal for the Study of Interpersonal Processes, 42,* 362–373.

Utsey, S., Bolden, M. A., Lanier, Y., & Williams, O. III (2007). Examining the role of culture-specific coping as a predictor of resilient outcomes in African-Americans from high-risk urban communities. *Journal of Black Psychology, 33*(1), 75–93. New York: Wiley.

Whitney, C. (2006). Intersections of identity—Identity development among queer women with disabilities. *Sexuality and Disability, 24,* 39–52. doi: 10.1007/s11195-005-9002-4

Wise, S. J. (2001). Redefining Black masculinity and manhood: Successful Black gay men speak out. *Journal of African American Men, 5*(4), 3–23.

Wynn, R., & West-Olatunji, C. (2008). Culture-centered case conceptualization using NTU psychotherapy with an African American gay male client. *Journal of LGBT Issues in Counseling, 2*(4), 308–325. doi: 10.1080/15538600802501995

Wynn, R., & West-Olatunji, C. (2009). Use of culture-centered counseling theory with ethnically diverse LGBT clients. *Journal of LGBT Issues in Counseling, 3*(3–4), 198–214. doi.org/10.1080/15538600903317218

Zamboni, B. D., & Crawford, I. (2007). Minority stress and sexual problems among African American gay and bisexual men. *Archives of Sexual Behavior, 36,* 569–578. doi: 10.1007/s10508-006-9081-z

4 Addressing Spirituality When Counseling Gay Boys, Adolescents, and Men

Samuel Sanabria & Joffrey S. Suprina

The Importance of Spirituality When Counseling Gay Men

Although spirituality is an important aspect of people's lives, it is often overlooked in discussions of gay boys, adolescents, and men. This is surprising when one considers how gay men view their faith. For example, research by the Barna Group (2009) found that 72% of heterosexuals listed their faith as "very important" to them while 60% of gay men listed their faith as "very important" to them. Whether the significance of spirituality is an integral part of everyone's wellness as exemplified in the Wheel of Wellness (Myers & Sweeney, 2005) or moderated by group identification as supported by Taylor and Chatters (2010) or Cohen (2002), spirituality and religion are worthy of exploration in the counseling process. Exploring spirituality and religion may be even more important when working with gay boys, adolescents, and men as many have experienced rejection from the religion of their upbringing.

Religion vs. Spirituality

Much has been written about religion and spirituality and its place in counseling and psychotherapy. Some human service professionals feel that religion and spirituality have no place in the counseling process, while others consider religion and spirituality a cultural consideration that must be included (Helminiak, 2008). For many years the terms spirituality and religion were used interchangeably and considered by many to be synonymous (Spilka & McIntosh, 1997). In recent times, religious professionals have begun to understand a more complex relationship between spirituality and religion. In their 2006 study, Hyman and Handal attempted to clarify the meanings of religion and spirituality using a qualitative study with a variety of religious professionals. Their participants defined religion as objective and external, based on ritualized organizational practices. Spirituality was defined as subjective, internal, and representing a personal relationship with God. They understood the two terms to be distinct but overlapping.

Religion

Religion exemplifies a group perspective and group relationship with the universe that is based on common beliefs agreed to by the group that are supported by rituals and practices. Inclusion in the religious group is often determined by membership and commitment of time, energy, and resources such as money or tithes. Exclusion from the group may be represented by a rejection of non-believers or excommunication of challenging believers. Some may argue that religion is a group's mission to promote individual spiritual development within its group members. However, religion is often connected with an Earthly organization that includes a hierarchy, board members, facilities, and finances. Such organizational structures emulate those of corporate entities. As such, the business of religion may sometimes interfere with the mission of religion with a potential to stifle the spiritual development of its members.

Spirituality

In contrast to the objective, externally based ritualized organizational practices of religion, spirituality is often understood to be more subjective, internal, and representing a personal relationship with something greater than one's self (Hyman & Handal, 2006). The Association for Spiritual, Ethical and Religious Values in Counseling (ASERVIC; 1996) defined spirituality as:

> Spirit may be defined as the animating life force, represented by such images as breath, wind, vigor, and courage. Spirituality is the drawing out and infusion of spirit in one's life. It is experienced as an active and passive process. Spirituality is also defined as a capacity and tendency that is innate and unique to all persons. This spiritual tendency moves the individual toward knowledge, love, meaning, peace, hope, transcendence, connectedness, compassion, wellness, and wholeness. Spirituality includes one's capacity for creativity, growth, and the development of a value system. Spirituality encompasses a variety of phenomena, including experiences, beliefs, and practices. Spirituality is approached from a variety of perspectives, including psychospiritual, religious, and transpersonal. While spirituality is usually expressed through culture, it both precedes and transcends culture.
>
> (para. 3–4)

Such an expansive definition seems to encompass the personal aspects of religion while being much more broad and inclusive. Although many mental health professionals understand a client's spirituality to be an important aspect of wellness, too many neglect assessing its influence or addressing it in treatment planning. However, a more recent finding suggested that counseling professionals may have addressed spirituality in counseling at greater rates than previously reported (Morrison, Clutter, Pritchett, & Demmitt, 2009).

Whether philosophically or politically motivated, it is clear that a differentiation between religion and spirituality is in progress and is therefore noted in the counseling literature. Weaver, Pargament, Flannelly, and Oppenheimer (2006) found a significant rise in the rate of articles in behavioral science literature that dealt with spirituality, or spirituality and religion, but found a downward trend for those that only address religion. If religious and counseling professionals are coming to understand a differentiation between religion and spirituality, what about gay men?

Religion, Spirituality, and Gay Men

In their 2009 study, Halkitis et al. found that lesbian, gay, bisexual, and transgender (LGBT) persons defined religion "largely in terms of communal worship and in terms of its negative influences in the lives of individuals and communities" (p. 1). They expressed an understanding of religion as a human-made institution that is concerned with power and wealth that results in negative influences such as divisiveness, deception, greed, hatred, and war. However, the same participants perceived spirituality as a personal relationship with God and self, related to interconnectedness with others and the world around them. They linked spirituality to concepts like respect, compassion, kindness, insight, and wisdom. With such contrasting perceptions of religion and spirituality, it is understandable that participants self-identified as more spiritual than religious. The religion/spirituality struggle between the group and individual as well as between corporate versus personal can be profound for LGBT persons including gay men. Effective counseling of gay men may require an exploration of the differentiation between religion and spirituality including some education about the potential differences in the terms and concepts involved.

Homosexuality and World Religion

A broad survey of world religions' teachings on homosexuality is beyond the scope of this chapter. However, it is important to have an understanding of the impact that historical and current religious teachings have on the perception of homosexuality and the present lives of gay men (Helminiak, 2008). *The Diagnostic and Statistical Manual of Mental Disorders* (*DSM*) classified homosexuality as a mental disorder up until 1973 when it was removed (APA, 1999). Since then, the field of psychology has accepted homosexuality as a normal part of sexual and affectional expression; however, many religious institutions have been slow to gain this acceptance (Helminiak, 2008). Although certain religious institutions (i.e., Metropolitan Community Church, Dignity USA, . . .) have moved toward a more tolerant position of lesbian, gay, and bisexual individuals, religion as a whole still holds to the tenets that homosexuality is a sin.

Teachings on homosexuality not only differ by religion, but may also differ significantly between cultures and geographic regions within a single religion. While it would not be possible to apply the content of this summary universally, important information can still be ascertained through the common teachings of these religions. The following is a brief overview of the teachings of homosexuality from the perspective of Christianity, Judaism, Islam, and others.

Conservative Judaism generally has a negative view of homosexuality. Biblical teachings have focused on male-to-male sexual encounters. In Leviticus 18:22 (King James Version), it is written: "thou shall not lie with mankind, as with womankind; it is an abomination," and in Leviticus 20:13, it is written: "If a man also lies with mankind as he lieth with woman, both of them have committed an abomination; they shall surely be put to death; their blood shall be upon them." Orthodox Jews tend to hold the position that homosexuality is unnatural and that anyone who engages in the acts has given into his or her unnatural desires. The largest branch of Judaism in North America, the Reform Judaism, has embraced lesbian, gay, and bisexual individuals as rabbis (Black, 2008). They tend to view the Levitical text as referring to prostitution, which is forbidden. The Restructionist movement has accepted lesbian, gay, and bisexual individuals and even encourages its members to officiate same-sex marriages. Despite the growing acceptance of lesbian, gays, and bisexuals in Judaism there are still significant disagreements that can resonate within the culture.

There are over 33,000 different Christian denominations in the world (Barnett, Kurian, & Johnson, 2001), each holding a different position regarding homosexuality that ranges from condemnation to complete acceptance. Even within denominations attitudes differ. At this time the Eastern Orthodox Church, the Roman Catholic Church, Seventh-Day Adventists Church, The Church of the Latter-Day Saints, and many Evangelical Protestant Churches hold the position that homosexuality is a sin. The Roman Catholic Church takes the stand that sex is for procreation and for married different gender couples. Any sexual activity outside of this is considered sinful. Most of these Christian churches view acceptable sex as that which occurs between a man and a woman within the confines of marriage. Like Judaism, Christians follow Old Testament scriptures including the Leviticus scriptures referring to homosexuality. Christian churches also follow New Testament scriptures that have passages addressing homosexual behaviors including Roman I: 26, 27, and I Corinthians 6:8–10. I Corinthians 6:8–10 (New American Standard) reads as follows:

> No, you yourselves do wrong and cheat, and you do these things to your brethren! Do you not know that the unrighteous will not inherit the kingdom of God? Do not be deceived. Neither fornicators, nor idolaters, nor adulterers, nor homosexuals, nor sodomites, nor thieves, nor covetous, nor drunkards, nor revilers, nor extortioners will inherit the kingdom of God.

Roman I:26, 27 reads:

> Even their women exchanged natural relations for unnatural ones. In the same way the men also abandoned natural relations with women and were inflamed with lust for one another. Men committed indecent acts with other men, and received in themselves the due penalty for their perversion.

There are several gay-affirming churches that view same-sex relationships as a natural part of human sexuality. Many mainline Protestant churches have accepted same-sex relationships and even allow for same-sex marriages.

Islamic law specifically condemns homosexuality. In this way Islam resembles Judaism and Christianity. The Qur'an explicitly rejects homosexuality as a sin against God and nature. Like many of the traditional Christian churches Islam views acceptable sex as that between a man and a woman, although sex can be done for the sake of pleasure. Most Muslim majority countries criminalize same-sex activities, which may lead to the death penalty. The Qur'an contains several references to sexual misconduct in the story of Lot, which refers to the residents of Sodom and Gomorrah. Their destruction was explicitly associated with their sexual practices. In the Qur'an 7:80–84 it states:

> And (We sent) Lut when he said to his people: What! do you commit an indecency which anyone in the world has not done before you? Most surely you come to males in lust besides females; nay you are an extravagant people. And the answer of his people was no other than that they said: Turn them out of your town, surely they are a people who seek to purify (themselves). So We delivered him and his followers, except his wife; she was of those who remained behind. And We rained upon them a rain; consider then what was the end of the guilty.

Historically there have been homoerotic themes present in poetry and other literature written by some Muslims from the medieval period onwards that celebrated love between men (Schmidtke, 1999). It is believed by many that attitudes toward homosexuals changed through Euro-American influences. At this time there is a small movement within Islam to accept homosexuality; however, it is uncertain whether this movement will influence the position of Islam on homosexuality.

Many of the non-Abrahamic world religions say little about same-sex activities. In some aboriginal religions of Africa and North America homosexual relationships were an important part of life (Baum, 1993; Jacobs, 1997). In some cultures, homosexuality was honored and seen as an important part of the development of the community (Cameron, 2005). Hinduism tends to view homosexuality mainly from its karmic effect on the individual. What the karmic effect will be is undetermined and would vary for individuals. Despite this position Hinduism is not generally supportive of homosexuality. Buddhism on the other hand is relatively neutral depending on the culture in which one practices. Cabezón (1993) noted that early Buddhism did not have any specific stigma associated with homosexuality. Buddha, himself, is believed by many to have had an intense and possibly sexual relationship with his servant Ananda. The Buddhist position on homosexuality differs from region to region. For example, Buddists from India tend to be less tolerant of homosexuality than those in China, Japan, and Tibet (Helminiak, 2008).

Confucianism and Taoism also say very little about homosexuality (Wawrytko, 1993); however, there have been many references to homoeroticism in Chinese history and literature. There is a well-known story in Chinese culture of the Emperor Ai-ti, who cut off the sleeve of his garment in order not to wake up his male lover, Tung Hsien. Homosexuality in Confusianism is often referred to as the "cut sleeve." There is an emphasis in Confucianism to procreate; however, Confucianism is accepting of homosexuality provided that the individual attends to society's obligations (Helminiak, 2008).

The Impact Religious Discrimination Has on Gay Men

Religious communities differ in their attitudes toward homosexuality and in the degree to which they affirm and embrace gay men. There are four approaches that religious communities can take in their attitudes toward homosexuals (Yakushko, 2005). The first is a "rejecting punitive" approach in which homosexuality is outright condemned. Conservatives and literalists of religious texts tend to be the most condemning toward homosexuals. The second is a "rejecting non-punitive" approach in which homosexuality is seen as sinful; however, homosexuals are accepted as members of the religious organization. The third position is one in which the religious community accepts homosexuality but it is seen as inferior to heterosexuality. This is called "qualified acceptance." The final position is more inclusive. This is where the religious community has a complete acceptance toward homosexuality and it is seen as a normal part of sexual expression. This is called "full acceptance." Those individuals who were part of a full acceptance religious community have a higher sense of self and stronger spiritual identity. They are better able to successfully integrate their sexual and religious identities. By comparison, those gay individuals who grew up in a conservative religious community that was more condemning of homosexuals are more likely to experience conflicts with their sexual identity and/or their religious identity. Although some gay individuals who have experienced this environment have worked toward an integrative identity, many gay individuals have not been so fortunate. As a result of the negative experiences they have had with their religious community, many have worked toward rejecting their sexual identity or separating their religious identity from their sexual identity (Kocet, Sanabria, & Smith 2011; Rodriguez & Ouellette, 2000). These experiences can have a strong negative impact on the development of gay boys into gay men.

Identity Development

Just as there can be stages to the coming out process, it may be beneficial to consider one's stage of development of both sexual identity and spiritual identity development. Although one can use separate identity development models such as Cass (1979) for sexual identity or Peck (1987) for spiritual identity development, using the Atkinson, Morten, and Sue (1989) Racial/Cultural Identity Development Model (R/CID) can be more efficient.

- Stage 1: *Conformity* (with them) is when the individual completely embraces the dominant culture's beliefs and customs while rejecting his own culture, which is incongruent with the dominant culture. For sexual identity development (SID) this can manifest as a denial of any homosexual tendencies. For spiritual/religious development (SRD) this can manifest as a blind acceptance of the religious practices of one's caregivers.
- Stage 2: *Dissonance* (unlike them) is characterized by conflicting messages and observations that are inconsistent with the view of one's own culture and the dominant culture. For SID this can manifest as the person understands that he is somehow different. For SRD this can manifest in feeling incongruence between the religion or beliefs of one's caregivers and one's self.
- Stage 3: *Resistance and immersion* (we vs. them) is when one completely embraces one's own culture's values and beliefs and rejects those of the dominant culture. For SID this can result in "gay pride" but also a version of cultural encapsulation in which one only associates with other gay men and organizations that are owned and operated by gays and lesbians. Likewise for SRD the individual can isolate his interaction with only those who believe as he does, feeling condemnation for those with other beliefs.

- Stage 4: *Introspection* (we like them?) is when the individual attempts to understand herself or himself better, tries to become more objective about the culture's views and attitudes, and strives to integrate the values of the minority and dominant group. For SID the individual may be expanding his associations and feel less disconnected from the dominant culture while retaining gay pride. For SRD the individual begins to understand the value in other spiritual and religious perspectives.
- Stage 5: *Integrative awareness* (we and them) is when one, rather than seeing conflict between one's culture and that of the dominant group, realizes that there are acceptable and unacceptable factors from both. A strong desire to end all forms of oppression exists in the individual. For SID this can manifest as a broad network of associations that include a variety of individuals including heterosexuals without a hierarchical preference. For SRD this can manifest in an acceptance of all spiritual beliefs without judgment, understanding that each person's spiritual path can be different without being wrong or threatening one's own chosen spirituality. Identifying the client's development and meeting the client within that developmental stage can be integral to successful counseling.

Gay Boys

One of the first stages of coming out is the awareness that one is gay. The age at which this occurs differs among individuals. Research has shown that the average age at which a youth identifies as being gay is between 8 and 11 years old (Savin-Williams & Diamond, 2000). This is a central period for any young gay boy who has not yet developed his sexual identity. This is a time in which young boys begin to formulate identifications and develop a sense of being "different" from others. Young boys are often inundated with social messages about what are acceptable and unacceptable behaviors and feelings. Young boys receive messages from a variety of credible resources including family, teachers, and religious leaders. If a young boy is raised in a conservative religious household in which anti-gay sentiments are expressed he will quickly learn to suppress his feelings and socially isolate (Hillier, Mitchell, & Mulcare, 2008). Young boys learn that being gay is unnatural and undesirable and that if one is gay then one is a deviant. The child can also learn negative associates including that gays are lonely and child molesters. They also face the fear of being ostracized, rejected, and giving up any meaningful intimate relationships. This can inhibit further growth as a child enters into early adolescence, when social relationships and sexual interests come together in the development of an adult identity. By this time a child learns to deny same-sex feelings and behaviors from themselves and others. They also learn to develop fear and hatred toward homosexuals, and in turn develop internalized homoprejudice (Williamson, 2000).

Adolescence

The second stage of sexual identity development is the identification of being gay. Studies have shown that the average age a gay young man begins the process of coming out is approximately 16 (Cianciotto & Cahill, 2003), a period in which the adolescent male begins to have increased awareness of sexual thoughts and feelings. This age average has reduced since the 1980s when the average age young men came out was between 19 and

23 (Shilo & Savaya, 2011). At the age of 16, gay adolescents are still in school and under the care of parental figures.

Gay adolescents need a lot of emotional support as they decide to come out. Unfortunately they are often undermined by significant people in their life and by the community at large (Riley, 2010). For example, ministers, priests, and other religious leaders may express anti-gay messages, which can cause adolescents to feel immoral, ashamed, and marginalized and thus less likely to come out. Religious leaders may also influence parents as to how they perceive gay people in general and their gay child in particular. Unlike their non-gay peers, gay adolescents are more likely to navigate through this important developmental step alone and without guidance from loved ones. Although other minority youth (i.e., racial/ethnic minorities) are the recipient of stigma and prejudice, they still have the support and guidance from their parents and community. They receive affirming messages that help develop coping skills that allow them to develop their self-esteem and their cultural identity. This support is extremely helpful in reducing the emotional impact from the prejudice they receive from the larger society. Often times, gay adolescents will hide their sexual identity at this stage in order to avoid any of the stigma and prejudice (Riley, 2010). They may also develop maladaptive coping skills that may lead to self-destructive behaviors and increase their risk for depression, anxiety, substance abuse, and HIV/AIDS, which can persist into adulthood.

Adults

The third and fourth stages of coming out are coming out to self and to others. This is a very important part of a person's sexual identity development. Individuals who grew up during the 1950s and 1960s may have remained "closeted" into their late years. During those times, gay-affirming religious organizations were not as prevalent as they are today. Religious attitudes toward homosexuals were more stringent and gay men had fewer options in finding a community that would help in their identity integration. Many adult gay males who experience religious discrimination and oppression feel a great sense of loss, either to their sexual identity or their religious identity (McQueeney, 2009). Reconciling their sexual and spiritual identities can be difficult since many gay men have received anti-gay messages from their religious community since they were children. Failing to reconcile their identities can result in a variety of stressors including depression, low self-esteem, and anxiety (Love, Bock, Jannarone & Richardson, 2005), as well as relational problems including alienation from family and friends (Love et al., 2005; McQueeney, 2009).

Despite negative experiences from religious organizations, many gay men continue to develop their spiritual identity. Gay men may feel the need or desire to examine their core religious beliefs and work toward an identity that brings their sexual and spiritual selves together. This journey may be an important part of their healing process. Yakushko (2005) has noted different approaches that religious organizations take on homosexuality; from absolute rejection to absolute acceptance. Gay men who attended non-gay-affirming religious organizations experienced more difficulty in their identity development, whereas gay men who attended gay-affirming religious organizations encountered little to no conflict in the development of their identities. For example, Helminiak (2006) revealed that while gay Catholics mostly received anti-gay messages from their churches, members of Dignity (a gay-affirming Catholic organization) had higher self-acceptance that was similar to that of non-gay Catholics. Gay-affirming religious organizations offer a sense of community for many gay men as well as an opportunity to create their own social support group and family.

SACRED Model

In 2008, through an analysis of supervision literature, Ross, Suprina, and Brack developed the SACRED Model as a structure to guide integration of spirituality into counseling supervision (Ross, Suprina, & Brack, 2013). This model consists of six stages: *Safety, Assessment, Conceptualization, Reflection, Emerging Congruence,* and *Development,* and serves as an effective structure for integrating spirituality into counseling. Each stage accommodates the unique challenges experienced by gay boys, adolescents, and men when dealing with religion and spirituality:

- Stage 1: Establishing *Safety* consists of encouraging an environment, timing, and relationship that is conducive to an open, explorative discussion of spirituality and religion. This is particularly important when working with gay males who, through experience with religious oppression, are cautious when talking about their religious experiences.
- Stage 2: *Assessment* requires assessing the counselor's and client's spiritual and religious definitions and perspectives and their relationship to the presenting issue(s). Gay males may have a different idea of what religion means for them. Gay men are less likely to identify themselves with a religion despite indicating the importance their faith is to them (Barna Group, 2009).
- Stage 3: *Conceptualization* entails exploration of the relationships between the identified spiritual and religious perspectives, the individual's worldview, the theoretical orientation, and the problem/solution. This is an especially pertinent stage when working with gay males who may have conflicts between their worldview and religious perspectives.
- Stage 4: *Reflection* necessitates identification of how the client's belief system and cultural diversities interact with self, others, and the world. Using Cass's sexual identity model and Peck's spiritual identity model would be useful in helping the client better understand how their separate identities shape their sense of self and how the integration of these identities can encourage growth.
- Stage 5: *Emerging Congruence* promotes synthesis between the religious and spiritual beliefs of the client, the client's worldview and the client's perceptions of the presenting issue(s).
- Stage 6: *Development* encourages ongoing development as the client learns to use the insights gained to promote continued spiritual growth and development to promote holistic wellness. This could include a process for developing identity pride and coming out to family and friends.

For understanding in how to apply the concepts in this chapter to a counseling client, a case study is presented.

Case Study: Tom

Tom is a 48-year-old Caucasian male who reports to a psychiatric clinic with suicidal ideation. He is accompanied by his 50-year-old Caucasian male life partner. Tom appears pale and gaunt with a distant gaze and is shy and reserved, hovering in the back of the room. His partner speaks for him during much of the initial contact session until the counselor requests to speak directly with Tom. Tom shares that he has been diagnosed with HIV since he was 16 years old. He also identifies as having addiction issues (mostly alcohol, but additional recreational drugs from time to time) and persistent depression. He has been seeing a psychiatrist for over 20 years for different medications but has never received counseling. He discloses that suicidal ideation is fairly common, happening every few weeks on average. He agrees to counseling and begins a treatment plan based in part on the SACRED Model.

Applying the SACRED Model

As spirituality and religion issues can be prominent with gay men, the counselor set the stage by asking what the client's spiritual and religious history was during the initial intake session. Making sure not to react to derogatory comments such as "I'm gay, I worship alcohol" helped to establish *safety* in the discussion. Having the discussions as a routine part of the client intake also reinforced that such exploration was normal. The client disclosed that he was the son of a Baptist minister and his mother was the self-proclaimed "first lady of the church." To further *assess* the client's spiritual and religious beliefs, the counselor explored the client's coming out stage, which appeared to be trapped between *Identity Confusion* (a gay male or heterosexual Christian) and *Identity Assumption.* An assessment of his identity development revealed being stifled between *Dissonance* and *Resistance and Immersion* in his sexual identity development and stuck at the *Dissonance* stage in his spiritual development (R/CID; Atkinson, Morten, & Sue, 1989). The counselor further inquired with, "Tell me about your religious experiences growing up." The client shared that in his youth he attended church every Sunday and really enjoyed most of the "rituals and socialization." He expressed feeling at home on some level, but also ill at ease. He shared that his father was not "preachy" at home or condemning in any way but did seem somewhat inaccessible. His mother was described as quite rigid in her interpretation and application of religious teachings. He felt loved by his mother but felt that her love was at least partially conditioned on his religiosity. Asking, "How have your religious practices changed over the years?" identified that he had not attended church since coming out as gay and that this was due to his feeling that he was condemned and would not be welcome in any church. When asked if he had explored other religious or spiritual avenues, he admitted that he had not. He also shared that he was unable to stay involved in Alcoholics Anonymous because of discomfort with the "religious" nature of the group.

It was at this point in the counseling process that an exploration of the difference between religion and spirituality was encouraged. The differentiation enabled the client to begin to disempower the religious dogma that was blocking his development of a personal relationship with his higher power. All of this was easily *conceptualized* from a psychodynamic perspective as an issue related to feeling belonging (to the church as a child) and lack of belonging (as an adult). Interestingly, research has linked feeling a lack of belonging to addiction for gay men when the Belonging Model of addiction was developed (Suprina, 2006).

For *reflection,* the client was asked to articulate his current beliefs about religion, spirituality, and belonging. This included a discussion of his relationships with his partner, parents, siblings, and other important people or groups. A pattern was identified in which the client had interactions with his partner, siblings, and parents, but did not feel connected to any of them. His closest sense of belonging or connection was to his bar friends when he was "high." He began to understand that the sense of belonging he felt while "high" was an illusion and not a true connection. He also began to understand that he was hungry for connection and, despite his repeated efforts, had not succeeded in connecting to anyone or anything other than drugs and alcohol.

Through this exploration, a pattern finally emerged of the client reaching out to his mother, her condemning him to Hell for his homosexuality, the client becoming drunk for solace and sense of connection, and, after coming down from the "high," becoming depressed and suicidal. This pattern was illuminated for the client and led to an exploration of how that same pattern of interaction may be playing out spiritually. The client acknowledged that he wanted a connection with "God" but felt thwarted in this desire to connect as he was thwarted in attempts to connect with his mother several days each week. However, the client admitted feeling a genuine connection with the counselor. With that safety foundation, the counselor suggested that the client cut off contact with his mother for just a week to see how that might disrupt the pattern. However, the client refused as he "is her favorite child (later it was discovered that he was the only one of his three siblings who had not cut off communication with his mother) and it would kill her to not have contact." As an alternative way to break the destructive pattern, the client was taught to say, "Don't go there, mother" when she turned their interaction to one of condemnation.

It is important to work within the client's worldview, boundaries, and timetable to alleviate resistance. After two weeks, the client reported that the intervention effectively prevented his downward spiral reaction to his mother, but did little to address his internalized homophobia related to negative messages from religion. To encourage some *emerging congruence* between the client's desire for connection with the God of his upbringing and the messages of condemnation from his religion and mother, the client was reminded of the concept of omnipresence (God is everywhere or in and of everything) contained in his childhood religion. In other words, the client was approached from his worldview and religious belief perspective. The omnipresence concept supported that he was a part of God and so opened a door to a sense of belonging with God. In working with this concept, the client began to feel connected to something greater than him.

To encourage continued *development,* further sessions explored how his body, as a piece of God, was to be cherished and maintained. This rather naturally led to him voluntarily diminishing his alcohol consumption and other self-destructive behaviors that he exchanged for healthful alternatives such as exercising and working in his garden. Eventually he attended a local church service of Metropolitan Community Church, a gay-affirming religious institution, to regain some group connection to spirituality and religion that was affirming. As exemplified by the Wellness Model of Myers and Sweeney (2005), the work on his spirituality seemed to have a positive influence on many areas of his life: his addictive behaviors diminished significantly while his physical health, mental health, self-esteem, and relationships were also enhanced.

Although this is a brief overview of some of the most pertinent interventions related to this chapter, additional interventions were included in the client's treatment such as couple's sessions with his life partner; however, the integration of spirituality and religion into his sessions was the most profound influence on his ultimate wellbeing. Although likely accentuated by his parents' roles within the religious institution, his story is not that different from those of many gay men, boys, or adolescents who may feel condemnation from their religion. If left unattended, those issues can become debilitating and cause a lifetime of negative symptoms. Although the SACRED Model can be just as effective with boys and adolescents, the counselor needs to be aware of the current knowledge and development of the client and be sure to adapt accordingly. For example, a boy or adolescent is more likely to revert to a Pre-Awareness stage on the Spiritual Development Model (Poll & Smith, 2003) that recommends the client be guided toward spiritual experiences that are affirming and welcoming. Providing spiritual resources that are developmentally appropriate will be most beneficial. No matter what age the client, processing of the client's past religious experiences and messages and separating religious teachings and dogma from one's personal relationship with the Higher Power of his choosing can go far to help the client develop a positive spirituality that supports wellness.

Clinicians can familiarize themselves with the gay-affirming religious organizations in their community in order to build a network of resources for their clients. This can be done by visiting different religious communities and interviewing the religious leaders on their position on homosexuality. It is also important for clinicians who are working with gay males to familiarize themselves with the special issues faced by this population. Clinicians need to be aware of their own religious and spiritual assumptions, biases, and beliefs about gay individuals in order to effectively work with this population.

References

American Psychological Association (APA) (1999). Answers to your questions about sexual orientation and homosexuality [Online]. Available: www.apa.org/topics/sexuality/orientation.aspx (accessed January 15, 2014).

Association for Spiritual, Ethical and Religious Values in Counseling (ASERVIC). (1996). *Summit on spirituality white paper.* Alexandria, VA: Author.

Atkinson, D. R., Morten, G., & Sue, D. W. (1989). A minority identity development model. In D. R. Atkinson, G. Morten, and D. W. Sue (Eds), *Counseling American Minorities* (pp. 35–52). Dubuque, IA: W. C. Brown.

Baum, R. M. (1993). Homosexuality and the traditional religions of the Americas and Africa. In A. Swindler (Ed.), *Homosexuality and the world religions* (pp. 1–46). Valley Forge, PA: Trinity Press International.

Barnett, P. B., Kurian, G. T., & Johnson, T. M. (2001). *World Christian encyclopedia: A comparative survey of churches and religions in the modern world volume 1: The world by countries* (2nd ed.). Oxford: Oxford University Press.

Black, J. K. (2008). Believe what you will, but this is the way it is: Religions and the spirituality of GLBTIQ people. *Gay & Lesbian Issues and Psychology Review, 4*(1), 48–55.

Cabezón, J. I. (1993). Homosexuality and Buddhism. In A. Swindler (Ed.), *Homosexuality and world religions* (pp. 81–101). Valley Forge, PA: Trinity Press International.

Cameron, M. (2005). Two-spirited Aboriginal people: Continuing cultural appropriation by non-Aboriginal society. *Canadian Woman Studies, 24,* 2/3, 123– 127.

Cass, V. C. (1979). Homosexuality identity formation: A theoretical model. *Journal of Homosexuality, 4,* 219–235.

Cianciotto, J., & Cahill, S. (2003). *Education policy: Issues affecting lesbian, gay,bisexual, and transgender youth.* New York: The National Gay and Lesbian Task. Force Policy Institute.

Cohen, A. B. (2002). The importance of spirituality in well-being for Jews and Christians. *Journal of Happiness Studies, 3*(3), 287–310.

Halkitis, P. E., Mattis, J. S., Sahadath, J. K., Massie, D., Ladyzhenskaya, L., Pitrelli, K., Bonacci, M., & Cowie, S-A. E. (2009). The meanings and manifestations of religion and spirituality among lesbian, gay, bisexual, and transgender adults. *Journal of Adult Development, 16*(4), 250–262.

Helminiak, D. A. (2006). The role of spirituality in formulating a theory of the psychology of spirituality. *Zygon, 41,* 198–224.

Helminiak, D. A. (2008). Homosexuality in world religions: A case study in the psychology of spirituality. *Journal of Individual Psychology, 64*(2), 137–160.

Hillier, L., Mitchell, A., & Mulcare, H. (2008). I couldn't do both at the same time: Same-sex attracted youth and negotiation of religious discourse. *Gay & Lesbian Psychological Review, 4*(2), 80–93.

Hyman, C., & Handal, P. J. (2006). Definitions and evaluation of religion and spirituality items by religious professionals: A pilot study. *Journal of Religion and Health, 45*(2), 264–282. doi: 10.1007/s10943-006-9015-z

Jacobs, S.-E. (Ed.) (1997). *Two-spirit people: Native American gender identity, sexuality, and spirituality.* Urbana-Champaign: Illini Books.

Kocet, M., Sanabria, S., & Smith, M. R. (2011). Finding the spirit within: Religion, spirituality, and faith development in gay, lesbian, and bisexual individuals. *Journal of LGBT Issues in Counseling, 5,* 163–179.

Love, P., Bock, M., Jannarone, A., & Richardson, P. (2005). Identity exploration: Exploring the spiritual experiences of lesbian and gay college students. *Journal of College Student Development, 46,* 193–209.

McQueeney, K. (2009). "We are God's children, y'all": Race, gender, and sexuality in lesbian-and-gay affirming congregations. *Social Problems, 56*(1), 151–173.

Morrison, J., Clutter, S., Pritchett, E., & Demmitt, A. (2009). Perceptions of clients and counseling professionals regarding spirituality in counseling. *Counseling and values, 53,* 183–194.

Myers, J. E., & Sweeney, T. J. (2005). *Counseling for wellness: Theory, research, and practice.* Alexandria, VA; American Counseling Association.

Peck, M. S. (1987). *The different drum: Community making and peace.* New York: Simon & Schuster.

Poll, J., & Smith, T. (2003). The spiritual self: Toward a conceptualization of spirituality identity development. *Journal of Psychology & Theology, 31,* 129–142.

Riley, B. H. (2010). GLB adolescent's "coming out." *Journal of Child and Adolescent Psychiatry, 23,*1, 3–10.

Rodriguez, E., & Ouellette, S. (2000). Gay and lesbian Christians: Homosexual and religious identity integration in the members and participants of a gay positive church. *Journal for the Scientific Study of Religion, 39,* 333–347.

Ross, D. K., Suprina, J. S., & Brack, G. (2013). The spirituality in supervision model (SACRED): An emerging model from a meta-synthesis of the literature. *The Practitioner Scholar: Journal of Counseling & Professional Psychology, 2,* 68–83.

Savin-Williams, R. C., & Diamond, L. M. (2000). Sexual identity trajectories among sexual-minority youths: Gender comparisons. *Archives of Sexual Behavior, 29,* 607–627.

Schmidtke, S. (1999). Homoeroticism and homosexuality in Islam: A review article. *Bulletin of the School of Oriental and African Studies, University of London, 62*(2), 260–266.

Shilo, G., & Savaya, R. (2011). Effects of family and friend support on LGB youths' mental health and sexual orientation milestones. *Family Relations, 60*(3), 318–330.

Spilka, B., & McIntosh, D. (Eds) (1997). *The psychology of religion: Theoretical approaches.* Boulder, CO: Westview/Harper.

Spiritual Profile of Homosexual Adults Provides Surprising Insights. www.barna.org/barna-update/article/13-culture/282-spiritual-profile-of-homosexual-adults-provides-surprising-insights (accessed January 23, 2012) The Barna Group, Ltd, 2009.

Suprina, J. S. (2006). A quest to belong: A qualitative study of gay male recovering alcoholics. *Journal of LGBT issues in counseling, 1,* 95–114.

Taylor, R., & Chatters, L. (2010). Importance of religion and spirituality in the lives of African Americans, Caribbean Blacks and Non-Hispanic Whites. *Journal of Negro Education,* 3, 280. Retrieved from http://elibrary.bigchalk.com.libproxy.edmc.edu

Wawrytko, S. A. (1993). Homosexuality and Chinese and Japanese religions. In A. Swindeler (Ed.), *Homosexuality and world religions* (pp. 199–230). Valley Forge, PA: Trinity Press International.

Weaver, A. J., Pargament, K. I., Flannelly, K. J., & Oppenheimer, J. E. (2006). Trends in the scientific study of religion, spirituality, and health: 1965–2000. *Journal of Religion and Health, 45*(2), 208–214. doi: 10.1007/s10943-006-9011-3

Williamson, I. R. (2000). Internalized homophobia and health issues affecting lesbians and gay men. *Health Education Research, 15*(1), 97–107.

Yakushko, O. (2005). Mental health counseling in Ukraine. *Journal of Mental Health Counseling, 27,* 161–167.

Part III

Developing Integral Partnerships in the Treatment of Gay Men, Adolescents, and Boys

5 Assessment and Treatment of the Medical Needs of Gay Men, Adolescents, and Boys

James E. Leone, Elizabeth M. Mullin, & Shan Mohammed

Males experience the poorest overall health outcomes in all demographic subpopulations (Porche, 2010; Wilkins, 2010). With so many health risks, it is vital to appreciate from a holistic view how to best assess and treat disparate male populations. Males clearly have health-related disparities that warrant further investigation as to how to close the gap via programs and interventions that better target their medical needs. Assessing medical needs is important; however, data clearly indicate that subgroups are at most risk for morbidity (Liao et al., 2004). The term "minority" often connotes racial/ethnic groups (i.e., black, Hispanic/Latino, Asian, and other non-white groups); however, sexual minority populations also have poorer health outcomes (as a whole) compared with the general male population and the population as a whole (Boehmer, Miao, Linkletter, & Clark, 2012). Many of these outcomes result from preventable behaviors (such as unprotected sex), but persist due to unmet psychosocial needs.

Understanding the unique medical challenges and needs of gay boys, adolescents, and men is vital for healthcare personnel to properly assess and treat them (Bauer & Wayne, 2005). Therefore, the purpose of this chapter is to: identify and explain excess gay male morbidity and mortality in light of all males using epidemiology; present and discuss health-related issues specific to gay males; discuss current medical practice when assessing and treating health issues in gay males; and identify best practices for future assessment and treatment.

Defining Health in Gay Boys, Adolescents, and Men

Traditionally, health has been conceptualized as "the absence of disease"; however, this definition has evolved to encompass a more holistic view (WHO, n.d.). In short, health is a relative balance among physical, spiritual, emotional, intellectual, occupational/financial, and social aspects of wellness (Roscoe, 2009). Health is variable and exists in degrees. Gay males are no different in that they experience varying degrees of health and wellness. However, having a sexual orientation other than heterosexual can carry different and elevated health risks based on behaviors and perceptions (Boehmer et al., 2012; Fredriksen-Goldsen & Muraco, 2010; Koblin, Chesney, Husnik, et al., 2003; Silberstein, Mishkind, Striegel-Moore, Timko, & Rodin, 1989). Health opportunities and challenges vary and change as males get older (Fredriksen-Goldsen & Muraco, 2010); to appreciate the former, it is helpful to first operationalize the stages of the lifespan of males. The term "male" biologically refers to people who have an XY chromosome pattern. Certainly, there are unique challenges for males born with various chromosomal anomalies (i.e., XXY syndrome), intersexed individuals, and female to male transsexuals/ transgender people; however, discussing these populations is beyond the scope of this chapter. Gay boys, adolescents, and men are people who identify their sexual orientation as other than heterosexual and may include orientations as exclusively homosexual as well as bisexual and "queer" (Young & Meyer, 2005). Development of sexual identity is important to understand in the context of age and timing due to inherent physical and psycho-emotional risks. For example, hormonal development and identity may precede sexual education, placing gay males at risk for negative health outcomes (e.g., unprotected anal intercourse).

In the context of this chapter, men are considered 20 years and older, adolescents 13–19 years old, and boys 9–12 years old. Because some sources (see Calzo, Antonucci, Mays, & Cochran, 2011; Rieger, Linsenmeier, Gygax, & Bailey, 2008; Savin-Williams, Joyner, & Rieger, 2012) postulate sexual orientation is fairly consistent by age 9 or 10, we present medical needs, assessment, and treatment from this perspective.

Issues Specific to Gay Boys, Adolescents, and Men

No health issues are specific to gay males; however, there is greater prevalence (overall magnitude of cases) and incidence (number of new cases) of several diseases and causes of death in this population (Boehmer et al., 2012; Dean et al., 2000). Only in recent years has a better understanding of the health of sexual minority populations become apparent. Inclusion of sexual orientation and gender identity on medical assessments (e.g., screenings, questionnaires) has allowed the medical community greater insight into the specific issues of gay males (Wolitski, Valdiserri, & Stall, 2008). In order to properly assess and treat gay males for health-related issues, it is important to understand the nature of prevalent health problems. The following sections present a major health topic, explain the topic in the context of gay-specific issues and concerns, and briefly discuss best practice in terms of how to deal with (attenuate) these medical issues in gay male populations.

Major Health-Related Issues

Eating Disorders and Somatic Disorders

Major forms of eating disorders include anorexia nervosa and bulimia nervosa, as documented in the *Diagnostic and Statistical Manual of Mental Disorders* (5th ed.; *DSM-5;* American Psychiatric Association, 2013). The hallmark of anorexia nervosa is severe self-imposed weight loss through a variety of methods, such as dieting, food restriction, excessive exercise, use of stimulants, and purging (vomiting), among others. Bulimia nervosa is characterized by excessive periods of bingeing on food followed by purging via the use of vomiting or cathartics (i.e., laxatives) in order to remove food from the body (American Psychiatric Association, 2013). Combinations of these disorders are possible as in the case of "bulimorexics" (Jones & Morgan, 2012). According to the *DSM-5,* both eating disorders are said to originate from obsessive thoughts that lead to compulsive episodes and therefore are treated as valid psychiatric disorders (American Psychiatric Association, 2013). Other forms of eating disorders do exist, though not formalized in the *DSM-5*, one of which is muscle dysmorphia. Also known as "reverse anorexia" or "bigorexia," muscle dysmorphia is characterized by an obsessive preoccupation with one's level of muscularity and leanness (Chung, 2001; Leone, Sedory, & Gray, 2005; Pope, Katz, & Hudson, 1993). The following sections will briefly present, discuss, and offer approaches to the assessment and treatment for these eating disorders in gay males.

For decades, the specter of eating disorders largely has rested upon the shoulders of women, particularly in the Westernized world (Steinhausen, 2002). While rates of anorexia nervosa are highest among wealthy to middle class Caucasian females, rates in all males has been said to account for up to 10% of the population diagnosed (Raudenbush & Zellner, 1997; Steinhausen, 2002). However, the latter figure conflicts with recent data suggesting 0.3% of males report anorexia nervosa, 0.5% bulimia nervosa, and 2% binge eating disorder (Hudson, Pope, & Kessler, 2007). Several authors have noted that the former rates are likely *underreported* due to gender bias in terms of males seeking and receiving treatment (Leone et al., 2011; Mangweth et al., 2004; McCabe & Ricciardelli, 2003). Gay males in particular are more likely to experience, report, and receive treatment for an eating disorder than are their heterosexual counterparts (Blashill & Vanderwal, 2009; Feldman & Meyer, 2010). Reasoning as to why gay males experience higher rates is not well understood; however, several theories exist. Objectification theory has been used with girls and women and states the former group has become acculturated to internalize an outside observer's perspective as representative of their physical self (Fredrickson & Roberts, 2006). This experience may be different for gay males as compared with heterosexual males due to the fact that heterosexual males often are not as objectified by females as gay males are by fellow gay males. For example, Wiseman and Moradi (2010) found higher levels of body surveillance, body shame, and eating disorder symptoms in sexual minority males who experience higher levels of body objectification. Another popular theory pertaining to gay males' experiences with eating disorders is gender role conflict (GRC). The masculine gender norm is typically one of restricted emotions—functionality, stoicism, and dominance among others (O'Neil, 2008). Gay males often are at odds with gender norms and stereotypical male hegemony, which can manifest in issues with control (Heasley, 2005). Because eating disorder etiology is strongly linked to emotional issues of control (American Psychiatric Association, 2013), gay males may express control, restrictive emotions, and GRC through body image distortions.

Gay Males and Anorexia Nervosa

As previously detailed, anorexia nervosa involves a severe restriction of calories as well as possibly exercise dependence (American Psychiatric Association, 2013). A confluence of genetic, nutritional, social, environmental, psychobehavioral, and neurobiological influences likely underpin the disorder (Steinhausen, 2002). There may be a genetic predisposition toward clinical depression and similar genes that control eating regulation and emotions (Strober, Freeman, Lampert, Diamond, & Kaye, 2000). Aside from genetic factors, social influences (e.g., peers, media, internalization) often play a large role in eating disorders, particularly anorexia nervosa (Steinhausen, 2002). Gay males have been reported to be more "appearance concerned" than heterosexuals (Marino-Carper, Negy, & Tantleff-Dunn, 2010). As in mainstream society, several desirable body types exist in gay culture. For example, older males are referred to as "daddies," heavier set men with body hair are termed "bears," and younger, thin, youthful-looking males are referred to as "twinks." The latter body type may provoke some gay males to restrict eating and adopt negative (excessive) exercise behaviors. Certainly media images, specifically images targeted toward gay males, further perpetuate the idealism of male attractiveness. Marino-Carper and colleagues (2010) found gay males scored higher on measures of drive for thinness, body dissatisfaction, and body image anxiety than heterosexual males. Media influence also was cited to be higher in gay males pertaining to body image dissatisfaction. Similar research also corroborates the previous study's findings, suggesting that eating disorders are likely resultant from gay males' internalization of media images as well as social expectations in gay community and culture (Siconolfi, Halkitis, Allomong, & Burton, 2009). Both studies authors' concluded that gay men may be more vulnerable to media and social influences, which may help to explain their higher rates of eating disorder pathology, particularly anorexia nervosa (Marino-Carper et al., 2010; Siconolfi et al., 2009).

Gender role conflict also may manifest in gay males as it pertains to eating and anorexia nervosa. Some gay males may take on more of a stereotypically feminine role and thus may view a heavier/larger body as being in conflict with their norm. To maintain a smaller, more feminine (or youthful) body appearance, some males may restrict eating and use exercise to reduce body mass and size (Blashill & Hughes, 2009). These behaviors can parlay into obsessions, control, and restrictions, which may affect the development of anorexia nervosa. Another factor that may impact restrictive eating in gay males pertains to sexual behavior, namely anal sex/intercourse. Although not unique to gay males, anal intercourse is a common sexual practice. In efforts to prepare for receptive anal intercourse, some males defer eating for extended periods of time so as to purge their bowels of feces. Suppository enemas and douching also may be used to prepare for anal intercourse. Restricting one's eating in preparation for sexual intercourse serves a practical purpose (cleanliness/hygiene); however, it also may fulfill an intrinsic body image need (Allensworth-Davies, Welles, Hellerstedt, & Ross, 2008).

Gay Males and Bulimia Nervosa

Hallmarked by episodes of binge eating followed by purging via various methods (e.g., vomiting, laxatives, exercise), bulimia nervosa likely results from anxiety disorders and depression (American Psychiatric Association, 2013). In fact, unlike anorexia nervosa, bulimia may serve a dual role in gay males; eating large quantities often is an expected and even celebrated part of masculinity (Meyer, Blissett, & Oldfield, 2001; Ruby & Heine, 2011) and purging allows the male to exert control over what he eats (thus addressing the shame, guilt, and anxiety that may develop from over-eating). Binging and purging can become an addictive pattern that carries with it physical and emotional consequences (Mitchell et al., 2004). Estimates in males are relatively low at 0.1% to 2.1%; however, as previously stated, eating disorder estimates in gay males are likely much higher (> 10%) due to underreporting and given that many people may practice bulimia nervosa but do not seek treatment (Feldman & Meyer, 2007; Raudenbush & Zellner, 1997).

Because people with bulimia look normal in terms of weight, intervention and diagnosis may present a particular challenge. Some individuals may not purge but use excessive exercise to help attenuate guilt from consuming excess calories and some even undergo extended periods of fasting prior to a bingeing episode. Essentially, any abnormal attitudes or eating practices in gay males may warrant further attention/questioning by qualified medical/health professionals (Mitchell et al., 2004). A particular issue, however, may be intervening in a community/culture that may subconsciously condone abnormal eating practices and behaviors such as anorexia nervosa and bulimia nervosa. Specific interventions should be designed with the gay community, its collective attitudes, practices and behaviors, and receptivity in mind. For example, embedding eating disorder resources (websites, hotlines, literature) in gay-friendly "safe spaces" and including discussions in school programming, such as gay straight alliances and clubs, also may prove helpful.

While health risks of bulimia nervosa are less severe than anorexia nervosa, there are high rates of physical and psychiatric morbidity. Purging behaviors such as self-induced vomiting can cause oral and esophageal disorders, such as erosion of tooth enamel, irritation of the esophagus (esophagitis), chronic gastric reflux, and inflamed salivary glands. Systemic issues also are common; chronic dehydration, loss of electrolytes, and small intestine and peristalsis movement also may become dysfunctional (Walsh, Wheat, & Freund, 2000). With bulimia nervosa likely to be more common in gay males, assessments, interventions, and treatments should take sexual orientation into consideration.

Gay Males and Muscle Dysmorphia

Relative to more well-known eating disorders such as anorexia nervosa and bulimia nervosa, muscle dysmorphia is currently classified as a psychosomatic spectrum disorder (Baghurst & Kissinger, 2009; Cafri, Olivardia, & Thompson, 2008). Formally identified in the literature by Pope and colleagues (1993), it was noted that muscle dysmorphia overwhelmingly affects males and presents with very clear signs and symptoms. Although not formally included in the *DSM-5* (American Psychiatric Association, 2013), Pope et al. (1997) proposed that characteristics consistent with muscle dysmorphia include:

- a preoccupation that one's body is not sufficiently lean and muscular—associated behaviors include long hours of lifting weights and excessive attention to diet. The preoccupation causes social distress, impaired function, and avoidance behaviors;
- use of substances (legal and illegal), such as sports supplements and/or androgenic-anabolic steroids;
- a primary focus on being too small or inadequately muscular with respect to one's physique.

Muscle dysmorphia likely fits within the previously described body-control pathway; however, other proposed causes include: a history of physical or mental abuse, genetic susceptibility, gender role conformity, media influences and pressure, and social desirability/Expectancy Theory, among others (Tucker, Watkins, & Cardinal, 2011). Specifically, Expectancy Theory proposes that individuals select a behavior expecting that the result will be positive and align with their motivation (Oliver, 1974).

Research on muscle dysmorphia in gay male populations presents yet another layer as to why it occurs. Expressing a strong drive for muscularity and leanness may be used to enhance self-esteem, convey masculinity to others, attract partners, and demonstrate health and virility. Chaney (2008) found that gay males with lower self-esteem and higher reported loneliness were more likely to report muscle dysmorphia symptoms. Similarly, Brennan, Craig, and Thompson (2012) found gay males to have higher body dissatisfaction and greater internalization of homophobia, and suggested that muscle dysmorphia and drive for muscularity may be used to moderate such feelings. Tylka and Andorka (2012) assert a three-factor model for the development of muscle dysmorphia in gay men with a particular focus on socio-cultural pressures to achieve an "ideal" physique, especially as it pertains to one's self perception of masculinity. Moreover, using one's muscularity to attract a partner and demonstrate health and virility in the gay community also has been noted (Kane, 2010).

Stigma associated with HIV/AIDS in the gay community also may prompt some males to pursue a muscular physique. For example, muscle "wasting" is likely with HIV/AIDS infected individuals; therefore, it is theorized that gay males may pursue a muscular physique so as to alleviate stigma or to communicate health to potential partners (Kane, 2010). Clearly attributing one causative factor to muscle dysmorphia in gay males is not only near sighted, but it also is illogical. The confluence of genetic, intrapersonal, interpersonal, and social factors likely underpins the true cause for this disorder (Baghurst & Kissinger, 2009; Leone et al., 2005). Gay culture, and society in general, may perpetuate muscle dysmorphia in males due to evolving ideals of the male physique. Because males with muscle dysmorphia often look fit and healthy and generally do not want help, efficacy of interventions and treatment are problematic. Coupled with the unique intersection of masculinity and sexuality in the gay community, muscle dysmorphia likely will be difficult to address without proper recognition, assessment, and treatment (Leone et al., 2005).

Helping Gay Males with Eating Disorders

As previously noted, gay males are more likely to experience, report, and receive treatment for an eating disorder than are heterosexuals (Blashill & Vanderwal, 2009; Feldman & Meyer, 2010). However, eating disoders are difficult to address due to the fact that many people deny them and suffer in silence (American Psychiatric Association, 2013). It is important to avoid confrontation but also to provide opportunities for open and honest communication. People often revert to secrecy and withdrawal when directly confronted with the aforementioned disorders (Mitchell et al., 2004). Guiding a person to recognize their behaviors are detrimental to their physical, emotional, and social health, among others, can be an extensive and extended process due to the individual's lack of rational thought. Lock and Le Grange (2005) recommend allowing people to discuss with family, friends, and healthcare personnel what they feel comfortable with, and having these people serve as non-judgmental advocates in their recovery process. A primary step in eating disorder treatment includes awareness, and then breaking the cycle of thought and action. For example, breaking the binge–purge cycle in people with bulimia nervosa is paramount. The latter can be addressed with cognitive behavioral therapy (CBT), possibly in combination with antidepressant medication such as selective serotonin reuptake inhibitors (SSRIs).

Focusing on and addressing the fears and expectations in a gradual, but progressive manner is practiced in CBT (Mitchell et al., 2004; Walsh, Wheat, & Freund, 2000). Working with gay males presents both opportunities and challenges for the practitioner. On one hand, gay males may be more apt to openly discuss feelings and emotions surrounding eating and body image; however, stigma and threatened masculinity also exist (Heasley, 2005). A skilled practitioner will go beyond the simple "cookie-cutter" approach toward eating disorders, and tailor assessments, interventions, and treatments with the personal and social pressures of gay males in mind.

Drug Use and Substance Abuse

Licit and illicit drug use in gay communities is prevalent and reportedly higher than in non-homosexual populations. A variety of theories as to why gay males use and abuse alcohol and drugs exist, ranging from psychiatric issues to social norming behavior and exposure (Halkitis & Parsons, 2002). Although there are many drugs that gay males may use, the following sections will primarily focus on the medical and health issues related to drug use and abuse.

Severe health issues can result from drinking and smoking, some in the short-term and others long-term. For example, smoking can lead to chronic bronchitis and other respiratory disorders (e.g., emphysema and chronic obstructive pulmonary disorder), in addition to severe consequences such as heart disease and lung cancer (Storholm, Halkitis, Siconolfi, & Moeller, 2011). Long-term effects of alcohol include organ damage/failure such as the kidneys and liver; similarly, cirrhosis of the liver is quite common in long-term heavy alcohol users (Barrett et al., 1995). However, of note are the short-term consequences of alcohol use by gay males. Psychiatric effects of alcohol on the brain can lead to depression and other psycho-emotional issues. Impaired cognitive function due to alcohol also presents several health issues; for example, drinking and driving and engaging in risky sexual behaviors (i.e., unprotected sex), thus increasing the likelihood for contracting and/or transmitting sexually transmitted infections (STIs). Research has demonstrated that, when under the influence, people have more sexual experiences, are less likely to use condoms, and are more likely to use them incorrectly when used (Boehmer et al., 2012; Halkitis & Parsons, 2002).

Recreational drug use also is higher in gay males (Boehmer et al., 2012). Studies have demonstrated that gay males are more likely than heterosexuals to report using methamphetamine, cocaine, marijuana, heroin, amyl nitrate ("poppers"), and other drugs (Barrett et al., 1995). One particular drug that has become popularized over the past 10–15 years in gay communities is the PDE5 inhibitors also known as erectile dysfunction drugs. Brand names such as Viagra™, Levitra™, and Cialis™ flood the market with claims of helping males with potency issues. However, some research (Prestage et al., 2009) suggests that otherwise healthy gay males may use these drugs not as indicated, but for hypersexual experiences. The desire for prolonged and/or multiple sexual experiences may be aided by using these drugs; however, side effects and other health consequences such as problems with blood pressure, visual and hearing disturbances, fainting, and damage to the penis due to prolonged erections exist (Prestage et al., 2009). Public health efforts need to be tailored to gay males and their communities to lessen/curb substance use and abuse.

Reducing Risk for Substance Abuse in Gay Males

The self-medicating properties of addiction have been shown to combat the physical and emotional pain associated with being a gay male in a society that does not readily accept homosexuality (Blackwell, 2011). Primary prevention should supersede other initiatives being that this is the most salient and cost-effective approach. Secondary prevention (screening) should be used to lessen the health burden from alcohol and drug use and may focus on: discussing limits (knowing when to stop drinking), understanding what alcohol poisoning is; providing alternative locations for gay men to meet (versus bars); creating and supporting gay-friendly alcohol treatment programs; and providing multi-level interventions that target where gay males live and socialize, but also working with organizations that provide care (i.e., healthcare providers).

By linking mental health services and medical treatment with health promotion and public health efforts, rates of substance abuse likely will decrease as well as related comorbidities such as STIs, violence and abuse, and drug dependence issues. Last, tertiary prevention (keeping existing health issues from getting worse) should be offered to offset additional health risks and costs, such as teaching intravenous (IV) drug users ways to minimize exposure to infections as well as keeping other people safe (other IV drugs users, partners, etc.) (Sowadsky, 1998, "Health Concerns for Gay Men"). The involvement of the community, stakeholders, partner organizations, academia, and other interested parties can be used to develop multilevel, creative solutions to alcohol and drug use issues that actually work!

Infectious Diseases, Vaccinations, and Gay Males

All populations are susceptible to infectious diseases (IDs), which account for significant levels of morbidity and mortality (Wolfe, Dunavan, & Diamond, 2007); however, gay males may be at greater risk for certain infections. Infection rates in gay males are higher for STIs; these infections, such as the human papillomavirus (HPV) and the human immunodeficiency virus (HIV), which causes acquired immune deficiency syndrome (AIDS), cause long-term consequences. This section will briefly detail some of the more commons IDs and STIs in gay males and ends in a discussion of prevention and risk reduction strategies.

Sexually transmitted infections are caused by a variety of biological organisms, such as bacteria, viruses, fungi, and parasites among others. Most are transmitted via intimate contact involving the exchange of bodily fluids/secretions such as blood, blood plasma, and semen. Identification and treatment of IDs and STIs have come a long way in recent decades, however, rates continue to remain stable, with some IDs on the rise in gay male populations (Wolitski & Fenton, 2011). Bacterial infections such as chlamydia and gonorrhea are easily identified and treatable with antibiotics, whereas viral infections (e.g., HPV, HIV, herpes) can take longer to diagnose and therapies only can suppress outbreaks versus providing a cure. Moreover, some infections, such as HIV, weaken the host's immune system making them more susceptible to opportunistic infections (e.g., pneumonia) as well as developing rare and specific cancers. The more prevalent IDs in gay males include hepatitis A, B, and C, tuberculosis, gonorrhea, chlamydia, syphilis, HPV, HIV, and each will be briefly presented and discussed (Mayer, 2011).

Hepatitis is an inflammatory condition of the liver. The liver functions to clean the blood, process chemicals, and aid in digestion. Hepatitis infections, particularly A, B, and C, often present with mild to moderate "flu-like" symptoms including fatigue, muscle and joint aches, low-grade fever, and headache. Pain in the upper right quadrant of the abdomen as well as yellowing of the skin and eyes (jaundice) also may be noticeable (Ryder & Beckingham, 2001). Hepatitis A is generally transmitted via the fecal–oral route through contaminated food and/or water; due to varied sexual practices in gay males, hepatitis A may be transmitted via anilingus (i.e., rimming) or not appropriately sanitizing penetrative anal devices. Hepatitis B is caused by exposure to bodily fluids, such as blood; therefore, it is considered a blood-borne pathogen. Rates of hepatitis B infections (worldwide) are rising, even though a three-shot vaccination series is available. This infection is more likely in gay males due to penetrative, receptive anal sex, particularly when protection (condoms) is not used (e.g., barebacking) (Sowadsky, 1998, "Health Concerns for Gay Men"). Tears to the sensitive tissues in the anus and rectum increase hepatitis B transmission between partners. Last, hepatitis C often presents as asymptomatic; therefore, detection can be an issue. Similar to hepatitis B, hepatitis C is transmitted via blood and bodily fluids, particularly in people who share needles to inject drugs (Ryder & Beckingham, 2001). The close relationship in some gay venues and drug culture makes hepatitis C infection a notable concern.

Bacterial STIs, such as gonorrhea, chlamydia, and syphilis are more prevalent in gay male populations. Signs and symptoms in males often are subtle, making early diagnosis and treatment a challenge (Mayer, 2011). While antibiotics are highly efficacious in treating bacterial STIs, subtle symptoms often preclude prevention and partner infections occur at fairly rapid rates before treatment can work. Gonorrhea typically is transmitted via unprotected anal and/or oral intercourse and is found in the rectum, penis, and throat. With rates of gonorrhea on the rise, public health and counseling professionals need to be aware that high-risk sexual behaviors are likely increasing as well (Wolitski & Fenton, 2011). Chlamydia rates also are higher in gay male populations, particularly infections of the anus/rectum. Transmission through high-risk behavior (e.g., unprotected anal intercourse) and outcomes are similar to gonorrhea. Treatment for chlamydia includes antibiotics, but issues with consistent testing and changing high-risk behaviors continue to be a public health concern in gay males (Marcus et al., 2010). Syphilis rates are on the rise in men who have sex with men (MSM), accounting for 64% of all cases in the U.S. (Mayer, 2011; Wolitski & Fenton, 2011). Although treatable with antibiotics and other medications, a main challenge is enhancing awareness, promoting consistent testing, encouraging positive behavior change, and achieving consistent re-testing and follow-up in at-risk groups of MSM.

Viral STIs common in gay males include HPV and the HIV (Mayer, 2011; Reiter, Brewer, McRee, Gilbert, & Smith, 2010). Unlike bacterial STIs, viruses cannot be cured, but, rather, controlled and suppressed via medication. Human papillomavirus is spread through intimate contact, but exposure to bodily secretions is not necessary for transmission to occur. Skin to skin exposure to the virus allows for cells to shed, which contain a viral load. Much attention to HPV has come by way of cervical cancer in females; however, HPV infection in males can cause genital and anal warts and, in some cases, oral and throat cellular changes (dysplasia). Genital warts on the penis often are not thought to be a major cause for concern, being that penile cancer is rare; however, transmitting HPV to a receptive partner (anally or orally) is a concern. Anal warts and HPV infection in the rectum can cause anal and rectal cancers leading to significant morbidity and mortality in males (Reiter et al., 2010). Recently, a rise in oral and facial cancers in gay males suggests a need for education and behavior change strategies to help reduce risky sexual behaviors (Gilbert, Brewer, & Reiter, 2011).

Perhaps one of the most well known viral infections in the gay community is HIV, the virus that causes AIDS. Gay males continue to have the highest incidence of HIV infection in the U.S. and other westernized nations and rates remain stable (not decreasing) (Chakravarty, Hoff, Neilands, & Darbes, 2012). HIV is transmitted via several media, such as blood and bodily secretions (semen), as well as through sharing needles in IV drug users. Unprotected sex, especially receptive anal intercourse, is likely an activity that poses the greatest risk for transmission (Chakravarty et al., 2012; Sowadsky, 1998, "Health Concerns for Gay Men"). Condoms and other barrier methods are highly effective in reducing infection, however, risk still persists. Serosorting can help reduce new infections in the gay community. Serosorting is a practice where a person who knows their serostatus (HIV-positive or HIV-negative) only engages in sexual activity with people with a similar serostatus (Chakravarty et al., 2012). With random sexual partners (hook-ups, one-night-stands, etc.) fairly likely in gay culture, practicing safer sex through the consistent use of condoms is the best method to reduce infection as well as to protect others. Knowing one's serostatus is effective, but literature suggests many males do not know this (Chakravarty et al., 2012; Wolitski & Fenton, 2011; Sowadsky, 1998, "Health Concerns for Gay Men"). While complete protection is not possible during sexual activity, risk reduction practices are highly effective in decreasing the chances of transmitting HPV and HIV.

Prevention and Helping Males with Infectious Diseases

Infectious disease rates in gay males are elevated relative to the general population (Mayer, 2011). There are several possible reasons as to why this is true, but primarily riskier behaviors and social norms toward behaviors keep IDs high. The nature of gay male sexual practices involves a distinct likelihood of sharing of bodily fluids (blood, semen) and if unprotected, IDs, STIs, and other problems are likely to develop. For example, unprotected anal intercourse (UAI) elevates risk for STIs, particularly HIV, whereas casual sexual exposure can lead to TB and HPV. In terms of social norms, it is more common in gay culture for men to have multiple partners (particularly when younger), use substances that may alter good judgment, have the expectation to get some type of infection/disease (i.e., fatalism), and not consistently use condoms (Halkitis & Parsons, 2002; Sowadsky, 1998, "Health Concerns for Gay Men").

Education efforts need to start early targeting young males (pre-teen and adolescents) so as to prevent infections in the first place. Age appropriate sexuality education classes should be stressed and taught with diversity of the audience in mind. Many classes on the topics of STIs and HIV are taught from a heterosexual perspective often leaving gay males feeling left out; they may even feel that the information does not pertain to them, putting them at greater risk (Sowadsky, 1998, "Health Concerns for Gay Men"). Keeping information relevant and engaging is tremendously important. Before hormonal influences take over boys' minds and bodies, they need to be armed with knowledge and attitudes to keep them safer sexually. Parents may be opposed to sexual education, but the rates do not lie; discussions by parents with their son as well as with their primary care physician also need to be encouraged and facilitated. Education and awareness can be promoted through schools' GSAs, health courses, or other appropriate outlets. Of course, education is only one prong of this multi-pronged issue. Inculcating young males with preventative measures, such as consistent condom use, needs to be a primary and concerted effort. Helping gay males relate to these topics will make it a more meaningful experience and may prompt healthier attitudes and behaviors.

Teaching responsible behaviors needs to be stressed in gay communities; for example, being that sexual activity is commonly performed under the influence of alcohol or other drugs, efforts focusing on reducing drug use and teaching responsible use needs to be a priority (Sowadsky, 1998, "Health Concerns for Gay Men"). Counselors in particular are a vital resource in designing and facilitating strategies for at-risk groups. Additionally, counselors should be prepared to assess whether if sexual violence/assault (i.e., rape) occurred, it places a man at risk for infection.

Primary prevention in helping to curb new infections includes vaccinations. Effective vaccinations exist for hepatitis A and B; however, despite availability, vaccination rates remain low (Reiter & Brewer, 2011). This could be due to lack of awareness or perceived less susceptibility, particularly in younger males. Recently, vaccination for HPV in males was recommended; however, in order to be effective, boys need to be vaccinated before their first sexual experience (i.e., oral or anal intercourse) (Reiter et al., 2010). The aforementioned barriers exist for HPV vaccinations, but also parental discontent. Parents may not want to acknowledge that their boy is sexually active or ready to become sexually active, thereby precluding early vaccination. Additionally, vaccinating for HPV can help reduce anal and rectal cancers in males but, again, boys struggling with their sexual orientation may not get the counseling needed to prevent future infection.

Secondary prevention through screenings is important for sexually active males. Rapid HIV testing has come a long way and results are highly sensitive and specific. Gay males are strongly encouraged to seek routine HIV testing, especially if they are IV drug users, have multiple sexual partners, or do not consistently use condoms (Chakravarty et al., 2012). Anal Papanicolaou (pap) smear tests can be used to identify dysplasic (abnormal) anal and rectal tissue, which may show early signs of anal and rectal cancer. When found early, survival rates and quality of life are much higher than in people who delay diagnosis and treatment (Reed, Reiter, Smith, Palefsky, & Brewer, 2010). All in all, a confluence of education, early intervention, screening, diagnosis, treatment, and follow-up along with sensitivity to gay culture are needed to limit IDs and enhance male health.

Cancer and Gay Males

The word "cancer" is ubiquitous in today's world and with people living longer; rates of cancer are expected to increase (Jemal et al., 2009). Some forms of cancer are more prevalent in gay males such as lung, anal/rectal, liver, and certain types of lymphomas (Boehmer, Miao, & Ozonoff, 2011). Most of the previously mentioned cancers are preventable through behavioral modification. Smoking has been linked to various forms of cancer, but particularly lung cancer and other cardiorespiratory diseases (e.g., chronic obstructive pulmonary disease, emphysema, and heart disease). With gay males smoking at higher rates than non-gays likely due to social norms, interventions, including education and behavioral modification counseling, need to be targeted at these groups (Storholm et al., 2011). Cancer of the anus and rectum in gay males is likely preceded by infection from strains of HPV. Penile and anal warts are signs that the immune system is battling HPV; frequent anal/rectal screenings should be performed along with anal Pap smears to rule out later stage cancers (Reiter et al., 2010). HPV can cause penile cancer as well, but rates are low and it is considered a rare form of cancer (Backes, Kurman, Pimenta, & Smith, 2009). Most important, proper sexual education and safer sexual practices (i.e., condoms) need to be stressed to reduce new infections that can lead to cancer.

Liver cancer is more common in gay males due to higher rates of hepatitis infection, drug use and alcohol consumption, and long-term damage (i.e., cirrhosis) (Gilbert, Levandowski, Scanlon, & Peterson, 2010). Again, safer sexual practices and limiting drug and alcohol consumption can reduce the chances of hepatitis infections (Sowadsky, 1998, "Health Concerns for Gay Men"). Some cancers, namely lymphomas, are more common in immune-compromised gay males, such as HIV-positive men. Kaposi's sarcoma is another rare cancer that is only seen in HIV-positive individuals as well as people who have progressed to full-blown AIDS (Wolitski & Fenton, 2011). While cancer is common in today's population, specific cancers continue to remain prevalent in gay males largely due to behavioral practices. Education and sexual orientation sensitive medical counseling likely can reduce risky behaviors in males.

Risky Sexual Behaviors

Serostatus and the acquisition of HIV/AIDS has been a major health-related concern of the gay community for decades. After the AIDS epidemic of the 1980s and 1990s that resulted in increased education of safer sexual behaviors, a relaxed mentality from this vigilance has occurred in recent years (Beckerman, Heft-LaPorte, & Cicchetti, 2008). Younger generations of MSM that did not experience the fear their older counterparts did, are engaging in risky sexual behaviors. With improvements in medical care, HIV/AIDS is no longer considered to be the same "death sentence" it once was. Researchers report that younger gay men know few, if any, other individuals who are HIV positive or at least perceived as so. Consequently, researchers have reported an increase in risk taking behaviors such as not disclosing serostatus or not using a form of a barrier (e.g., condom) (Beckerman et al., 2008; Halkitis et al., 2008).

Engaging in unprotected anal intercourse (i.e., barebacking) is considered an extremely risky sexual behavior for the transmission of HIV and other STIs (Halkitis et al., 2008).

While approximately 75% of individuals disclose their serostatus when engaging in anal sex (Moskowitz & Seal, 2011), the percentage needs to be increased to diminish the transmission of STIs. Increased risk taking has been associated with negative sexual experiences, such as childhood sexual abuse. Men who engaged in barebacking reported having sexual experiences at a young age, sometimes spurred on by parents or other guardians (Halkitis et al., 2008). Barebackers have described themselves as lonely and isolated. Most have experienced significant loss or abandonment and participants also reported alcohol and drug use. These qualities are important to understand from a counseling perspective to devise therapeutic approaches.

Some individuals have purposely sought out opportunities to become HIV-positive through risky sexual experiences (Beckerman et al., 2008). Some men in the gay community have reported experiencing fatigue and anxiety worry with practicing safer sex to avoid HIV transmission. Mental fatigue can lead to burnout for the individual. For gay men in a relationship where one individual is HIV-positive and another is HIV-negative, fear of contracting HIV can prove strenuous for the relationship. Some HIV-negative individuals reported that they felt they would be able to have a closer relationship with their partner if they both were HIV-positive.

Reducing Risky Sexual Behaviors

Reducing the number of risky sexual behaviors one engages in plays a critical role in diminishing the physiological consequences of STIs. In a therapeutic relationship, counselors should engage in and encourage an open discussion regarding the thoughts and feelings that surround safer sex (Beckerman et al., 2008). This should open the corridor to discussing the emotional fatigue and worry associated with avoiding the transmission of STIs. The therapist should help the client make connections between fantasy and reality of seroconversion through reflection and behavioral modification techniques (Beckerman et al., 2008). Behavior modification techniques where the client practices serostatus disclosure can decrease the anxiety inhibiting the behavior previously, which may increase safer sex behaviors in the future (Moskowitz et al., 2011). Additionally, counselors should emphasize the bolstering of self-confidence in the therapeutic relationship. Research has shown that individuals with higher levels of self-confidence are more likely to disclose their serostatus (Moskowitz & Seal, 2011).

Feeling connected to a peer network has been strongly associated with safer sex behaviors. Counselors should help the client focus on close friends and family who support them remaining sero-negative (Beckerman et al., 2008; Darbes & Lewis, 2005; Mutchler & McDavitt, 2010; Satterfield & Crabb, 2011). For young males, best friends (males or females) have been shown to be effective advocates for safer sex behaviors. By emphasizing reliance on a close friend, a young male may be less likely to engage in risky sexual behaviors because the friend serves as a constant reminder that someone else cares (Mutchler & McDavitt, 2011). One of the most important peers to consider is one's partner. Open dialogue between partners is critical, especially if one partner is sero-negative and the other is sero-positive. Constant communication regarding safer sex should provide the support a sero-negative individual needs to overcome the shame, guilt, and frustration associated with being in a relationship with a sero-positive partner (Darbes & Lewis, 2005).

The role of the counselor is pivotal, particularly when it intersects (or coincides) with medical issues. Close discussion and collaboration with medical providers (and vice versa) is important in treating the client in a holistic manner. The unique circumstances of gay males and their health concerns may afford the counselor and medical provider opportunity to develop an integrated healthcare model, which can benefit the population at-large as well as advance socially just health principles.

Clinical Applications

During their lifespan, gay males have a variety of opportunities to engage with health professions that can address many of the health disparities previously mentioned. It is critical that the health profession is educated on the needs specific to the gay male population to identify warning signs for health disparities. Historically, homosexuality was considered a mental illness. While it was removed from the *Diagnostic and Statistical Manual of Mental Disorders* in 1973, health professions may still harbor ingrained intolerance and/or ignorance of the health needs of the gay community. LGBT individuals have repeatedly reported instances of discrimination and ignorance when engaging with health professionals (Hughes, 2009).

Health professionals must first examine their own biases and determine methods to engage their gay male patients in a professional and educated manner without pathologizing their sexual orientation or falling victim to cultural stereotypes of gay males (Boysen, Fisher, DeJesus, Vogel, & Madon, 2011; Casey, 2009). Common stereotypes of gay men are that they are: (i) mentally ill, (ii) perverted, (iii) closeted, (iv) flamboyant, (v) feminine, (vi) involved in activism, and (vii) cross-dressers. These stereotypes can be harmful to providing equitable and effective care for patients. Medical professionals should be aware of the sexual orientation development process, noting the key mental and physiological changes.

Additionally, addressing one's biases should allow for the professional to create a more open experience with his or her clients or patients. Sexual orientation is one component of many that a healthcare practitioner must account for when considering proper care (Satterfield & Crabb, 2010). Few medical histories include sexual orientation as a recorded variable and, historically, gay male patients may be reluctant to provide that information to their healthcare professional to avoid the potential for discrimination. It is critical that the professional provides an atmosphere that demonstrates respect and cultural sensitivity to all individuals. Increased appreciation for one's unique attributes should foster open communication regarding sexual orientation.

We have identified a number of different health professionals who may be in a position to recognize the health disparities that gay male patients face and provide necessary care. They include: general practitioners, physicians (specialists), physician assistants, nurses, psychologist, counselors, and social workers, among others. While this list is in no way comprehensive, it demonstrates a need in allied health professions to engage in education of the health disparities specific to gay men's health. Health providers who treat gay male patients should have materials available regarding common morbidities for this population, such as literature on substance abuse treatment or the importance of practicing safer sex.

Because of the increased risk for a variety of morbidities, both mental and physical, it is important that practitioners learn to recognize warning signs and refer if necessary. For example, it is critical that a doctor who is treating a gay male for HIV/AIDS is aware of the correlation between a positive serostatus and drug abuse or depression. Medical schools also can take a lead role in the healthcare of sexual minority populations by introducing/incorporating evidence-based and relevant physical and psychological care guidelines for emerging professionals. Collaboration between medical and mental health professionals should be a natural team-based dynamic. Viewing one's health as holistic, medical and mental health professionals are encouraged to collaborate, sharing resources and best practice outcomes in order to provide the highest level of care to all clients or patients. Health problems cannot be treated in a silo. By engaging the patient from a variety of health perspectives, the gay male is more likely to achieve positive health outcomes. Individuals working in Emergency Care situations also should be keen to the health disparities among gay males as they may treat gay men in the emergency department.

Other Windows for Intervention

Healthcare for gay males often will go beyond routine healthcare visits. Because of the prevalence of substance abuse, addiction, depression, and suicide ideation, gay males may seek treatment in the form of mental health therapy, substance abuse rehabilitation, and support groups.

Support groups are critical to positive health outcomes in the gay male community (Casey, 2009; Darbes & Lewis, 2005; Masten, Kochman, Hansen, & Sikkema, 2007; Vincke & Bolton, 1994). During adolescence, researchers have shown that students are more likely to do well in school and report a sense of belonging if the school has a Gay–Straight Alliance (Heck, Flentje, & Cochran, 2011; Kosciw, Greytak, Diaz, & Bartkiewicz, 2009). Gay–Straight Alliances (GSAs) typically are student-run organizations that educate on issues related to LGBT student life and can act as a voice in the school against gay hate speech, bullying, and victimization. They are however, more common among liberal, high income, suburban communities (Heck et al., 2011). We recommend greater efforts to establish more programs. Students who attend schools with a GSA are less likely to report being the victims of verbal and physical abuse. A school nurse or health educator may play a key mentorship role in a GSA. By being a part of a GSA, health professionals may be better able to spot the warning signs of victimization and bullying that lead to the health disparities that gay boys and men experience.

For adults, a wide array of support groups exist for members of the gay community. While general support, such as friends and relatives, can play a critical role, domain-specific support groups may be more effective in dealing with certain issues. Darbes and Lewis (2005) found that individuals who participated in an HIV-specific support group had more positive health outcomes than did individuals who either did not have any support or did have a general support system. A coping group model intervention demonstrated positive outcomes for gay male childhood sexual abuse survivors (Masten et al., 2007). Gay male smokers indicated a preference for participating in smoking cessation services tailored to their sexual orientation status over a general cessation program (Schwappach, 2009). Additionally, there are gay-male Alcoholics Anonymous meetings and gay-male substance abuse support groups. Having support groups specific to the health issues results in more effective and positive health outcomes (Casey, 2009).

As the aging process continues, concerns for quality healthcare are important to older LGBT adults. Aging LGBT adults have reported that they are most concerned about general decline in health, loss of independence, and decrease in cognitive abilities (Hughes, 2009). Healthcare of the aging gay male needs to be tailored to the group's unique needs and concerns (Reisner et al., 2011). Older LGBT adults share many of the same concerns about living in older adulthood as heterosexuals, such as being alone and loss of respect (Boehmer et al., 2012; Reisner et al., 2011; Satterfield & Crabb, 2010). LGBT individuals have noted important opportunities for healthcare, such as the lack of LGBT community organizations for older adults. Assisted living care housing situations often are of mixed sexual orientation. With loss of autonomy and a diminishing population, LGBT individuals may feel that they are without an LGBT community to engage with during their later years (Hughes, 2009). Currently, few resources exist specifically for older gay male adults that provide the sense of community, self-respect, autonomy, and potential for a high quality of life. Recognizing specific windows for intervention, such as annual preventative health appointments, health screenings, or colonoscopies, among this population is important to mitigating the loneliness and depression often associated with this group.

Assessing Current Practices in Medical Assessment and Treatment of Gay Males

As previously noted, the healthcare community does provide services specific to gay males, but often not in an integrated and gender-sensitive manner (Boysen et al., 2011). Treatments for a variety of physical and emotional concerns in gay males are available; however, awareness, accessibility, and overcoming stigma associated with treatment continue to be a barrier (Wolitski et al., 2008). Advances in healthcare accessibility through the Patient Protection and Affordable Care Act (PPACA) may serve to advance care and integration of services in all groups, but care needs to be taken to advocate for equality of services to marginalized, higher-risk groups, such as gay males.

Evidence-based best practices need to be planned and delivered at earlier ages during the lifespan of gay males. Evidenced by higher rates of morbidity and mortality in gay male health outcomes throughout the lifespan (Boehmer et al., 2012; Wolitski et al., 2008), earlier interventions through careful gender and sexual orientation specificity need to be planned and implemented. If we hope to reduce health-related disparities and ensure a vibrant citizenry, medical care and treatment of gay males need to be included in the lexicon of healthcare in the U.S.

Toward a Future of Best Practices in the Assessment and Treatment of Gay Males

Health does not occur in a vacuum, nor does the delivery of healthcare to individuals. Appreciating the holistic nature of health in diverse populations and communities *and* delivering appropriate care that takes individual and community values into account, likely will yield the best results. Allowing gay males to comfortably interact with healthcare professionals in welcoming environments may strengthen the patient–professional relationship and dynamic, and ensure that patients receive optimal care. Building an open and trusting relationship is of paramount concern for healthcare providers; gay patients who feel threatened or stigmatized, or fear they will be unfairly judged by their provider, are less likely to divulge health concerns and practices and are less likely to follow up for future care (Coker, Auston, & Schuster, 2010). The latter is so critical due to many physical and emotional conditions in gay males that warrant consistent follow up, such as HIV-positive men, those with depression/anxiety disorders, and those with substance abuse issues.

Training of healthcare practitioners needs to begin as soon as a formal education begins. Inclusivity in the provision of medical care should be stressed in professional preparation programs, such as medical school. For example, understanding how to best take a sexual history without undue judgment or bias is a critical skill for healthcare providers so as to not ostracize gay males. For clinicians already in practice, continuing education and in-services delivered by community partner organizations sensitive to the needs of gay males can help raise awareness and help structure a welcoming environment for gay individuals. Continuous assessment and evaluation of the care provided to sexual minority males needs to continue to better inform healthcare practitioners; however, we first need to provide a welcoming, friendly, and inclusive environment in which they are served.

References

Allensworth-Davies, D., Welles, S. L., Hellerstedt, W. L., & Ross, M. W. (2008). Body image, body satisfaction, and unsafe anal intercourse among men who have sex with men. *Journal of Sex Research, 45*(1), 49–56.

American Psychiatric Association. (2000). *Diagnostic and statistical manual of mental disorders* (text revision IV; DSM–TR IV). Washington, DC: American Psychiatric Publishing.

American Psychiatric Association (2013). *Diagnostic and statistical manual of mental disorders* (5th ed.). Arlington, VA: American Psychiatric Publishing.

Backes, D. M., Kurman, R. J., Pimenta, J. M., & Smith, J. S. (2009). Systematic review of human papillomavirus prevalence in invasive penile cancer. *Cancer Causes and Control, 20*(4), 449–457. doi: 10.1007/s10552-008-9276-9

Baghurst, T., & Kissinger, D. B. (2009). Perspectives on muscle dysmorphia. *International Journal of Men's Health, 8,* 82–89.

Barrett, D. C., Bolan, G., Joy, D., Counts, K., Doll, L., & Harrison, J. (1995). Coping strategies, substance use, sexual activity, and HIV sexual risks in a sample of gay male STD patients. *Journal of Applied Social Psychology, 25*(12), 1058–1072.

Bauer, G. R., & Wayne, L. D. (2005). Cultural sensitivity and research involving sexual minorities. *Perspectives on Sexual and Reproductive Health, 37*(1), 45–47.

Beckerman, N. L, Heft-LaPorte, H., & Cicchetti, A. (2008). Intentional seroconversion in the gay community: The social work role in assessment and intervention. *Social Work in Health Care, 47*(4), 502–518. doi: 10.1080/00981380802173640

Blackwell, C. W. (2011). Reducing alcohol abuse in gay men: Clinical recommendations from conflicting research. *Journal of Social Service Research, 38*(1), 1–8. doi: 10.1080/01488376.2011.583836

Blashill, A. J., & Hughes, H. M. (2009). Gender role and gender role conflict: Preliminary considerations for psychotherapy with gay men. *Journal of Gay & Lesbian Mental Health, 13,* 170–186. doi: 10.1080/19359700902914300

Blashill, A. J., & Vanderwal, J. S. (2009). Mediation of gender role conflict and eating pathology in gay men. *Psychology of Men and Masculinity, 10,* 204–217.

Boehmer, U., Miao, X., Linkletter, C., & Clark, M. A. (2012). Adult health behaviors over the life course by sexual orientation. *American Journal of Public Health, 102*(2), 292–300.

Boehmer, U., Miao, X., & Ozonoff, A. (2011). Cancer survivorship and sexual orientation. *Cancer, 117*(16), 3796–3804. doi: 10.1002/cncr.25950

Boysen, G. A., Fisher, M., DeJesus, M., Vogel, D. L., & Madon, S. (2011). The mental health stereotype about gay men: The relation between gay men's self-stereotype and stereotypes about heterosexual women and lesbian. *Journal of Social and Clinical Psychology, 30*(4), 329–360.

Brennan, D. J., Craig, S. L., & Thompson, D. E. A. (2012). Factors associated with a drive for muscularity among gay and bisexual men. *Culture, Health and Sexuality, 14*(1), 1–15. doi: 10.1080/13691058.2011.619578

Cafri, G., Olivardia, R., & Thompson, J. K. (2008). Symptom characteristics and psychiatric comorbidity among males with muscle dysmorphia. *Comprehensive Psychiatry, 49,* 347–379.

Calzo, J. P., Antonucci, T. C., Mays, V. M., & Cochran, S. D. (2011). Retrospective recall of sexual orientation identity development among gay, lesbian, and bisexual adults. *Developmental Psychology, 47*(6), 1658–1673. doi: 10.1037/a0025508

Casey, M. (2009). Addressing key theoretical approaches to gay male sexual identity: Issues and insights for practitioners of mental health. *Critical Public Health, 19*(3–4), 293–305.

Cass, V. C. (1979). Homosexuality identity formation: A theoretical model. *Journal of Homosexuality, 4,* 219–235.

Centers for Disease Control and Prevention. (n.d.). Leading causes of death in males United States, 2007. Available at: www.cdc.gov/men/lcod/index.htm (accessed January 8, 2014).

Chakravarty, D., Hoff, C. C., Neilands, T. B., & Darbes, L. A. (2012). Rates of testing for HIV in the presence of serodiscordant UAI among HIV-negative gay men in committed relationships. *AIDS and Behavior* [online]. doi: 10.1007/s10461-012-0181-6

Chaney, M. P. (2008). Muscle dysmorphia, self-esteem, and loneliness among gay and bisexual men. *International Journal of Men's Health, 7*(2), 157–170.

Chung, B. (2001). Muscle dysmorphia: A critical review of the proposed criteria. *Perspectives in Biological Medicine, 44,* 565–574.

Coker, T. R., Austin, S. B., & Schuster, M. A. (2010). The health and healthcare of lesbian, gay, and bisexual adolescents. *Annual Review of Public Health, 31,* 457–477. doi: 10.1146/annurev.publhealth.012809.103636

Darbes, L. A., & Lewis, M. A. (2005). HIV-specific social support predicts less sexual risk behavior in gay male couples. *Health Psychology, 24*(6), 617–622.

Dean, L., Mayer, I. H., Robinson, K., Sell, R. L., Sember, R., Silenzio, V. M. B., et al. (2000). Lesbian, gay, bisexual, and transgender health: Findings and concerns. *Journal of the Gay and Lesbian Medical Association, 4*(3), 102–151. doi: 10.1023/A:1009573800168

Feldman, M. B., & Meyer, I. H. (2007). Eating disorders in diverse lesbian, gay, and bisexual populations. *International Journal of Eating Disorders, 40*(3), 218–226. doi: 10.1002/eat.20360

Feldman, M. B., & Meyer, I. H. (2010). Comorbidity and age of onset of eating disorders in gay men, lesbians, and bisexuals. *Psychiatry Research, 180*(2), 126–131.

Fredrickson, B. L., & Roberts, T. A. (2006). Objectification theory: Toward understanding women's lived experiences and mental health risks. *Psychology of Women Quarterly, 21*(2), 173–206. doi: 10.1111/j.1471-6402.1997.tb00108.x

Fredriksen-Goldsen, K. I., & Muraco, A. (2010). Aging and sexual orientation: A 25-year review of the literature. *Research in Aging, 32*(3), 372–413.

Friedman, M. S., Marshal, M. P., Stall, R., Cheon, J., & Wright, E. R. (2008). Gay-related development, early abuse and adult health outcomes among gay males. *AIDS Behavior, 12,* 891–902. doi: 10.1007/s10461-007-9319-3

Gilbert, L. K., Levandowski, B. A., Scanlon, K. E., & Peterson, R. S. (2010). A comparison of hepatitis A and hepatitis B measures among vaccinated and susceptible online men who have sex with men. *International Journal of STD & AIDS, 21*(6), 400–405. doi: 10.1258/ijsa.2009.009010

Gilbert, P. A., Brewer, N. T., & Reiter, P. L. (2011). Association of human papillomavirus-related knowledge, attitudes, and beliefs with HIV status: A national study of gay men. *Journal of Lower Genital Tract Disease, 15*(2), 83–88.

Halkitis, P. N., & Parsons, J. T. (2002). Recreational drug use and HIV-risk sexual behavior among men frequenting gay social venues. *Journal of Gay & Lesbian Social Services, 14*(4), 19–38.

Halkitis, P. N., Siconolfi, D., Fumerton, M., & Barlup, K. A. (2008). Risk bases in childhood and adolescence among HIV-negative young adult gay and bisexual male barebackers. *Journal of Gay & Lesbian Social Services, 20*(4), 288–314. doi: 10.1080/10538720802310709

Heasley, R. (2005). Queer masculinities of straight men: A typology. *Men and Masculinities, 7*(3), 310–320. doi: 10.1177/1097184X04272118

Hudson, J. I., Pope, H. G., & Kessler, R. C. (2007). The prevalence and correlates of eating disorders in the national comorbidity survey replication. *Biological Psychiatry, 61*(3), 348–358.

Hughes, M. (2009). Lesbian and gay people's concerns about ageing and accessing services. *Australian Social Work, 62*(2), 186–201. doi: 10.1080/3124070902748878

Jemal, A., Siegel, R., Ward, E., Hao, Y., Xu, J., & Thun, M. J. (2009). Cancer statistics, 2009. *CA: A Cancer Journal for Clinicians, 59,* 225–249.

Jones, W. R., & Morgan, J. F. (2012). Eurotophilia in bulimia nervosa: A clinical feature. *International Journal of Eating Disorders, 45*(2), 298–301. doi: 10.1002/eat.20919

Kane, G. D. (2010). Revisiting gay men's body image issues: Exposing the fault lines. *Review of General Psychology, 14*(4), 311–317. doi: 10.1037/a0020982

Kassel, P., & Franko, D. L. (2000). Body image disturbance and psychodynamic psychotherapy with gay men. *Harvard Review of Psychiatry, 8,* 307–317.

Koblin, B. A., Chesney, M. A., Husnik, M. J. Bozeman, S., Celum, C. L., Buchbinder, S., et al. (2003). High-risk behaviors among men who have sex with men in 6 U.S. cities: Baseline data from the EXPLORE study. *American Journal of Public Health, 93*(6), 926–932.

Kosciw, J. G., Greytak, E. A., Diaz, E., M., & Bartkiewicz, M. J. (2009). The 2009 national school climate survey. New York: Gay, Lesbian, and Straight Education Network.

Leone, J. E., Fetro, J. V., Kittleson, M., Welshimer, K. J., Partridge, J. A., & Robertson, S. L. (2011). Predictors of adolescent male body image dissatisfaction: Implications for negative health practices and consequences for school health from a regionally representative sample. *Journal of School Health, 81*(4), 174–184. doi: 10.1111/j.1746-1561.2010.00577.x

Leone, J. E., Sedory, E. J., & Gray, K. A. (2005). Recognition and treatment of muscle dysmorphia and related body image disorders. *Journal of Athletic Training, 40,* 352–359.

Liao, Y., Tucker, P., Okoro, C. A., Giles, W. H., Mokdad, A. H., & Harris, V. B. (2004). REACH 2010 Surveillance for Health Status in Minority Communities—United States, 2001–2002. *Morbidity & Mortality Weekly Report Surveillance Summary, 53*(6), 1–36.

Lock, J., & Le Grange, D. (2005). Family-based treatment of eating disorders. *International Journal of Eating Disorders, 37,* Suppl, S64–S67.

Mangweth, B., Hausmann, A., Walch, T., Hotter, A., Rupp, C. I., Biebl, W., et al. (2004). Body fat perception in eating-disordered men. *International Journal of Eating Disorders, 35,* 102–108.

Marcus, J. L., Bernstein, K. T., Stephens, S. C., Snell, A., Kohn, R. P., Liska, S., et al. (2010). Sentinel surveillance of rectal chlamydia and gonorrhea among males—San Francisco, 2005–2008. *Sexually Transmitted Diseases, 37*(1), 59–61. doi: 10.1097/OLQ.0b013e3181b76c42

Marino-Carper, T. L., Negy, C., & Tantleff-Dunn, S. (2010). Relations among media influence, body image, eating concerns, and sexual orientation in men: A preliminary investigation. *Body Image, 7*(4), 301–309.

Masten, J., Kochman, A. E., Hansen, N. B., & Sikkema, K. J. (2007). A short-term group treatment model for gay male survivors of childhood sexual abuse living with HIV/AIDS. *International Journal of Group Psychotherapy, 57*(4), 475–496.

Mayer, K. H. (2011). Sexually transmitted diseases in men who have sex with men. *Clinical Infectious Diseases, 53*(supplement 3), S79–S83. doi: 10.1093/cid/cir696

McCabe, M. P., & Ricciardelli, L. A. (2003). Sociocultural influences on body image and body changes among adolescent boys and girls. *Journal of Social Psychology, 143,* 5–26.

Mitchell, J. E., Agras, W. S., Wilson, G. T., Halmi, K., Kraemer, H., & Crow, S. (2004). A trial of a relapse prevention strategy in women with bulimia nervosa who respond to cognitive-behavior therapy. *International Journal of Eating Disorders, 35,* 549–555. doi: 10.1002/eat.10265

Moskowitz, D. A., & Seal, D. W. (2011). Self-esteem in HIV-Positive and HIV-Negative gay and bisexual men: Implications for risk-taking behaviors with casual sex partners. *AIDS Behavior, 15,* 621–625. doi: 10.1007/s10461-010-9692-1

Mutchler, M. G., & McDavitt, B. (2011). 'Gay boy talk' meets 'girl talk': HIV risk assessment assumptions in young gay men's sexual health communications with best friend. *Health Education Research, 26*(3), 485–505.

Oliver, R. (1974). Expectancy Theory predictions of salesmen's performance. *Journal of Marketing Research, 11,* 243–253.

O'Neil, J. (2008). Summarizing 25 years of research on men's gender role conflict using the Gender Role Conflict Scale: New research paradigms and clinical implications. *The Counseling Psychologist, 38,* 358–445.

Pope, H. G., Gruber, A. J., Choi, P., Olivardia, R., & Phillips, K. A. (1997). Muscle dysmorphia: An underrecognized form of body dysmorphic disorder. *Psychosomatics, 38,* 548–557.

Pope, H. G., Katz, D. L., & Hudson, J. I. (1993). Anorexia nervosa and 'reverse anorexia' among 108 male bodybuilders. *Comprehensive Psychiatry, 34,* 406–409.

Porche, D. J. (2010). Healthy men 2020. *American Journal of Men's Health, 18*(3), 18.

Prestage, G., Jin, F., Kippax, S., Zablotska, I., Imrie, J., & Grulich, A. (2009). Use of illicit drugs and erectile dysfunction medications and subsequent HIV infection among gay men in Sydney, Australia. *The Journal of Sexual Medicine, 6*(8), 2311–2320. doi: 10.1111/j.1743-6109.2009.01323.x

Raudenbush, B., & Zellener, D. A. (1997). Nobody's satisfied: Effects of abnormal eating behaviors and actual and perceived weight status on body image satisfaction in males and females. *Journal of Social and Clinical Psychology, 16,* 95–110. doi: 10.1521/jscp.1997.16.1.95

Reed, A. C., Reiter, P. L., Smith, J. S., Palefsky, J. M., & Brewer, N. T. (2010). Gay and bisexual men's willingness to receive Papanicolaou testing. *American Journal of Public Health, 100*(6), 1123–1129. doi: 10.2105/AJPH.2009.176446

Reisner, S. L., O'Cleirigh, C., Hendriksen, E. S., McLain, J., Ebin, J., Lew, K., & Mimiaga, M. J. (2011). "40 & forward": Preliminary evaluation of a group intervention to improve mental health outcomes and address HIV sexual risk behaviors among older gay and bisexual men. *Journal of Gay & Lesbian Social Services, 23,* 523–545. doi: 10.1080/10538720.2011.611113

Reiter, P. L., & Brewer, N. T. (2011). Hepatitis vaccination among a national sample of gay and bisexual men. *Sexually Transmitted Diseases, 38*(3), 235–238. doi: 10.1097/OLQ.0b013e3181f422bb

Reiter, P. L., Brewer, N. T., McRee, A. L., Gilbert, P., & Smith, J. S. (2010). Acceptability of HPV vaccine among a national sample of gay and bisexual men. *Sexually TransmittedDiseases, 37*(3), 197–203. doi: 10.1097/OLQ.0b013e3181bf542c

Rieger, G., Linsenmeier, J. A. W., Gygax, L., & Bailey, M. J. (2008). Sexual orientation and childhood gender nonconformity: Evidence from home videos. *Developmental Psychology, 44*(1), 46–58. doi: 10.1037/0012-1649.44.1.46

Roscoe, L. J. (2009). Wellness: A review of theory and measurement for counselors. *Journal of Counseling and Development, 87*(2), 216–226.

Ruby, M. B., & Heine, S. J. (2011). Meat, morals, and masculinity. *Appetite, 56*(2), 447–450.

Ryder, S., & Beckingham, I. (2001). ABC of diseases of liver, pancreas, and biliary system: Acute hepatitis. *BMJ, 322,* 151–153.

Satterfield, J. M., & Crabb, R. (2010). Cognitive-behavioral therapy for depression in an older gay man: A clinical case study. *Cognitive and Behavioral Practice, 17,* 45–55.

Savin-Williams, R. C., Joyner, K., & Rieger, G. (2012). Prevalence and stability of self-reported sexual orientation identity during young adulthood. *Archives of Sexual Behavior, 41*(1), 103–110. doi: 10.1007/s10508-012-9913-y

Schwappach, D. L. B. (2009). Queer quit: Gay smokers' perspectives on a culturally specific smoking cessation service. *Health Expectations, 12,* 383–395.

Siconolfi, D., Halkitis, P. N., Allomong, T. W., & Burton, C. L. (2009). Body dissatisfaction and eating disorders in a sample of gay and bisexual men. *International Journal of Men's Health, 8*(3), 254–264. doi: 10.3149/jmh.0803.254

Silberstein, L. R., Mishkind, M. E., Streigal-Moore, R. H., Timko, C., & Rodin, J. (1989). Men and their bodies: A comparison of homosexual and heterosexual men. *Psychosomatic Medicine, 51*(3), 337–346.

Sowadsky, R. (1998). "Health concerns for gay men." Available at: www.thebody.com/content/art2282.html (accessed January 8, 2014).

Steinhausen, H. C. (2002). The outcome of anorexia nervosa in the 20th century. *American Journal of Psychiatry, 159,* 1284–1293.

Storholm, E. D., Halkitis, P. N., Siconolfi, D. E., & Moeller, R. W. (2011). Cigarette smoking as part of a syndemic among young men who have sex with men ages 13–29 in New York City. *Journal of Urban Health, 88*(4), 663–676. doi: 10.1007/s11524-011-9563-8

Strober, M., Freeman, R., Lampert, C., Diamond, J., & Kaye, W. (2000). Controlled family study of anorexia nervosa and bulimia nervosa: Evidence of shared liability and transmission of partial syndromes. *American Journal of Psychiatry, 157,* 393–401.

Tucker, R., Watkins, P. L., & Cardinal, B. J. (2011). Muscle dysmorphia, gender role stress, and sociocultural influences: An explorative study. *Research Quarterly in Exercise and Sport, 82*(2), 310–319.

Tylka, T. L., & Andorka, M. J. (2012). Support for an expanded tripartite influence model with gay men. *Body Image, 9*(1), 57–67.

Vincke, J., & Bolton, R. (1994). Social support, depression, and self-acceptance among gay men. *Human Relations, 47*(9), 1049–1062. doi: 10.1177/001872679404700902

Walsh, J. M. E., Wheat, M. E., & Freund, K. (2000). Detection, evaluation, and treatment of eating disorders. *Journal of General Internal Medicine, 15,* 577–590.

Wilkins, D. (2010). Men's health. *Perspectives in Public Health, 130*(50), 201.

Wiseman, M. C., & Moradi, B. (2010). Body image and eating disorder symptoms in sexual minority men: A test and extension of objectification theory. *Journal of Counseling Psychology, 57*(2), 154–166. doi: 10.1037/a0018937

Wolfe, N. D., Dunavan, C. P., & Diamond, J. (2007). Origins of major infectious human diseases. *Nature, 447,* 279–283.

Wolitski, R. J., & Fenton, K. A. (2011). Sexual health, HIV, and sexually transmitted infections among gay, bisexual, and other men who have sex with men in the United States. *AIDS and Behavior, 15*(1 supplement), 9–17. doi: 10.1007/s10461-011-9901-6

Wolitski, R. J., Valdiserri, R. O., & Stall, R. (2008). Health disparities affecting gay and bisexual men in the United States: An introduction. In R. J. Wolitski, R. Stall, and R. O. Valdiserri (Eds.), *Unequal opportunity: Health disparities affecting gay and bisexual men in the United States.* New York: Oxford University Press.

World Health Organization. (n.d.). Defining Health. Available at: www.who.int/en/ (accessed January 8, 2014).

Young, R. M., & Meyer, I. H. (2005). The trouble with "MSM" and "WSW": Erasure of the sexual-minority person in public health discourse. *American Journal of Public Health, 95*(7), 1144–1149.

6 The Mental Health and Counseling Needs of Gay Men, Adolescents, and Boys

Larry D. Burlew, Nicole Pacheco Pulliam, & Kathleen L. Grant

In this chapter, the common mental health (MH) issues of gay men and youth are reviewed. However, the issues cannot be understood fully without acknowledging the role of the "stigmatizing social and cultural context" (D'Augelli, Grossman, Hershberger, & O'Connell, 2001, p. 150) in which gay men and youth develop their sexual identity. For example, if all religions affirmed homosexuality as staunchly as heterosexuality, religious gay men and youth would not have a spiritual crisis. But, this is not the case; instead many religions condemn homosexuality, so gay men and boys experience distressful thoughts about being gay and can feel ostracized from their inherited religion (Barret & Barzan, 1996; Kubicek et al., 2009).

For gay men and youth, the consequences of encountering pervasive cultural and societal stigmatization are a double-edged sword. This *double edge* can produce positive personal attributes such as resiliency and adaptability, but it can also produce negative attributes such as an increased risk for suicide, periods of self-hate and lower self-esteem, and loneliness (Barney, 2003; Berg, Mimiaga, & Safren, 2008; Bybee, Sullivan, Zielonka, & Moes, 2009).

Most gay youth and men exhibit strong resiliency and adaptability in confronting the powerful social/sexual norm of heterosexuality. Gay youth and men violate social norms about masculinity and male sexual practices with which heterosexual youth and men also struggle in their gender identity development (Addis, Mansfield, & Szydek, 2010; Blazina, Settle, & Eddins, 2008; Chae & Ayala, 2010). Therefore, the mental health (MH) issues that gay men and youth experience may be typical or normative developmental responses (although not always productive) to gender norm transgression and hostile heterosexist environments.

Developmental Counseling for Gay Youth and Men

Helping gay boys, adolescents, and men reach their potential with respect to their sexual identity requires both preventative and direct intervention treatment strategies. Through genuine gay-affirming counseling we can help gay youth and men address their sexual identity crises, as well as enhance their development before a crisis occurs. Providing effective developmental counseling to clients includes preventative strategies that help gay youth and men face experiences such as coming out, discrimination, and social alienation. Developing skills to address these issues before they cause an identity crisis is paramount. Developmental counseling also involves direct intervention strategies to help gay clients and students deal directly with issues that are creating barriers to successful sexual identity development. For direct intervention the MH practitioner must accurately access the crisis; for example, a suicidal gay adolescent needs crisis counseling for the suicidal ideation, and then other types of interventions for issues related to the suicidal behavior (e.g., being bullied at school or feeling alone in his attraction to other boys).

MH practitioners need to extend their services beyond their counseling offices to public arenas like schools, colleges, community centers, institutions (e.g., assisted living), and state and national government offices with psychoeducational, social justice, and advocacy interventions. These types of interventions help create healthier gay-affirming environments so that gay boys and men eventually will have socio-cultural contexts (i.e., social and cultural norms and behaviors from society and community like respect for diversity) equal to what heterosexual boys and men experience in their sexual identity development.

Individual/Group Counseling

Many personal/behavioral/emotional issues may occur for gay youth and men during their sexual identity development and coming out experience requiring individual or group counseling. For example, social alienation is often one of the issues gay youth and men experience; therefore, a gay client or student may need individual counseling using a Cognitive Behavior Therapy (CBT) approach because the client has maladaptive thoughts about nobody liking him due to his sexual identity, and he lacks the social skills to initiate friendships. On the other hand, the same client could also be included in a support group of other gay clients, particularly if multiple minority identities are involved.

Psychoeducational Interventions

Gay youth, in particular, are often unaware of issues that can occur in their sexual identity formation, like risky sexual behaviors or the use of drugs and alcohol to self-medicate. Therefore, during individual or group counseling, they may need educational interventions related to potential maladaptive and/or destructive behaviors that can occur in the coming out process. On the other hand, providing education and support to parents, school and community staff, and peers is needed to create a less stigmatizing environment for gay youth and men within which to form their sexual identity safely.

Programming Interventions

Many programming interventions can be initiated to help gay men and youth with the coming out process and potential subsequent reactions from their communities. Additionally, programming interventions can be initiated in the communitiy to help community members be more accepting of individuals who are sexual minorities. For example, MH practitioners, school counselors, and other professionals need specific in-service training to provide gay-affirming service environments to their gay clients and students.

Reviewing concrete gay-affirming practices such as the therapeutic stance, linguistic practices, the general office environment, and resources specific to gay youth and men will help clients feel more comfortable in working with them. Additionally, specific programs such as observation of LGBT history month, GSA groups in schools, or creating gay-friendly college campuses, hospitals, churches, and nursing homes are needed to "foster environment[s] that encourage and support openness about sexual orientation" (Bybee et al., 2009, p. 153).

Social Justice and Advocacy Interventions

Gay youth and men live in a society that is often unjust and unkind to their minority sexual identity status. Therefore, professionals should be alert to where injustices such as discrimination, bullying, or harassment occur in their own communities and advocate for social equality. They should initiate projects that help gay youth and men increase their ability to naturally become an integrated part of our society. This may require attending PTA meetings to change policies in schools so that LGBT history month can be celebrated as readily as Black history month or to allow Safe Spaces to be created in schools. Professionals can fight for equal rights to legal marriage or stronger anti-gay hate crimes so that such acts are punished to the full extent. Advocating for changes in our legal, educational, and religious institutions, as well as workplaces, should help create safer environments for gay youth and men to experience their sexual identity development formation in less stigmatized environments.

Mental Health Issues

In America, gay men and youth of all races are vulnerable to MH issues largely due to society's intolerance and negativity toward their sexual minority status (Barney, 2003; Bybee et al., 2009; Huebner, Rebchook, & Kegeles, 2004). Additionally, racial differences exist with respect to frequency, intensity, and extent of risk for certain MH problems, which is partly related to experiencing multiple minority identities, thus multiple sources of minority stressors (Barney, 2003; Grov, Bimbi, Nanin, & Parsons, 2006; Negy & Eisenman, 2005). Age and stage of development, both in the coming out process and stage of life, can also impact a gay youth's or man's experience with MH problems, at-risk behaviors, and homonegativity (D'Augelli et al., 2001; David & Knight, 2008; Huebner et al., 2004). Finally, life experiences, such as homelessness, poverty, and HIV, contribute a separate dimension to the stressors that gay men and youth can experience, even though we do not discuss these at length in this chapter (Diaz, Ayala, Bein, Henne, & Marin, 2001; Meris, 2001).

Societal Conditions Leading to Psychological Distress

Gay men and youth are often faced with a variety of negative societal conditions that directly affect their overall MH. Discrimination, stigma, victimization, and homophobia as they pertain to sexual orientation often result in an increase of emotional and psychological issues (Diaz et al., 2001; Wong, Weiss, Ayala, & Kipke, 2010).

Gay men and youth who have multiple minority identities (e.g., race[s], nationality, ethnicity, religion) face additional stressors, particularly within their own cultures and even within the gay culture. As MH professionals, it is critical to understand the ways in which negative societal conditions lead to psychological distress and, consequently, maladaptive behaviors.

Stigma

Perhaps one of the most prevalent societal conditions affecting gay men and youth is stigma. *Sexual stigma* relates to "the negative regard, inferior status, and relative powerlessness that society collectively accords to any non-heterosexual behavior, identity, relationship, or community," often referred to as heterosexism at the societal level (Parrott & Peterson, 2007, p. 306). Religion, language, the legal system, and the media have directly impacted the heterosexist attitude maintained by society. Gay men and youth experience sexual stigma from many different areas of life including the work environment, school, and within community organizations. As a result, it is a difficult task to remain an active member of society without experiencing sexual stigma and, in turn, this directly impacts the decision to identify as gay (D'Augelli et al., 2001; Saewyc et al., 2006). Sexual stigma can also become internalized by heterosexuals as sexual prejudice, which can result in aggression and discrimination toward gay men and youth as a way of expressing such prejudice (Parrott & Peterson, 2007). Gay youth face constant societal struggles at school via anti-gay comments by peers and are impacted by a lack of anti-gay bullying laws enforcement by parents and school administrators (Rosario, Hunter, Maguen, Gwadz, & Smith, 2001; Saewyc et al., 2006).

HIV-related stigma and discrimination also continue to be negative societal conditions affecting the MH needs of gay men and youth. "HIV-related stigma and discrimination are often associated with preexisting fears, ignorance and misunderstanding about issues such as sexuality, gender, race, ethnicity, culture, and drug use" (Brooks, Etzel, Hinojos, Henry, & Perez, 2005, p. 737). In addition to the emotional/psychological issues related to HIV-related stigma, both preventative efforts and quality of life issues can be affected by discriminatory beliefs about those living with HIV. Some men note fear of negative social consequences as a primary reason for not getting tested. Denial of care by medical providers and housing facilities for older persons living with HIV have been identified as negative consequences. In particular, gay youth from ages 13–24 are currently a major population of concern due to the significant increase in the number of HIV/AIDS cases reported by the CDC (Radcliffe et al., 2010; Wong et al., 2010).

Anti-gay Harassment/Violence/Hate Crimes

Harassment, in both the verbal and physical forms, and hate crimes are considered major factors in the mental health of gay men and youth. Often leading to anger, fear, and sadness, many gay men and youth who have been harassed due to sexual identity often struggle with behavioral issues such as social alienation and engagement in risky sexual practices. Hate crime survivors experience higher and more intense psychological distress as compared with individuals who experience non-bias crimes (Nakamura & Zea, 2010; Willis, 2008). Parrott and Peterson (2007) cited three possible theories for anti-gay aggression, which are based on: *sexual prejudice,* the negative beliefs about the deviation from prescribed gender roles; *peer dynamics,* the need to prove toughness and heterosexuality to friends; and *thrill seeking,* the need to attack gay men out of boredom and amusement. These theories of anti-gay aggression are described as primary motivations that are "justified by broader heterosexist societal norms" (Parrott & Peterson, 2007, p. 308).

Youth who choose to identify as gay often report experiences of homophobia and harassment in the verbal and physical form by family and peers. Numerous studies (e.g., Lock & Steiner, 1999; Wong et al., 2010) report the relationship between experiences of homophobia/harassment and an increase in drug use/abuse and high sexual risk-taking behaviors amongst gay youth in particular. Consequences (e.g., Post-Traumatic Stress, constant fear, anxiety, depression, suicidal ideation) of such experiences can lead to a variety of MH concerns, of which MH professionals need to remain aware. Gay youth can often experience homophobia at increased levels due to the "lack of independence and control of their lives" and with their peers acting as the primary perpetrators (Huebner et al., 2004).

The MH concerns of gay men and youth who have experienced various forms of harassment and/or hate crimes can be mitigated by focusing on meaning-making of such experiences. For gay men and youth who lived through these intense negative experiences, an increased sense of purpose/value in life and need to educate and advocate are often noted as positive consequences despite their struggles (Willis, 2008).

Racism/Multiple Minority Identity Issues

For gay men and youth from ethnic minority groups, the prevalence of homophobia, stigmatization, and reports of verbal/physical harassment tend to be more prevalent (Brooks et al., 2005; Diaz et al., 2001; Greene, 1994). The overlap of ethnic minority status with sexual minority status can, consequently, lead to an increase in MH issues. For ethnic minority groups in particular, family and social support are of great significance for healthy identity development. Therefore, strong cultural norms and gender role attitudes and expectations influence the ways in which ethnic minority families and communities respond to homophobia and sexual stigma (Brooks et al., 2005).

For example, within the African American culture, homosexuality is often considered prohibited, conflicting with religious beliefs and gender role expectations. From an early age, or even as an adult, African American gay men and youth can experience feelings of embarrassment, shame, anxiety, and depression when faced with the decision of whether or not to come out. Because the family and community play such integral roles in healthy development and overall MH for African Americans, coming out is difficult for fear of rejection by family and friends (Brooks et al., 2005; Graham, Braithwaite, Spikes, Stephens, & Edu, 2009; Pitt, 2010).

Members from Latino groups may face similar challenges. Homosexuality is often seen as an embarrassment to the community and considered a sign of weakness for gay men. This reaction may primarily occur because it goes against the *machismo* belief that men should be the strong, dominant members of society. Conflicting beliefs about their ethnic minority status and sexual identity can lead to feelings of shame, guilt, and fear of rejection by their communities and family members, often forcing them to hide their sexual identities (Brooks et al., 2005; Glassgold, 2009; Greene, 1994).

Asian Americans, Pacific Islanders, and Native Americans tend to face similar negative societal conditions, although there still remains a lack of supporting research for these groups. For gay men and youth from these cultures, going against established gender and cultural norms is often seen as disobedient and shameful. For example, there is an expectation to carry out the family lineage by starting families of their own. Additionally, sex in general is not often discussed and is considered taboo as a topic (Barney, 2003; Greene, 1994). Like African American and Latino communities, family support and the continuation of cultural norms and practices often conflict with sexual identity development. Members from the Asian American and Pacific Islander groups have also been identified as having increased levels of emotional/psychological symptoms (Yoshikawa, Wilson, Chae, & Cheng, 2004).

Although gay men and youth from non-ethnic minority groups face challenges due to their sexual identity, the struggles resulting from multiple levels of minority stressors (e.g., racism, heterosexism, classism) seem to pose additional challenges for gay men and youth from ethnic minority groups. However, we are aware that the experiences vary among racial and ethnic cultures and can differ greatly when considering MH concerns and interventions, even though common themes exist. Awareness of these themes can assist MH practitioners with culturally appropriate interventions and in providing the needed support for minority gay men and youth.

Case Study: Joseph

Joseph, a 19-year-old African American male is a sophomore in college living in an all-male residence hall. Joseph is self-identified as gay but has not come out to any of his family or any of his peers at college. Joseph is an active member in several clubs on campus, including the Culture Club, Organization of African American Unity, and Campus Christian Coalition. Recently, Joseph's roommate, Tim, and some of his other peers, have started to question Joseph's sexuality due to disinterest he has shown toward females at any of the parties or other social events they attend on campus. Tim has also started to question Joseph's sexuality due to Joseph's newly formed friendships with two members of the campus Gay/Straight Alliance club and has heard that Joseph has attended some of the club's general meetings. Soon thereafter, Joseph overheard a conversation between Tim and another friend where they were making rude remarks, calling Joseph and his friends from the Gay/Straight Alliance "sissies," "freaks," and "weirdoes." About a week later, Joseph began to receive comments on his room door that stated "MOVE OUT QUEER" and "FAGS GO TO HELL." Joseph also found out from his R.A. that Tim recently requested a room change. Joseph's grades are beginning to suffer; he has lost interest in any campus activities, and has started to travel home throughout the week and every weekend more frequently. Although he has not come out to his family, primarily because of their religious beliefs, his core group of friends back home who are aware that he is gay seem to provide good support for him.

Intervention Recommendations

Joseph struggles with stigma and discrimination from his peers and family and is distancing himself from college campus life and feeling hopeless that the situation will change. To aid with Joseph's struggles with discrimination and stigma faced by his peers, psychoeducational-based programming led by Resident Assistants in the residence halls could be effective in educating the campus and residential community about the LGBT community and concerns surrounding homophobia. This could also allow Joseph to feel supported and empowered on campus. However, for this to occur, Joseph must feel comfortable enough with a student affairs staff member to share what has happened, and this will more likely occur if residence life has created a gay-friendly campus feeling.

Joseph could participate in a mentorship program (i.e., an older undergraduate or graduate student who has successfully confronted similar issues), which would allow him to connect with others who have also faced stigma/discrimination. By working with a mentor, Joseph may be able to develop a healthy gay identity and could gain insight into coping mechanisms to mitigate MH concerns (Dooley, 2009). While working with a mentor, Joseph could be involved in group counseling with a group of LBGT students or young adults within the community. He can learn from others how to deal with discriminatory remarks about gay people, and gain a sense of community with other young gay people who are having similar experiences. Additionally, the group members can share how they approach coming out to friends, parents, and others, and how to identify when coming out is appropriate and safe. Joseph will have an opportunity within the group to discuss his reaction to homophobia and homonegativity and to identify how he can develop resilience and an internal locus of control in these situations.

Once Joseph comes out to his family, most likely with guidance and help from his mentor, individual or group counseling, or support from the LGBT center on campus, supportive services providing resources to educate family members about the LGBT population could be effective. Also, additional resources may be needed to educate family members on open and accepting religious institutions in their local area to ease feelings of stigma from their local community (Saewyc et al., 2006).

Maladaptive and Adaptive Behaviors

Gay men live in stressful social environments due to the stigma and prejudice that they face (Meyer, 2003), and they may develop maladaptive/destructive behaviors to cope with this stress. These less constructive behaviors include concealment, issues related to the coming out process, body image and eating disorders, and more destructive behaviors such as substance abuse, suicide, and risky sexual practices. However, gay youth and men also develop adaptive, healthy, or constructive behaviors due to the challenges they face in their sexual minority identity formation.

Concealment

Larson and Chastain (1990) defined concealment as "a predisposition to actively conceal from others personal information that one perceives as distressing or negative" (p. 440). There are varying levels of concealing or being *in the closet:* a gay man may hide his sexual identity from his family, acquaintances, and even himself. Hiding his sexual orientation requires a gay man to conceal information about his non-sexual life activities such as the people with whom he takes a vacation, celebrates a holiday, or spends a weekend. In this way, many sexual and non-sexual domains of his life are censored and hidden from others (Drescher, 2002; McAndrew & Warne, 2010; Potoczniak, Aldea, & DeBlaere, 2007). Gay men may conceal their sexual identity for a variety of reasons. In particular, Meyer (2003) noted that a man may conceal his sexual orientation to protect himself from real harm (e.g., being attacked, getting fired from a job, etc.), out of shame and guilt, or rejection of family and friends.

Long-term concealment of one's sexual identity has deleterious effects on an individual's mental and physical health. Concealment can lead to: i) increased depression, higher anxiety, and physical symptoms; ii) the loss of the opportunity for positive, supportive, and affirming social relationships; iiii) a negative effect on self-esteem; and iv) substance abuse (Berger, 1990; Bybee et al., 2009; D'Augelli et al., 2001; Larson & Chastain, 1990). Overall, Bybee et al. (2009) reported, "Attendant lies [from concealment], cover-ups, and hiding secrets can lead to harmful, ongoing feelings of guilt and shame, serving to further undercut mental well-being" (p. 145), even though concealment can also be a helpful way for gay men and youth to avoid harassment and homonegative actions.

Coming Out Process

Coming out is described as "acknowledging openly, to one's self first then to others, either selectively or generally, that one is gay" (Amadio & Perez, 2004, p. 368). While coming out is usually identified with greater feelings of comfort with being homosexual and ultimate mental wellbeing, gay men and youth can experience negative outcomes and maladaptive behaviors in the process of coming out (Bybee et al., 2009; D'Augelli, 2002; Penn, 1997).

In adolescence, parental reaction to sexual-orientation disclosure has a significant effect on an adolescent's mental health. When both parents are rejecting, the gay adolescent is significantly more likely to experience MH issues than if at least one parent is accepting (D'Augelli, 2002). If an adolescent is alienated from his parents, he loses the opportunity for support, and particularly in minority cultures, family rejection causes intense psychological distress for gay youth and men (Brooks et al., 2005; Cain, 1991; Glassgold, 2009). In extreme cases, a young man may be thrown out of his house, which is linked to numerous negative outcomes such as loss of financial support and the possibility of prostitution in order to survive (Rivers, 2000).

Victimization is prevalent among gay young men who have come out. According to D'Augelli (2002), more than 75% of his LGB youth participants had been verbally abused because of their sexual orientation, and 15% reported physical attacks. Study participants who suffered from victimization were more likely to report MH symptoms. Additionally, young people who suffer from victimization are more likely to display negative school-related behaviors, including poor academic performance and school truancy (Rivers, 2000).

Gay adolescents and men are at risk for social isolation during the coming out process. It is not unusual for gay men to lose a friend when they disclose their sexual orientation or not to disclose due to concerns about rejection or to avoid stigma (D'Augelli, 2002; Pachankis & Goldfried, 2006). The rejection experienced during this time can lead to a social retreat or regression in gay men; for example, older Black men reported disengaging as a coping mechanism over perceived homonegativity or racism (David & Knight, 2008; Lock, 1998). While being out as a gay youth or man ultimately correlates with later stages of gay pride and integration (Cass, 1984), the journey itself can be dangerous, and coming out to people is a life-long skill required for adult gay men.

Treatment Recommendations

School counselors must recognize that many gay adolescents may not disclose their sexual orientation to them. Therefore, school counselors must adopt a *gay-affirming* approach for all clients, which may help Joseph feel accepted and supported and be more likely to disclose his complex feelings to his counselor. A *gay-affirming* approach can be created by giving special consideration to the office environment, confidentiality, and linguistic practices (i.e., using language that is gay affirming such as, "Are you seeing anybody regularly?", rather than "Do you have a girlfriend?"; "gay" instead of "homosexual"). Counselors should ensure that their office environment is welcoming to gay youth by having posters, brochures, and information on bulletin boards that reflect topics relevant to gay adolescents and their families (Frankowski, 2004). Joseph might fear the counselor will reveal information about his sexuality to his parents, so the counselor should ensure that Joseph understands the confidential nature of the counseling relationship, as well as the limits to that confidentiality (Lock, 1998). Finally, the counselor should use gender-neutral, non-judgmental language such as *partner* and ask questions about romantic relationships in a gender-neutral manner, such as: "Have you ever had a romantic relationship with a boy or a girl?" (Frankowski, 2004).

Through individual counseling, Joseph can discuss issues related to his sexual orientation. As this is occurring, the counselor should assess Joseph's stage of sexual-identity formation with respect to the coming out process. The overall goal of therapy may be to support Joseph as he accepts his same-sex attraction, as well as create an identity as a gay man; however, the counselor must realize that this is a long and complex process (Medeiros, 2003). Coming out prematurely can have serious effects on Joseph's mental health, as this step can lead to victimization and alienation (Lock, 1998). The counselor can help Joseph explore his dreams and wishes for his life and can recommend developmentally appropriate literature and movies that are gay affirming (The Trevor Project, 2010). The counselor can help Joseph, at any stage of coming out, to learn how to communicate with others about his sexual orientation and examine the risks involved with when, how, and with whom to come out. During counseling, psychoeducational materials should be provided to and discussed with Joseph related to safe-sex, safe Internet chatting and dating, and community resources for meeting other young gay men.

As parental support has been correlated to MH outcomes in gay youth (D'Augelli, 1994), the counselor can work with Joseph in terms of deciding when and if he will come out to his parents. The counselor should carefully explore the consequences of Joseph coming out to his parents with respect to how supportive he thinks his parents will be. The counselor (with Joseph if he wants to be involved) can organize a GSA group in the school, which might make Joseph feel safer without having to disclose his sexual identity if he prefers not to. The counselor can also offer workshops on gay youth and families at PTA meetings. Of course, school administrators will have to be supportive of these activities, but if they are not then the counselor can advocate for social justice and equality for all students in the school.

Emotional/Psychological Issues

Psychological distress is an issue for gay men and youth as they continue their journey of sexual identity formation. Several common themes emerge with respect to gay clients' emotional and psychological issues. The severity and duration of any psychological distress somewhat depends on the resiliency and adaptability of the client, as well as other factors (e.g., stage of coming out, age, or support systems).

Depression

The most commonly reported MH problem for gay men and youth is depression. Bybee et al. (2009) reported that "gay individuals report higher levels of anxiety, depression, and hopelessness" (p. 144), even though much of this research was completed on adolescent and college-aged participants. While it is important to assess whether the depression is acute, chronic, or adjustment depression, identifying the underlying causes for the mood disorder is necessary for treatment.

Gay men and youth experience their sexual identity formation within a socio-cultural context of homonegativity. When part of your identity is so devalued by society and very likely by family members as well, shame and guilt for acting on those same-sex feelings can result in *depression.* Additionally, due to the typical internal struggles of sexual identity formation, gay youth and men may experience other factors that contribute to their depression. Examples of these factors include: concealment of their sexual identity, thus living a *double life* or what is sometimes referred to as *passing as heterosexual;* discomfort with being gay; social, work, or educational discrimination and oppression; victimization; internalized homonegativity; negative family reaction to being gay; self-hate, self-blame, and disgust with self; negative but internalized messages like *don't ask, don't tell;*

harassment; racism interacting with homophobia; and feeling vulnerable to verbal or physical abuse (Bybee et al., 2009; "Gays' mental health," 2006; Iwasaki & Ristock, 2007; Lock & Steiner, 1999; McAndrew & Warne, 2010; Russell & Keel, 2002; Rosser, Bockting, Ross, Miner, & Coleman, 2008). Finally, along with issues that are specific to developing a minority sexual identity, gay youth and men can experience depression like any other person related to failed relationships, couple discord, work-related problems, family history of depression, and financial distress (Iwasaki & Ristock, 2007).

Anxiety

Anxiety/stress is another emotional/psychological issue that gay men and youth commonly report. In a European study of 571 gay men, Wang, Hausermann, Ajdacic-Gross, Aggleton, and Weiss (2007) found that close to half of their respondents fit the diagnosis for a mental disorder and that 62.9% of those self-reporting a diagnosis experienced an anxiety disorder. Anxiety disorders produce emotional symptoms like excessive worrying, physical symptoms like sleep disturbances, and functional symptoms such as interference with social or occupational functioning (American Psychiatric Association, 2000). However, for gay men and youth, anxiety can present in the form of Generalized Anxiety Disorder, Posttraumatic Stress Disorder or Acute Stress Disorder, Substance-Induced Anxiety Disorder, Social Anxiety Disorder, or, in special cases, even a Panic Disorder (Alexander & Associates, 2002; Glassgold, 2009; Hatzenbuehler, McLaughlin, Keyes, & Hasin, 2010; Miranda & Storms, 1989; Pachankis & Goldfried, 2006; Wang et al., 2007). What form the anxiety and/or stress takes depends a great deal on the issues the gay man or youth is confronting. However, whatever the form, negative health effects are often the result when chronic or continuous anxiety and stress are not addressed in treatment (Iwasaki & Ristock, 2007).

Wang et al. (2007) claimed that anxiety disorders occur earlier in the life of gay youth and men than mood disorders. Generalized anxiety may develop sooner in the life of a boy or adolescent in the early stages of coming out simply by concealing his sexual identity (Alexander & Associates, 2002; Bybee et al., 2009). Along with the fear of rejection comes social anxiety, and Pachankis and Goldfried (2006) found that gay men and adolescents who were less open about their sexual identity and who felt less comfortable with homosexuality had higher social anxiety. In the later stages of coming out, gay youth and men become more visible as they become more open about their sexual orientation (Cass, 1984). This visibility makes them more vulnerable to victimization, verbal and physical harassment, and hate crimes, which can result in post-traumatic stress disorder or acute stress (Alexander & Associates, 2002; Huebner et al., 2004; Iwasaki & Ristock, 2007).

Personal life experiences and events can also contribute to anxiety. For example, Wang et al. (2007) found that gay men who were single and living alone experienced higher levels of anxiety; trying to adopt a child as a gay couple can produce anxiety (Goldberg & Smith, 2011); sexual dysfunction can produce concerns related to performance anxiety (Hirshfield et al., 2010); ethnic minority gay men may experience discrimination even within the gay community causing greater minority stress (Iwasaki & Ristock, 2007); older gay men may experience a sense of being excluded from the gay community or ageism, thus experiencing stress (D'Augelli et al., 2001); and financial, classism, career issues, death anxiety, and institutional discrimination may all produce anxiety responses (Diaz et al., 2001; Hatzenbuehler et al., 2010; Hintze, Templer, Cappelletty, & Frederick, 1993; Iwasaki & Ristock, 2007).

Practitioners tend to think of stress and anxiety only when it causes a client problems, but positive forms of stress for gay youth and men can also be identified. Stress or anxiety related to knowing how and when to deal with potential anti-gay verbal or physical attacks is a necessary skill for survival. Sometimes anger experienced in the pride stage of coming out allows gay youth and men to advocate for gay rights at individual, social, and institutional levels. Iwasaki and Ristock (2007) summarized this nicely: "Considering the positive effects of stress recognizes the strengths and resilience of lesbians and gay men, who may proactively, rather than reactively, deal with stress in an empowered way" (p. 301). Empowering gay clients during treatment may be an important way to combat less productive anxiety and stress.

Low Self-Esteem

Berk (2010) defined self-esteem as "the judgments we make about our own worth and the feelings associated with those judgments" (p. 258). As with any process of identity development, there are ebbs and flows with respect to evaluating one's own worth. Because gay youth and men are developing their overall identity within a socially stigmatized milieu, developing a positive and strong sense of self-esteem may have more challenges. However, it is clear that the self-esteem of adult gay men is stronger than that of adolescents (Bybee et al., 2009). Developmentally this makes sense as gay youth become gay men, move into the integrated and pride phase of coming out, experience successful work lives and relationships, and meet the challenges that being gay inherently presents.

While developing a healthy respect for self is important to avoid mental health issues like depression, suicidality, and destructive behaviors, there are factors that would contribute to a gay man or youth developing a sense of low self-esteem. These factors should be considered in the initial assessment of a gay client because they tend to predict lower self-esteem. Some of the factors include: negative attitude toward homosexuality and internalized homophobia; discomfort with sexual orientation; higher levels of minority stress; heavier reliance on external locus of control, thus believing the negative regard of others; greater concerns about negative social evaluations; overt self-hatred; lack of self-acceptance; perception of excessive amounts of negative life experiences; more reports of suicidal ideation or attempts; more loneliness with feelings of lack of control over loneliness; less openness about sexual orientation; and more experiences with anti-gay sentiments (D'Augelli et al., 2001; Diaz et al., 2001; Huebner et al., 2004; McAndrew & Warne, 2010; Pachankis & Goldfried, 2006; Rosario et al., 2001).

None of these factors in and of themselves necessarily developmentally culminate in a sense of lower self-esteem. However, in younger gay boys, adolescents, and men, it is important to identify if they are experiencing, or perceive that they are experiencing, a combination of these factors. If they are, then treatment can include focusing on developing an internal locus of control and on developing skills to avoid destructive behavior patterns.

Loneliness

The emotion of loneliness is a part of the human condition; by nature, humans are social beings (Berk, 2010; Rokach, 2011). However, for gay men and youth, loneliness is often intense enough that it is reported as one of the more frequent causes of psychological distress. Gay men and youth not only experience loneliness like their heterosexual counterparts might (e.g., longing to be in a relationship or be part of a social clique), but they also experience a unique form of loneliness stemming from societal rejection and stigmatization of homosexuality (D'Augelli et al., 2001; Kuyper & Fokkema, 2010; McAndrew & Warne, 2010).

Rokach (2011) described *intense loneliness* as painful as well as causing people to "[suffer] from a variety of emotional disorders" (p. 70). The *intense loneliness* of gay youth and men can begin to occur as soon as a boy accepts and understands his feelings of attraction to other boys because he realizes he is different and most likely does not know that other boys may feel the same. The feeling of loneliness can intensify when the boy understands the rejecting nature of society with respect to homosexuality and realizes he can even be victimized if he identifies as gay (Meyer, 2003; Pachankis & Goldfried, 2006). Therefore, concealing his sexual identity may become a coping strategy to keep him safe. In concealing his sexual identity, he becomes invisible, or at least his true sexual self, and he is constantly vigilant not to disclose his true identity. Then, every time a gay man or youth decides to come out there is always the stress that a friend, family member, co-worker, or acquaintance will reject him due to social discrimination and homophobia (McAndrew & Warne, 2010). Pachankis and Goldfried (2006) identified this experience as a social anxiety disorder, claiming that gay men have an "increased alertness and hyper-vigilance in relating to dominant group members" (p. 998).

As a natural progression, if a gay man or youth is hyper-vigilant in social interactions, feeling socially alienated because of his sexual identity, and concealing that for his own sense of self-worth and safety, then intense loneliness can occur. Chaney (2008) describes Kassel and Franko's (2000) theory that "pre-gay boys develop into young adults with damaged self-esteem. An overall feeling of inadequacy may lead some men to isolate themselves, leading to loneliness" (p. 165). Clearly, an ongoing feeling of loneliness can interact negatively with depression, low self-esteem, and even suicidal thoughts if not identified and treated.

Developmental and Cultural Considerations

Gay youth and men have common experiences with respect to the MH issues presented in this section of the chapter. However, they will not experience them at the same age, with the same intensity, or without additional cultural stressors; simply put, gay youth and men are not a homogenous population. While we do not review the developmental and cultural considerations in the MH of gay youth and men at length in this chapter, they should not be ignored in treatment.

Professionals working with gay youth and men must develop an understanding of the stage of coming out, the developmental stage/age, and specific cultural implications of their gay clients/students with respect to how these factors interact with their MH issues. For example, gay boys who identify in childhood are more likely to feel lonely and, therefore, may be more predisposed to depression in adolescence (Qualter, Brown,

Munn, & Rotenberg, 2010). While adolescents in general are at greater risk for suicide (Berk, 2010), gay adolescents may experience additional stressors, particularly if they are further along in the coming out process. If they are out, they are more visible, yet have less control over their lives, and therefore, may be environmentally at risk for victimization and negative experiences, putting them at an even greater risk for suicidality (Bagley & Tremblay, 2000; Lock & Steiner, 1999).

Ultimately, Bybee et al. (2009) reported that "with maturation during adulthood, parental expectations may recede in importance, self-esteem rises, and self-acceptance appears to increase" (p. 145). However, even in the adult stages of midlife and older adulthood, gay men have different experiences from younger gay men. For example, older gay men may feel more of a reduced sense of shame and guilt related to their sexual identity than younger gay men, yet they may feel isolated and invisible in the younger gay community of men (Bybee et al., 2009; Fokkema & Kuyper, 2009; Graneheim & Lundman, 2010).

Professionals must also take into consideration the unique cultural experiences of gay youth and men who are racial minorities, from lower socio-economic status populations, who are disabled, and those who belong to special needs populations such as the homeless, HIV/AIDS victims, and those with special diagnoses such as eating disorders or muscle dysmorphia. Racial minority gay men and youth experience sexual identity formation within a multiple identity formation process. Discrimination and oppression based on racism create a heightened level of minority stress with reactions of more intense depressive symptoms, anxiety, social alienation, and potential for family discord (Barney, 2003; Glassgold, 2009; Graham et al., 2009; Hillin, McAlpine, Montague, & Markham, 2007). Adding additional minority stressors (e.g., poverty or homelessness) or HIV/AIDS diagnosis to gay men or youth intensifies potential for psychological distress while dealing with other specific unique needs (e.g., grief for HIV/AIDS clients) (Diaz et al., 2001; Meris, 2001; Russell & Keel, 2002).

Case Study: Allan

Allan is a 58-year-old Caucasian gay man. He feels comfortable with his sexual identity, even though he compartmentalizes it. He is not out to his family, but he has a small group of friends he considers family. His partner of 20 years died two years ago, and he still feels lonely and sad. He tried getting into the bar scene again, but claims young gay men act as if he "doesn't exist." When he thinks of going out now, he feels anxious, like he's not able to breathe. This reaction began when a young gay man in a bar called him, "Grandpa"; he doesn't feel good about himself right now and doubts that he will ever find another lover. He feels his work is suffering, but hasn't said anything about his loss because he is a federal government employee and believes they abide closely, albeit not explicitly stated, with a "don't ask, don't tell" approach with respect to sexual identity. His friends are "tired" of hearing him crying about his partner, and they think he should have "moved on with his life by now." He's been drinking more than usual and does nothing on weekends but sleeps and watches TV.

Treatment Recommendations

Allan is experiencing complicated grief over the loss of his partner of 20 years. He has a limited number of people to process his grief feelings with because he has compartmentalized his life, thus most likely in the Identity Acceptance stage of Cass's (1984) coming out model. The small family of creation seems tired of listening to his grief, so he has nowhere else to express it. He is not out at work, so will not explain the effect of his grief to co-workers or supervisors. He perceives that discrimination could occur. He is lonely and tries to meet other gay men by going out to bars and is now feeling lower self-esteem with negative self-thoughts about ever being in another relationship. However, he claims to feel the affect of ageism in the younger gay community, and he is experiencing signs of panic attacks. Finally, he seems depressed and is coping by drinking more.

To start treatment, it is important to assess Allan's level of depression and, if necessary, refer him to a doctor for possible psychopharmacological treatment. Allan could use a combination of individual and group counseling. Allan could be in a grief group with other gay men of different ages and races/ethnicities. The group will help Allan meet other gay men who are experiencing a loss, identify how others deal with their grief, be able to discuss work and learn how others handled notifying supervisors and/or co-workers about the loss, learn other coping mechanisms for loneliness and grief besides drinking, and learn how to date again. This intervention would help with his loneliness, grief work, fear of discrimination, and feelings of low self-esteem.

During individual counseling, Allan can i) learn techniques to address his panic attacks; ii) be provided psychoeducational materials related to stages of coming out to understand how his stage (Identity Acceptance and compartmentalizing) contributes to his inability to address his loss at work or with other people; iii) learn more about his legal status at work and anti-discrimination laws; iv) be provided resources for networking with older gay men and lesbians; and v) address ageism in the gay culture and how to confront ageist remarks. Allan may even want to ask his family of creation to a couple of sessions so that they can find out more about complicated grief and learn new ways to support Allan work through the grief.

Finally, based on Allan's experience, community workshops for older gay men on loss of a long-term partner can be offered, which might prevent experiences like Allan is having. Additionally, workshops in the gay community on the effect of "—isms" can include discussions around ageism and racism in the gay community itself, which can also help in preventing future "—ism" experiences for other gay men and youth.

References

Addis, M. E., Mansfield, A. K., & Syzdek, M. R. (2010). Is "masculinity" a problem?: Framing the effects of gendered social learning in men. *Psychology of Men & Masculinity, 11*(2), 77–90.

Alexander, C. J., & Associates (2002). Homosexuality and risk for psychiatric disorders. *Journal of Gay & Lesbian Social Services, 14*(3), 103–107.

Amadio, D. M., & Perez, R. M. (2004). Affirmative counseling and psychotherapy for lesbian, gay, and bisexual clients. In C. Negy (Ed.), *Cross-cultural psychotherapy: Toward a critical understanding of diverse clients* (pp. 301–325). Reno, NV: Bent Tree Press.

American Psychiatric Association. (2000). *Diagnostic and statistical manual of mental disorders (DSM-IV-TR)*. Arlington, VA: American Psychiatric Association.

Bagley, C., & Tremblay, P. (2000). Elevated rates of suicidal behavior in gay, lesbian, and bisexual youth. *Crisis, 21*(3), 111–117.

Barney, D. D. (2003). Health risk-factors for gay American Indian and Alaska Native Adolescent males. *Journal of Homosexuality, 46,* 137–157.

Barret, R., & Barzan, R. (1996). Spiritual experiences of gay men and lesbians. *Counseling and Values, 41,* 4–15.

Berg, M., Mimiaga, M., & Safren, S. A. (2008). Mental health concerns of gay and Bisexual men seeking mental health services. *Journal of Homosexuality, 54,* 293–306.

Berger, R. M. (1990). Passing: Impact on the quality of same-sex couple relationships. *Social Work, 35,* 328–332.

Berk, L. A. (2010). *Development through the lifespan* (5th ed.). Boston, MA: Allyn & Bacon.

Blazina, C., Settle, A., & Eddins, R. (2008). Gender role conflict and separation-Individuation Difficulties: Their impact on college men's loneliness. *Journal of Men's Studies, 16*(1), 69–81.

Brooks, R. A., Etzel, M. A., Hinojos, E., Henry, C. L., & Perez, M. (2005). Preventing HIV among Latino and African American gay and bisexual men in a context of HIV-related stigma, discrimination, and homophobia: Perspectives of providers. *AIDS Patient Care and STDs, 19,* 737–744.

Bybee, J. A., Sullivan, E. L., Zielonka, E., & Moes, E. (2009). Are gay men in worse mental health than heterosexual men? The role of age, shame and guilt, and coming out. *Journal of Adult Development, 16,* 144–154.

Cain, R. (1991). Relational contexts and information management among gay men. *The Journal of Contemporary Human Services, 72,* 344–352.

Carlat, D. J., Camargo, C. A., & Herzog, D. B. (1997). Eating disorders in males: A report On 135 patients. *The American Journal of Psychiatry, 154,* 1127–1132. Retrieved from http://search.proquest.com/docview/220478352?accountid=12536

Cass, V. (1984). Homosexual identity formation: Testing a theoretical model. *The Journal of Sex Research, 20,* 143–167.

Centers for Disease Control and Prevention. (2011). *HIV and AIDS among gay and Bisexual men: CDC fact sheet.* Retrieved from: www.cdc.gov/nchhstp/newsroom/docs/fastfacts-msm-final508comp.pdf

Chae, D. H., & Ayala, G. (2010). Sexual orientation and sexual behavior among Latino and Asian Americans: Implications for unfair treatment and psychological distress. *Journal of Sex Research, 47,* 451–549.

Chernin, J. N., & Johnson, M. R. (2003). *Affirmative psychotherapy and counseling for lesbians and gay men.* Thousand Oaks, CA: SAGE.

Cochran, S. D., & Mays, V. M. (2000). Lifetime prevalence of suicide symptoms and Affective Disorders among men reporting same-sex sexual partners: Results from NHANES III. *American Journal of Public Health, 90,* 573–578.

D'Augelli, A. R. (1994). Identity development and sexual orientation: Toward a model of lesbian, gay, and bisexual development. In E. J. Trickett, R. J. Watts, and D. Birman (Eds.), *Human diversity: Perspectives on people in context* (pp. 312–333). San Francisco, CA: Jossey-Bass.

D'Augelli, A. R. (2002). Mental health problems among lesbian, gay, and bisexual youths ages 14 to 21. *Clinical Child Psychology and Psychiatry, 7,* 433–456.

D'Augelli, A. R., Grossman, A. H., Hershberger, S. L., & O'Connell, T. S. (2001). Aspects of mental health among older lesbian, gay, and bisexual adults. *Aging & Mental Health, 5,* 149–158.

David, S., & Knight, B. G. (2008). Stress and coping among gay men: Age and ethnic differences. *Psychology & Aging, 23,* 62–69.

Diaz, R. M., Ayala, G., Bein, E., Henne, J., & Marin, B. V. (2001). The impact of homophobia, poverty, and racism on the mental health of gay and bisexual Latino men: Findings from 3 U.S. cities. *American Journal of Public Health, 91,* 927–932.

Dooley, J. (2009). Negotiating stigma: Lessons from the life stories of gay men. *Journal of Gay & Lesbian Social Services, 21*(1), 13–29.

Drescher, J. (2002). Invisible gay adolescents. *Adolescent Psychiatry, 26,* 73–94.

Frankowski, B. L. (2004). American academy of pediatrics clinical report: Sexual orientation and adolescents. *Pediatrics, 113,* 1827–1832.

French, S. A., Story, M., Remafedi, G., Resnick, M. D., & Blum, R. W. (1996). Sexual orientation and prevalence of body dissatisfaction and eating disordered behaviors: A population-based study of adolescents. *International Journal of Eating Disorders, 19,* 119–126.

Fokkema, T., & Kuyper, L. (2009). The relation between social embeddedness and loneliness among older lesbian, gay, and bisexual adults in the Netherlands. *Archives of Sexual Behavior, 38,* 264–275.

Gays' mental health. New data (2006, June). *Harvard mental health letter.* Available from: www.health.harvard.edu/newsletters/Harvard_Mental_Health_Letter/2006/June (accessed January 10, 2014).

Goldberg, A. E., & Smith, J. Z. (2011). Stigma, social context, and mental health: Lesbian and gay couples across the transition to adoptive parenthood. *Journal of Counseling Psychology, 58,* 139–150.

Glassgold, J. M. (2009). The case of Felix: An example of gay-affirmative, cognitive-behavioral therapy. *Pragmatic Case Studies in Psychotherapy, 5*(4), 1–21. Retrieved from http://pcsp.libraries.rutgers.edu

Graham, L. F., Braithwaite, K., Spikes, P., Stephens, C. F., & Edu, U. G. (2009). Exploring the Mental health of Black men who have sex with men. *Community Mental Health Journal, 45,* 272–284. doi: 10.1007/s10597-009-9186-7

Graneheim, U. H., & Lundman, B. (2010). Experiences of loneliness among the very old: The Umea 85+ project. *Aging & Mental Health, 14,* 433–438. doi: 10.1080/13607860903586078

Greene, B. (1994). Ethnic-minority lesbians and gay men: Mental health and treatment issues. *Journal of Consulting and Clinical Psychology, 62,* 243–251.

Grov, C., Bimbi, D. S., Nanin, J. E., & Parsons, J. T. (2006). Exploring racial and ethnic differences in recreational drug use among gay and bisexual men in New York City and Los Angeles. *Journal of Drug Education, 36*(2), 105–123.

Hatzenbuehler, M. L., McLaughlin, K. A., Keyes, K. M., & Hasin, D. (2010). The impact of institutional discrimination on psychiatric disorders in lesbian, gay, and Bisexual populations: A prospective study. *American Journal of Public Health, 100,* 452–459.

Hillin, A., McAlpine, R., Montague, R., & Markham, R. (2007). Workers' learning needs regarding mental health in Aboriginal, same-sex attracted and culturally and linguistically diverse young people. *Australasian Psychiatry, 15,* S80–S84. doi: 10.1080/10398560701701254

Hintze, J., Templer, D. I., Cappelletty, G. G., & Frederick, W. (1993). Death depression and death anxiety in HIV-infected males. *Death Studies, 17,* 333–341.

Hirshfield, S., Chiasson, M. A., Wagmiller, R. L., Remien, R. H., Humberstone, M., Scheinmann, R., & Grov, C. (2010). Sexual dysfunction in an internet sample of U.S. men who have sex with men. *Journal of Sexual Medicine, 7,* 3104–3114.

Huebner, D. M., Rebchook, G. M., & Kegeles, S. M. (2004). Experiences of harassment, discrimination, and physical violence among young gay and bisexual men. *American Journal of Public Health, 94,* 1200–1203.

Iwasaki, Y., & Ristock, J. L. (2007). The nature of stress experienced by lesbians and gay men. *Anxiety, Stress, & Coping, 20,* 299–319.

Kubicek, K., McDavitt, B., Carpineto, J., Weiss, G., Iverson, E., & Kipke, M. D. (2009). "God made me gay for a reason": Young men who have sex with men's resiliency in resolving Internalized homophobia from religious sources. *Journal of Adolescent Research, 24,* 601–633. doi: 10.1177/0743558409341078

Kuyper, L., & Fokkema, T. (2010). Loneliness among older lesbian, gay, and bisexual adults: The role of minority stress. *Archives of Sexual Behavior, 39,* 1171–1180.

Larson, D. G., & Chastain, R. L. (1990). Self-concealment: Conceptualization, measurement, and health implications. *Journal of Social and Clinical Psychology, 9,* 439–455.

Lock, J. (1998). Treatment of homophobia in gay male adolescents. *American Journal of Psychotherapy, 52,* 202–214.

Lock, J., & Steiner, H. (1999). Gay, lesbian, and bisexual youth risks for emotional, physical, and social problems: Results from a community-based survey. *Journal of the American and Child and Adolescent Psychiatry, 38,* 297–304.

McAndrew, S., & Warne, T. (2010). Coming out to talk about suicide: Gay men and suicidality. *International Journal of Mental Health Nursing, 19,* 92–101. doi: 10.1111/j.1447-0349.2009.00644.x

Medeiros, D. M. (2003). Mom, dad. I'm gay: How families negotiate coming out. *Archives of Sexual Behavior, 32,* 488–489.

Medeiros, D. M., Seehaus, M., Elliott, J., & Melaney, A. (2004). Providing mental health services for LGBT teens in a community adolescent health clinic. *Journal of Gay & Lesbian Psychotherapy, 8*(3–4), 83–95.

Meris, D. (2001). Responding to the mental health and grief concerns of homeless HIV-infected gay men. *Journal of Gay and Lesbian Social Services, 13*(4), 103–111.

Meyer, I. H. (2003). Prejudice, social stress, and mental health in lesbian, gay, and bisexual populations: Conceptual issues and research evidence. *Psychological Bulletin, 129,* 674–697. doi: 10.1037/0033-2909.129.5.674

Miranda, J., & Storms, M. (1989). Psychological adjustment of lesbians and gay men. *Journal of Counseling & Development, 68,* 41–45.

Nakamura, N., & Zea, M. C. (2010). Experiences of homonegativity and sexual risk behavior in a sample of Latino gay and bisexual men. *Culture, Health & Sexuality, 12*(1), 73–85.

Negy, C., & Eisenman, R. (2005). A comparison of African American and White college students' affective and attitudinal reactions to lesbian, gay, and bisexual individuals: An exploratory study. *Journal of Sex Research, 42,* 291–298.

Pachankis, J. E., & Goldfried, M. R. (2006). Social anxiety in young gay men. *Journal of Anxiety Disorders, 20,* 996–1015.

Parrott, D. J., & Peterson, J. L. (2007). What motivates hate crimes based on sexual orientation? Mediating effects of anger antigay aggression. *Aggressive Behavior, 34,* 306–318.

Penn, R. E. (1997). *The gay men's wellness guide: The National Lesbian and Gay Health Association's complete book of physical emotional, and mental health and well-being for every gay male.* New York: Henry Holt and Company.

Pitt, R. N. (2010). "Killing the messenger": Religious Black gay men's neutralization of anti-gay religious messages. *Journal for the Scientific Study of Religion, 49*(1), 56–72.

Potoczniak, D. J., Aldea, M. A., & DeBlaere, C. (2007). Ego identity, social anxiety, social support, and self-concealment in lesbian, gay, and bisexual individuals. *Journal of Counseling Psychology, 54,* 447–457. doi: 10.1037/0022-0167.54.4.47

Qualter, P., Brown, S., Munn, P., & Rotenberg, K. (2010). Childhood loneliness as a predictor of adolescent depressive symptoms: An 8-year longitudinal study. *European Child & Adolescent Psychiatry, 19,* 493–501.

Radcliffe, J., Doty, N., Hawkins, L. A., Gaskins, C. S., Beidas, R., & Rudy, B. J. (2010). Stigma and sexual health risks in HIV-positive African American young men who have sex with men. *AIDS Patient Care and STDs, 24*(8), 493–499.

Rivers, I. (2000). Long-term consequences of bullying. In C. Neal and D. Davies (Eds.), *Issues in therapy with lesbian, gay, bisexual and transgender clients* (pp. 146–159). Buckingham, UK: Open University Press.

Rokach, A. (2011). From loneliness to belonging: A review. *Psychology Journal, 8*(2), 70–81.

Rosario, M., Hunter, J., Maguen, S., Gwadz, M., & Smith, R. (2001). The coming-out process and its adaptation and health-related associations among gay, lesbian, and bisexual youths: Stipulation and exploration of a model. *American Journal of Community Psychology, 29,* 133–160.

Rosser, B. R. S., Bockting, W., Ross, M. W., Miner, M. H., & Coleman, E. (2008). The relationship between homosexuality, internalized homo-negativity, and mental health in men who have sex with men. *Journal of Homosexuality, 55,* 185–203.

Russell, C. J., & Keel, P. K. (2002). Homosexuality as a specific risk factor for eating disorders in men. *Journal of Eating Disorders, 31,* 300–306. doi: 10.1002/eat.10036

Saewyc, E., Skay, C., Richens, K., Reis, E., Poon, C., & Murphy, A. (2006). Sexual orientation, sexual abuse, and HIV-risk behaviors among adolescents in the Pacific Northwest. *American Journal of Public Health, 96,* 1104–1110. doi: 10.2105/AJPH.2005.065870

The Trevor Project. (2010). *Books and films for LGBT young people.* Retrieved from: www.thetrevorproject.org/sites/default/files/ComprehensiveBookandFilmList.pdf

Wang, J., Hausermann, M., Ajdacic-Gross, V., Aggleton, P., & Weiss, M.G. (2007). High prevalence of mental disorders and comorbidity in the Geneva gay men's health study. *Social Psychiatry & Psychiatric Epidemiology, 42,* 414–420. doi: 10.1007/s00127-007-0190-3

Willis, D. G. (2008). Meaning in adult male victims' experiences of hate crime and its aftermath. *Issues in Mental Health Nursing, 29,* 567–584.

Wong, C. F., Weiss, G., Ayala, G., & Kipke, M. D. (2010). Harassment, discrimination, violence, and illicit drug use among young men who have sex with men. *AIDS Education and Prevention, 22,* 286–298.

Yoshikawa, H., Wilson, P. A.D., Chae, D. H., & Cheng, J. (2004). Do family and friendship networks protect against the influence of discrimination on mental health and HIV risk among Asian and Pacific Islander gay men? *AIDS Education and Prevention, 16,* 84–100.

7 The Impact of Substance Abuse and Addiction in the Lives of Gay Men, Adolescents, and Boys

Michael P. Chaney & Michael Brubaker

Introduction

It has become increasingly important among clinicians and researchers whose work has been focused on substance use disorders to better understand the factors that contribute to the etiology and maintenance of substance use disorders among specific cultural groups. Reasons for this trend include the need to develop culturally responsive treatment options and prevention efforts. Of particular concern is the impact of substance use disorders on the lives of gay male adults, adolescents, and boys. Because many gay men's, adolescents', and boys' experiences with substance abuse counselors and treatment programs tend to be negative and non-affirming (Matthews & Selvidge, 2005), a greater understanding of the dynamics of substance use disorders and treatment needs among this population is a must. Studies have shown that gay men in substance abuse treatment generally feel unsupported throughout the treatment process because of homonegativity expressed by other clients and treatment providers (Cheng, 2003). They also tend to feel disconnected from others while in treatment, report being dissatisfied with treatment, and are more likely to relapse at the end of treatment compared with their heterosexual peers (Senreich, 2009).

Prevalence Rates

It is estimated that one in every 12 adults either abuses alcohol or is alcohol dependent (National Council on Alcoholism and Drug Dependence, 2013). Based on a national survey, the lifetime prevalence of drug abuse among Americans is approximated to be 8% (Kessler, Berglund, Demler, Jin, Merikangas, & Walters, 2005). In terms of substance use among gay men, adolescents, and boys, the research has consistently shown that they are more likely than their heterosexual counterparts to engage in substance use or to be substance dependent (Dahan, Feldman, & Hermoni, 2007; McCabe, Hughes, Bostwick, West, & Boyd, 2009). For example, in a study by Theide et al. (2003), drug use within the past six months was commonplace among two out of three same-sex attracted men and adolescents who were between the ages of 15 and 22 years old. In the same study, it was discovered that 19% of gay males in several large cities within the United States used drugs on a weekly basis or even more frequently.

In order to effectively treat this population, competent clinicians should have knowledge about the types of substances commonly used by these men and youth, as well as trends associated with alcohol and drug use. In this section, we present a general overview of epidemiological trends of substance use among gay males.

Research has consistently demonstrated that same-sex attracted males are more likely than heterosexual men to use certain drugs. For example, gay and bisexual males (3.9%) are more likely than heterosexual men (1.2%) to use cocaine (Cochran, Ackerman, Mays, & Ross, 2004). In a study by McCabe, Hughes, Bostwick, and Boyd (2005), the researchers found that men who have sex with men (MSM) were more likely than men who have sex with women to have used marijuana within the past month. Gay males are also more likely to use methamphetamine compared with their heterosexual peers (Copeland & Sorenson, 2001). In an important study, The Urban Men's Health Study (Stall et al., 2001), alcohol and drug use among a total of 2,172 MSM in four large metropolitan cities (Chicago, Los Angeles, New York, and San Francisco) was examined. The researchers explored the prevalence of alcohol and/or drug use within the preceding six months and found the following: alcohol (87.7%), marijuana (42.4%), poppers (19.8%), cocaine (15.2%), crack cocaine (3%), Ecstasy (11.7%), speed/methamphetamine (9.5%), downers (8.8%), psychedelics (4.2%), opiates (3.2%), and other uppers (2.2%) were used by MSM (Stall et al., 2001). The percentages reflect the average number of men among the four cities who used the respective substances in the prior six months. Because substance abuse issues typically develop as a result of dynamic individual, environmental, and familial interactions, it is not surprising that McCabe, West, Hughes, and Boyd (2013) found non-heterosexuals compared with heterosexuals had more prominent histories of familial substance abuse issues. To get a better understanding of the meaning of the aforementioned substance abuse trends, the next section highlights several of the substances in more detail and their impact on gay males.

Alcohol Use Among Gay Males

A consistent theme that you will see throughout this chapter is that gay males are more likely to use and/or abuse substances compared with their heterosexual peers. A recent study that explored alcohol use among gay men found that 91% of the gay male participants used alcohol (Wong, Kipke, & Weiss, 2008). Of the men in this study who used alcohol, 40% were frequent binge drinkers. Not only are gay men less likely to abstain from alcohol compared with heterosexual men, but gay men are two times more likely than heterosexual men to experience drinking-related problems (Gruskin & Gordon, 2006). Alcohol-related problems include injuries and accidents, legal problems, sexually transmitted infections, or relationship problems. Although the majority of research that has investigated alcohol use among men has found discrepancies between the amount of alcohol consumed by MSM versus heterosexual men, a few studies have found no differences. For example, Trocki, Drabble, and Midanik (2005) found there are no differences in drinking patterns between gay and heterosexual men. Similarly, McCabe et al. (2005) reported that heterosexual men are more likely than MSM to engage in heavy episodic drinking, though results like these are not consistent with most of the research. It has been suggested that gay males consume more alcohol than heterosexual males because of the negative consequences and stress associated with being part of an oppressed population (Hughes, 2005).

Take a minute to think about a time when you went out with friends for a night on the town and cocktails. What did you notice about your friends' (or your own) behaviors after one or two drinks? Maybe they became louder and more talkative, laughed harder, or did something wild, crazy, and out of character. Although it may seem like alcohol is a stimulant, it is actually a depressant. Alcohol suppresses the parts of the brain that manage our inhibitions. As a result, a gay man under the influence of alcohol might do things that he typically would not do but for the introduction of alcohol. Initially, alcohol may also cause an individual to experience euphoric feelings. In this sense, for some gay men, adolescents, and boys, the feelings of exhilaration provided by alcohol provide a temporary escape from negative feelings and stress.

Smoking

Other substances prominently used by gay men, adolescents, and boys are nicotine and marijuana. Though these two substances are two distinct classes of drugs with very different pharmacological effects, for the purposes of this chapter, we chose to discuss them together because the majority of men ingest these substances in the same way; they are typically smoked.

Nicotine is a stimulant, and when initially ingested may cause an individual to feel more alert and energized. Over time, nicotine prevents specific neurons in the brain from generating chemical signals, which may cause an individual to feel a sense of relaxation. It may be these two dichotomous feelings that make smoking appealing to some gay males. As with other drugs, sexual minorities smoke more than heterosexuals (Lee, Griffin, & Melvin, 2009). It has been estimated that there are 45 million cigarette smokers in the United States (Kaufman, 2006). Approximately, 33% of gay men smoke cigarettes, compared with 24% of heterosexual men. Although gay men are more likely than heterosexuals to smoke cigarettes, heterosexual men are more likely than gay and bisexual men to smoke cigars (Gruskin, Greenwood, Matevia, Pollack, & Bye, 2007).

A new smoking trend that is emerging is hookah smoking. Meaning "jar" in Arabic, a hookah is a water pipe that is used for smoking flavored tobacco. Hookah lounges or bars can be found in many large cities, especially in trendy, "hipster" type neighborhoods. A recent study investigated the relationship between smoking (including hookah smoking), sexual orientation, and ethnicity (Blosnich, Jarrett, & Horn, 2011). The researchers found that regardless of ethnicity, lesbian, gay, and bisexual (LGB) college students smoked cigarettes at greater rates than their heterosexual peers. In general, LGB students who identified as multiracial or White smoked the most compared with other ethnicities, whereas Black students smoked the least. Hispanic and White LGB college students reported the highest rates of hookah smoking, and Black LGB students reported high rates of smoking hookah and cigars. Overall, Black LGB students reported the highest rates of all forms of smoking.

There are many reasons why gay men and youth might start smoking. One reason is to self-medicate negative feelings. Munafò, Hitsman, Rende, Metcalfe, and Niaura (2007) purported that depressive distress is associated with smoking initiation. Relatedly, higher rates of smoking have also been attributed to gay men who have experienced multiple AIDS-related losses (Stall, Greenwood, Acree, Paul, and Coates, 1999).

The social aspects of smoking might also draw some men to start smoking. Stall et al. (1999) found a relationship between smoking and regular attendance at gay bars. It will be interesting to see if, in the coming years, smoking rates among gay men decline due to stringent smoking bans in public places. Some have argued that there is a smoking disparity among gay males because of tobacco companies specifically targeting these communities (Smith, Offen, & Malone, 2005). It is not uncommon for tobacco companies to financially sponsor gay-related events, advertise in gay periodicals, and to pass out free packs of cigarettes at gay bars.

Another mood-altering substance that is typically abused by many gay men and adolescents is marijuana. Marijuana is a cannabinoid that is commonly smoked or ingested orally (typically incorporated into food products). The active ingredient in marijuana is delta-9-tetrahydrocannabinol (THC). After use of marijuana, individuals might experience a sense of anxiety, relaxation, enhanced or altered sense of perception, loss of coordination, laughter, impaired judgment, inhibition, and impulsivity. Marijuana use tends to be higher among gay men than heterosexual men (Cochran, Ackerman, Mays, & Ross, 2004).

Stimulant Use Among Gay and Bisexual Men

Drugs that stimulate the central nervous system are called stimulants. These drugs cause a person to feel alert, energized, and euphoric. Cocaine and methamphetamine are two commonly abused stimulants among some gay males. Cocaine use is especially high among gay men. Within the gay male communities, lifetime use of cocaine is almost twice as high as the general population. Use of methamphetamine (meth) among gay men is also problematic. In a national online study, 6% of gay and bisexual men reported using meth within the previous six months (Hirshfield, Remien, & Chiasson, 2006). This number is likely an underrepresentation of the actual number of men who use meth. Studies have consistently found that gay, bisexual, and even transgender men are more likely to use meth compared with other populations (Cochran & Cauce, 2006). For most gay men, meth is not typically a gateway drug. In other words, meth is not the first drug used by most men. It is typically used after the experimentation of other drugs (Parsons, Kelly, & Wesier, 2007).

One only need look at the some of the subjective effects of cocaine and meth to understand the reasons behind the dramatic use of these drugs among many gay individuals. Although the effects of the drugs depend on dose, administration, and purity, initially most men will experience an increase in sex-drive, energy, arousal level, alertness, and impulsiveness that can last for hours. In a culture that has historically socialized in bar and dance club settings, stimulants provide the needed energy for late-night partying and uninhibited interactions. In addition, because gay male culture tends to be sexualized, cocaine and meth are often integrated into sexual encounters to enhance the experiences (Semple, Patterson, & Grant, 2002). Similarly, these substances lower inhibitions around sexual behavior, leading men to engage in riskier behaviors.

Because cocaine and meth use is not uncommon within the gay community, it is not surprising that attitudes around their use are not necessarily unfavorable among some men. In a recent qualitative study (Fazio, Hunt, & Moloney, 2011), gay and bisexual men were interviewed about their perceptions of cocaine and meth use. In general, the men in this study had favorable attitudes about cocaine use. Not only did they perceive cocaine use to be acceptable in the gay and bisexual communities, but its use was also normalized as part of the club scene. In this sense, cocaine use is no different from alcohol use in terms of prevalence and acceptance (Fazio et al., 2011). On the other hand, meth use was viewed in much more negative terms. Meth use was viewed as shameful and dangerous. Some of the negative attitudes toward meth use are due to its connection to risk of contracting HIV. In sum, many gay men view cocaine as a social drug, whereas meth is viewed as problematic (Fazio et al., 2011).

Club Drugs

Substances that are commonly used in bar or dance club settings fall under the umbrella term, club drugs. Meth, cocaine, MDMA (Ecstasy), ketamine, GHB, and nitrite inhalants are commonly used club drugs. Gay males demonstrate higher use of all of the aforementioned club drugs compared with other groups (Degenhardt, 2005; Lampinen, McGhee, & Martin, 2006). In one study, over 50% of MSM reported use of Ecstasy, ketamine, or meth, and of these men, nearly half reported ongoing use (Clatts, Goldsamt, & Yi, 2005).

In the previous section, we briefly described cocaine and meth. Other club drugs include:

- MDMA (3,4-methylenedioxy-N-methylamphetamine), or Ecstasy, a hallucinogenic compound that is structurally similar to amphetamine. At low doses, the subjective effects include euphoria, feeling connected to others, increased energy, perception enhancement, a general sense of wellbeing, mild hallucinations, and increased self-confidence. At higher doses, someone is more likely to experience adverse effects including anxiety, panic attacks, or dissociative experiences.
- Ketamine is used as a surgical anesthetic. Ketamine in low doses can produce mild hallucinations, feelings of stimulation, and perceptual distortions of sight and sound. Higher doses can lead to intense hallucinations, dissociative experiences, and trance-like states.
- GHB (gamma-hydroxybutryic acid) is a central nervous system depressant. Odorless and colorless, at low doses an individual might feel mild euphoria, uninhibited, sociable, stimulated, and sexual enhancement. High doses can lead to visual distortions, sleep, coma, or death.
- Nitrite inhalants, more commonly known as "poppers," cause an immediate and intense, but very short "rush." Users typically feel light-headed and sexual. Because poppers relax the muscles in the body, they are often incorporated into sexual activities.

Gay males are more likely to engage in poly-club drug use rather than just using one drug at a time. For example, because the effects of combining ecstasy and GHB can be extremely pleasurable, this is a popular combination (Halkitis & Palamar, 2006). On the flip side, many men will not combine GHB with depressants due to undesirable effects; rather GHB is often combined with stimulants, such as meth (Halkitis, Palamar, & Mukherjee, 2007).

A major factor related to club drug use among gay males is their beliefs about their peers' drug use. In an informative study, Ramchand, Fisher, Griffin, Becker, and Iguchi (2013) explored club drug use among weekend circuit party attendees. The researchers found that one in five men had intentions to use GHB, marijuana, cocaine, erectile dysfunction drugs, and poppers, and one in ten men intended to use ketamine and meth while at the events. It was also discovered that men who had no intentions of using drugs while at the circuit parties were in fact more likely to use ketamine, GHB, cocaine, or erectile dysfunction drugs if they believed other attendees were using these drugs. In fact, men who attended the weekend circuit parties had a tendency to overestimate the amount of ecstasy, cocaine, erectile dysfunction drugs, and poppers used by peers. Thus, clinicians who work with gay men who attend dance clubs or weekend circuit parties will want to i) assess clients' intentions of use and what they believe to be true about others' drug use, and ii) educate clients about drug risks and debunk inaccurate beliefs related to others' drug use.

In summary, we have presented an overview of prevalence rates of alcohol and drug use among same-sex attracted males. We chose to highlight alcohol, smoking, stimulants, and club drugs because these are substances that many gay individuals seem to struggle with at disproportionate rates. Clearly, some sexual minority men and youth abuse other drugs that we did not discuss (i.e., opioids, barbiturates, etc.). Competent clinicians should make sure they know the pharmacological characteristics of the various drugs, understand their influence in the lives of gay males, and be versed in the reasons why drug use is rampant in this community. We now provide a few explanations as to why substance abuse and dependence is a major issue among sexual minority males.

Etiology of Substance Abuse and Addiction Among Gay and Bisexual Men and Boys

Understanding the causes of substance abuse and dependence among gay male adults and youth is important both for prevention and treatment measures. Counselors have a major role in providing direct therapeutic interventions for these populations with emerging substance use disorders; they also have the responsibility to prevent problematic substance use by lessening risk factors and promoting protective factors. Woodford (2012) explains that boys and men are "gendered beings" who are raised with societal expectations about what it means to be a man. Males who are taught very constricted, traditional notions of masculinity tend to grow up believing that they should be tough, avoid the expression of tender emotions that could make them appear vulnerable to others, and not ask for help when they are in distress. These notions of manhood can play a significant role in male substance abuse and addictive behaviors, which in turn can affect the development of the brain and erode important emotional bonds that men have with others. Thus, gender-sensitive counseling with gay boys, adolescents, and men who have substance abuse problems involves understanding the client's male socialization experiences, teaching him about how the brain works, and fostering his emotional awareness and communications and connections with others as he moves on the path to recovery. By understanding the etiology of addiction, they may do both.

General Theories of Addiction

There are numerous theories about how one becomes addicted, but more current research has emphasized an integrated pathway to becoming addicted to a chemical substance (Stevens & Smith, 2013).

Studies have indicated that genetics may influence as little as 30% or as much as 70% of addictive behaviors (Agrawal & Lynskey, 2008). In terms of environmental factors, behavioral theories and socio-cultural theories have largely guided the thought behind non-genetic contributors to addiction. Bandura's (1977) Social Learning Theory has been a particularly salient theory among those serving child and adolescent populations as it stresses the role of peer and family modeling, the media, and the norms and expectations surrounding young people. As children learn social norms about drinking and drug use through these various models, they too can be influenced to respond in like manner.

Socio-cultural theories are also important to consider, as they take into account the various risk and protective factors that are specific to particular cultural groups (Stevens & Smith, 2013). For instance, women typically use at lower rates than men, a fact that has been attributed to the social roles that women have in American society (Hughes & Eliason, 2002). Many women are shunned for their use of substances whereas men may be revered for their high tolerance. When considering lesbian women, these protective factors dissipate as these roles and expectations are less stringent (Hughes & Eliason, 2002). As previously mentioned, gay adult men have been known to use certain drugs at higher rates that heterosexual men. Meth, in particular, was more commonly used over the past decade, as some gay men alleviated the shame of sex with other men (Kurtz, 2005). This example shows one way that societal oppression, which can be internalized, leads to increased substance use.

It should be noted that different drugs vary in their addictive properties. The physiological dependence of alcohol, marijuana, cocaine, and heroin are all quite different. Furthermore, it has been proposed that the route of administration, that is, the way that one uses a drug, can impact the progression to becoming addicted to a substance (Barrio et al., 2001). For example, shooting heroin intravenously immediately impacts the user, rewarding them more quickly for their behavior. When snorted, the drug is used less efficiently and enters the bloodstream more slowly, thus providing less reward later than when taking in intravenously. While neither is safe, some believe these different pathways alter the addictive properties of the drug.

Contributing Factors Specific to Gay Males

Gay Bars and Clubs

Due to the long history of stigmatization and societal oppression of sexual minorities, venues in which these communities could socialize and interact were few. Typically bars, were venues that were secret gathering spots only known to members of the lesbian, gay, and bisexual communities. Today, bars continue to hold social relevance for many gay men and are believed to be a major contributor to substance use among these communities. Bars are an important part of gay culture because they provide a safe environment for men to meet other men where repercussions are limited. Historically, gay bars and clubs were established deep in the bowels of urban centers so that they would not be discovered by mainstream society. Over time, as the gay community began to better structure itself, gay individuals started forming communities in the areas in and around the locations of the bars, clubs, and other gay-related venues. In fact, gay men are more likely than other groups to live in these gay urban neighborhoods, also called "gay ghettos" (Black, Gates, Sanders, & Taylor, 2000) or "gayborhoods." By living in these gay areas, the men are able gain access to important resources, including the socialization associated with gay bars and clubs.

Gay men spend more time in gay bars than any other men, including bisexual men (Trocki et al., 2005). Although this may not be surprising, the reasons for this phenomenon help to explain the disproportionately high substance use rates among gay men. It is true that gay bars serve as a place for men to meet, but what results when a collective group of men gather is that a community is built and a cultural identity (including cultural norms) is formed (Ghaziani & Cook, 2005). In other words, in gay bars, many men learn what they were not taught by their families of origin, assimilation into gay culture including adoption of gay cultural norms. Unfortunately, some of these gay cultural norms endorse maladaptive behaviors such as alcohol and drug use.

Within the gay bar or club scene, there is a cultural norm of drug use, especially cocaine, ecstasy, and meth (Kelly, Parsons, & Wells, 2006). Klitzman, Greenberg, Pollack, and Dolezal (2002) found that gay men were 2.5 times more likely to use ecstasy if more than half of their friends were gay or bisexual. High levels of involvement with gay men and/or in a gay bar scene have been found to be related to alcohol and polydrug use (Lea, Reynolds, & de Wit, 2013). Interestingly, there is evidence that gay males who have diverse groups of friends are less likely to use drugs. With this information, counselors should explore the norms associated with the social networks or friendships of gay male clients and the meanings of gay bars and the gay community in the lives of clients.

Internalized Heterosexism and the Minority Stress Model

One of the strongest predictors for substance abuse and addiction among same-sex attracted men is internalized heterosexism (Amadio, 2006). Although some studies reported that there is no relationship between internalized heterosexism and substance abuse, a recent meta-analysis of studies spanning 20 years found that the majority of the research does in fact support that a relationship exists (Brubaker, Garrett, & Dew, 2009). One theory that helps to explicate this relationship is the Minority Stress Model.

One of the more commonly accepted socio-cultural theories that integrates the concepts of identity development is Myer's (2003) Minority Stress Model. It begins with the understanding that stress occurs due to one's minority status as well as the degree to which one embraces a minority identity. For gay males, heterosexism in the form of bullying, anti-gay remarks, institutional discrimination, and violence can occur in the school, family, or community. These external (distal) prejudicial events create stress that compromises mental health outcomes including substance use. In addition, there are various internal (proximal) stressors that gay individuals may experience as they become vigilant in preventing hostile events, worry about social rejection, internalize negative stereotypes (internalized heterosexism), and try to hide their identities. In like fashion, the internal stress can lead to higher substance use. To the degree that an individual can establish positive and affirming social supports, positive minority coping may occur and lessen substance abuse and other negative mental health outcomes.

Being out as gay may also have offsetting effects. Men who have disclosed their sexual orientation publicly may experience greater levels of harassment, but they also have greater psychological functioning. Indeed, individuals who are out generally have higher self-esteem, lower levels of depression, and a greater sense of belonging (Kosciw, Greytak, Bartkiewicz, Boesen, & Palmer, 2012). However, evidence suggests that, among same-sex attracted individuals who are out, more severe problems are experienced associated with their substance use compared with other populations (Cochran & Cauce, 2006). Similarly, gay males who are out to the majority of their social networks engage in higher amounts of drug use (Thiede et al., 2003). Among gay youth, those who are out and experience victimization have lower self-esteem and higher depression than those who are not victimized (Kosciw et al., 2012). These studies all underscore that gay males are more likely to experience various forms of discrimination and oppressive attitudes when others know about their respective identities. For individuals who are coming to terms with their sexual orientation, finding a safe and supportive environment is a priority, and one that may enhance psychological functioning, including lower substance use.

Sexual Enhancement and Sensation Seeking

Another factor that contributes to the high prevalence of substance abuse among gay men is related to enhancing sexual experiences and seeking higher levels of stimulation. For some gay men who may not be comfortable expressing their same-sex sexual desires, incorporating alcohol or drugs into the experiences may lessen anxiety and self-consciousness associated with the behaviors. While anxiety and shame may be temporarily minimized, the alcohol and drugs might cause an individual to experience a disinhibition effect. They may engage in behaviors they would not otherwise engage in but for the introduction of alcohol and drugs. The evidence that substance use leads to risky behaviors is staggering (Fazio et al., 2011; Operario et al., 2006). It is not uncommon for some gay men to incorporate stimulants into their sexual activities, especially cocaine or meth. Stimulants can intensely enhance sexual experiences, prolong sexual activity, and foster a drug-induced self-confidence.

Sensation seeking is characterized by a desire to seek out new, innovative, and exciting activities that lead to feelings of intense stimulation. In sexual situations, sensation seeking has been found to contribute to substance use and unprotected intercourse among MSM (Kalichman & Cain, 2004). Unfortunately, under the influence of alcohol or drugs, men may not have the capacity to think rationally and, as a result, put themselves at risk for contracting sexually transmitted infections (e.g., HIV/AIDS). Among HIV-negative MSM, alcohol, inhalants, amphetamines, and snorted cocaine have been linked to risk of HIV exposure (Colfax et al., 2004). Meth, cannabis, and Viagra have been found to contribute to high-risk sexual activity (i.e., unprotected sex) among HIV-positive men (Drumright et al., 2006). Informed clinicians will thoroughly assess to what extent clients are incorporating alcohol or drugs into sexual activities, if clients are engaging in high-risk behaviors, and the subjective meanings behind the use of alcohol or drugs while engaging in sexual behaviors.

Substance Use Among Gay Male Youth

Similar to the trends of gay male adults, evidence suggests that gay male youth are at greater risk for abusing substances than their heterosexual peers. Gay male youth are more likely to use meth, Ecstasy, ketamine, and marijuana compared with heterosexuals (Hegna & Rossow, 2007; Lampinen et al., 2006). Marshal et al. (2008) reported that same-sex attracted adolescents were two to five times more likely to use alcohol and other drugs compared with their heterosexual counterparts. The risk of abusing alcohol is not limited to early adolescence, but can carry on into emerging adulthood. Compared with heterosexual men, alcohol use increases more dramatically among MSM in their first year of college (Hatzenbuehler, Corbin, & Fromme, 2008). Cigarette smoking is also disproportionately high among same-sex attracted youth. It is estimated that 32–50% of lesbian, gay, and bisexual youth smoke compared with 8–35% of heterosexual youth (Lee et al., 2009). When compared with other same-sex attracted peers, smoking is still greatest among LGB youth compared with LGB adults (Lampinen et al., 2006).

The reasons for gay male youth being at greater risk for substance abuse are numerous. The risk is greatest for gay youth who have experienced bullying and victimization by their peers. Thus, it is probable that use might be a response to dealing with negative experiences and distress. Additional evidence that points to substance use being used as a coping strategy is that risk of substance use is greatest during developmental milestones specifically associated with same-sex attracted youth. These milestones include first awareness of being attracted to members of the same gender, first time same-sex sexual experience, and self-acknowledgment of a gay identity and disclosing this identity to others (Marshal et al., 2008).

As sexual orientation is such a highly stigmatized facet of a gay male adolescent's identity, the crisis that he experiences may be unlike any other he has experienced previously. Subject to gay slurs, a lack of positive role models in their schools, and verbal and physical harassment (Kosciw et al., 2012), these young people know that the stakes are high when coming out. Furthermore, as negative stereotypes persist, a self-discovering gay youth who has internalized these negative social messages must face the cognitive dissonance of discovering that he is the person whom he has learned to demean. Many of these boys find solace in trying to manage these stressors through the use of alcohol or other substances. By "fitting in" with prevailing substance using norms, a gay youth may feel more accepted by his peers. For those boys who have "come out," substance use is one way to manage the anxieties related living in a non-supportive environment (Rosario, Schrimshaw, & Hunter, 2006).

Gay-Affirming Social Supports for Youth

Gay-affirming supports for gay youth began as early as the 1960s, when youth collectively challenged the notions that their same-sex attraction was deviant (Cohen, 2005). These groups served many functions, including social activism, peer support, outreach, providing food and shelter, and public education. Since 1972, students have organized gay–straight clubs in schools. Over time, these organizations have expanded dramatically with over 4,000 gay–straight alliances registered with the Gay, Lesbian & Straight Education Network (GLSEN).

School Supports

As youth spend a large proportion of their time in the schools, it is no wonder that this is where many gay youth report extensive marginalization (Watson, Varjas, Meyers, & Graybill, 2010). In the *2011 National Climate Survey* (n = 8,584) taken by the Gay, Lesbian and Straight Education Network (GLSEN), 8,584 LGBTQ students answered an online survey to share their experiences of harassments and supports in their schools. Most of the sample (81.9%) reported being verbally harassed for their sexual orientation, with a third noting this harassment to occur frequently (Kosciw et al., 2012). Physical harassment is also commonplace among LGBTQ youth, with 38.3% reporting their being pushed, shoved, or similarly harassed in the last year due to their sexual orientation or gender expression. Assaults remain high as well, with 18.3% reporting being punched, kicked, injured by weapon, or similarly harmed because of their sexual orientation (Kosciw et al., 2012). The lack of safety, especially when caused by physical assault, has been linked to suicidal behaviors among LGBT youth (Goodenow, Szalacha, & Westheimer, 2006). The level of support and acceptance for LGTBQ youth in the school environment can have a significant role on the level of harassment, sense of belonging, and overall school attendance for LGBTQ youth.

Community Supports

Students without GSAs may have local community-based groups to address some of their needs for social support. As noted previously, some of the earliest organizations for gay youth were self-initiated advocacy groups. Gay youth have been at the forefront of activism since the 1960s, when a group of young hustlers organized in San Francisco to advocate for their civil liberties (Cohen, 2005). Since that time, a number of organizations have emerged to meet the political and social needs of young gay men, the families, and the society, that they wished to change. These youth can be a powerful force, and in the case of Massachusetts and California, they successfully advocated for state legislative changes to ban discrimination based on sexual orientation (Holmes & Cahill, 2004).

Twelve-Step Support Groups

Alcoholics Anonymous (www.aa.org), Narcotics Anonymous (www.na.org), and other Twelve-Step groups are known for having groups designated for certain populations, including youth and LGBT individuals. In larger communities, there may be groups that are designed for gay youth.

Helping gay youth to know about their local and national services is essential for those who need support through the various crises and concerns of their maturation. Counselors can serve gay youth by knowing about age-appropriate community resources and helping them to gain access.

Substance Abuse Treatment for Gay Youth

Much like the schools, treatment for gay youth may prove to be less affirming and helpful than one would hope. While the levels of harassment indicated in the schools have not been as visible in treatment settings, there remain discriminatory acts and neglect for the needs of gay communities. Such attention is important as treatment centers have a role in creating and eliminating barriers to treatment for gay youth.

Together, gay and bisexual men are more than three times as likely as heterosexual men to see a mental health provider and more than five times as likely to attend a self-help group (Cochran, Sullivan & Mays, 2003). Despite the higher utilization rates, clinicians and their treatment programs are not always accepting of LGBT consumers (Matthews, Selvidge, & Fisher, 2005). In fact, lesbian and gay adults have reported discrimination in treatment (Matthews, Lorah, & Fenton, 2006) and a general lack of sexual minority affirmation by both counselors and agencies (Matthews & Selvidge, 2005). Although not reported in the literature, gay youth are also likely to experience similar marginalization in traditional treatment settings.

Counselors without specialty training and agencies that fail to meet the needs of gay youth will likely be less effective in serving these clients. According to Berlin and Lawson (2011), adolescent treatment needs to meet at least three different areas of concerns, including: i) general life skills and motivational training; ii) coping skills to address high-risk situations; and iii) empowerment and self-esteem enhancement. In this process, youth learn stress management skills, behavioral self-control, social skills, and how to increase their motivation for change (Berlin & Lawson, 2011). As gay youth develop these skills, they need to discuss the stressors and supports in their home, school, and among friends, many of which relate to gay identity development and discrimination. Furthermore, as these youth develop coping skills, they will need to find positive social supports who understand how to enhance a youth's recovery and the triggers that threaten problematic substance use. Lastly, gay youth may find it difficult to develop self-esteem in an environment where support is lacking. Even if an agency states it does not discriminate, if it does not create an affirming environment through well-trained staff and affirming policies, it is likely creating a setting that embraces a "don't ask, don't tell" ethos, encouraging clients to remain silent about a significant portion of their lives. A few ways agencies can demonstrate that they are a gay-affirming are: providing regular educational trainings to their service providers on how to effectively work with gay clients; conducting regular safe-space trainings; displaying safe space stickers and posters visible to clients; and crafting non-heterosexist intake forms and documentation.

Applying evidence-based practices designed for the general population to gay youth can also be problematic. For example, family therapy approaches such as Multidimensional Family Therapy (MDFT) are becoming more commonly used with substance abusing adolescents and their families (Berlin & Lawson, 2011). Austin, Macgowan, and Wagner (2005), in a review of five well-established family approaches, found both MDFT and Brief Strategic Family Therapy (BSFT) to be efficacious when treating substance-abusing youth. Unfortunately, these approaches are not well studied with substance-abusing gay youth. In fact, there are no evidence-based programs for gay youth listed on the SAMHSA's National Registry of Evidence-based Programs and Practices (NREPP). This poses a problem for counselors who experience pressure to use evidence-based practices. As gay youth experience unique circumstances in their families and support systems, counselors need to exercise caution when applying such practices.

Specialized Services

Substance Abuse Treatment Programs are increasingly providing specialized services for LGBT clients, offering LGBT counseling groups such as coming-out groups (Adam & Guttierrez, 2011). In addition, counseling, medical, and social services staff members are receiving specialized training in order to better meet the emotional and physical health needs of LGBT clients. In some cases, treatment centers will exclusively serve the LGBT population but, more commonly, they are integrated within the general treatment milieu (Cochran, Peavy, and Robohm, 2007). There are many advantages to specialized treatment as gay youth have the ability to normalize their experiences in the presence of other clients with similar circumstances. These young men also have the ability to openly explore minority stress and develop queer social supports that might not avail themselves in traditional treatment settings.

Finding specialty treatment can often be a challenge. In a review of the nation's top 144 substance abuse treatment programs for adolescents, Brannigan, Schackman, Falco, and Millman (2004) scored them low on gender and cultural competence, noting that only 12% were meeting the specific needs of lesbian and gay clients. This compares similarly to Cochran et al.'s (2007) investigation of the Substance Abuse and Mental Health Services Administration's treatment listings ($n = 7{,}691$). The researchers found that even though 11.8% reported having specialized services, most of that subsample (70%) over-represented their services to the LGBT population. Furthermore, over half that were found to truly offer specialized services were from California and New York (Cochran et al., 2007). At the writing of this chapter, there are 131 programs listed on the SAMHSA Treatment Finder designated as offering specialty substance abuse treatment services for gay and lesbian youth (http://findtreatment.samhsa.gov). Those seeking services using this resource are advised to inquire directly with the agency about the type of specialty services offered, whether staff have been trained specifically to counsel LGBT clients, and the percentage of clients who identify as a sexual minority.

It should also be noted that specialty treatment is not always optimal for all gay youth. Counselors are served well by recognizing the intersectionality of gay identity with other primary identities (e.g., gender, race, ethnicity, culture) in their clients (Wynn & West-Olatunji, 2009). Gay men of color are often torn between their culture and their gay identity (Adam & Guttierrez, 2011). They may choose not to disclose their orientation to their family, but build support in other ways. Similarly, they may choose not to attend gay-specific treatment groups, especially if the groups are not ethnically diverse or meet their specific cultural needs.

Affirming Substance Abuse Treatment

Because of inexperience or lack of training, some clinicians hold negative attitudes toward gay men. As a result, gay men who desperately need treatment are reluctant to seek out services or receive inferior treatment that often leads to immediate relapse. For gay clients who have been in substance abuse treatment, the news about their experiences is generally discouraging. Clients often report that the programs are not gay affirming (Matthews & Selvidge, 2005), which can influence their treatment success and long-term sobriety. Thus, in order for gay men to have the best chances for successful treatment outcomes, counselors must have a solid understanding of elements of gay-affirming substance abuse treatment.

Gay-affirming substance abuse treatment for gay men involves counselors helping clients to accept their identities as gay men and to help clients understand any correlations between their sexual orientations and substance use. Starting with the initial contact, culturally responsive counselors will meet the client where he is in terms of his sexual identity as well as his recovery process. When establishing initial treatment goals, for some clients, complete abstinence may not be a primary goal. In situations such as these, service providers might need to put aside their own agendas and utilize harm reduction strategies and motivational interviewing skills to gently guide a client to a different stage of readiness. Another aspect of gay-affirming substance abuse treatment is the integration of gay cultural norms and values into traditional methods of substance abuse treatment. For example, Shoptaw et al. (2005) incorporated key principles of cognitive-behavioral substance abuse therapy with cultural aspects of gay male substance abusers. Specific references of gay culture (i.e., circuit parties, HIV risk, etc.,) were included in drug treatment-related psychoeducation (contingency management, relapse triggers etc.). In addition to incorporating gay cultural values and norms into treatment, gay-affirming substance abuse treatment should address the following topics throughout the recovery process. We recognize that the list below is not exhaustive, rather it is meant to serve as a starting point toward practicing as a gay-affirmative substance abuse provider.

Association and Socialization Issues

These include the influences of the gay community on a client's substance use included but not limited to the role of gay bars, circuit parties, and sex clubs. In addition to communal gathering places, counselors should also assess clients' use of the Internet, social media, and/or smart phone applications for the purposes of meeting potential sex partners where substance use might be part of these encounters.

Heterosexism and Internalized Heterosexism

Service providers should ask clients about previous experiences in treatment including experiences of discrimination or bias from providers and/or peers. Additionally, counselors should help clients understand the relationship between oppression, internalized heterosexism, and substance abuse.

Social Support

Gay-affirming substance abuse providers should work with clients to identify supportive, affirming social networks on which clients may rely throughout the recovery process. Such support circles may include gay or gay-friendly twelve-step groups, coming out support groups, HIV+ support groups, and friends who will be supportive of the client's recovery and sexual orientation.

Family Issues

In addition to asking about familial history of substance abuse and addiction, mental illness, and trauma, gay-affirming counselors will ask clients about familial reactions to a client's self-disclosure as gay, if a client has come out to family members. Counselors should also explore familial attitudes and beliefs toward a gay identity, from the client's perspective. Affirming counselors will assist clients to connect potential relationships between the aforementioned family issues and the client's substance use. Further, supportive family members need to be identified and integrated into the client's treatment. Affirming counselors should ask clients whom they consider to be "family." In *Guidelines for Psychological Practice with Lesbian, Gay, and Bisexual Clients,* The American Psychological Association (2012) suggested that competent clinicians will "recognize that that families of lesbian, gay, and bisexual people may include people who are not legally or biologically related" (p. 18).

Same-Sex Sexual Behavior

Gay-affirming substance abuse treatment must address the sexual behavior of gay male clients. Counselors should be comfortable asking clients about their specific same-sex sexual behaviors and how alcohol or drugs were part of those practices. Counselors should also educate clients about the relationship between substance use and high-risk sexual behavior. Gay-affirming counselors should not pathologize or shame same-sex sexual practices, rather affirming providers will educate themselves about the diverse sexual behaviors in which various subcultures of the gay male community engage. Counselors should recognize that sexual behavior is a major relapse trigger for many gay men and treatment plan accordingly.

Multiple Oppressed Identities

Gay-affirming counselors will identify the intersections of clients' various cultural identities including race, ethnicity, sexual orientation, gender identity and expression, ability, socio-economic status, spirituality, and other identities with which a client identifies. In addition, service providers will understand how oppression, based on any aspect of self, might contribute to substance abuse and dependence. Educating clients about this relationship should be part of treatment. Additionally, counselors should examine the meaning of a client's sexual orientation in terms of other aspects of his identity (e.g., what does it mean to be a gay man of color who is alcohol dependent?).

Religion and Spirituality

Due to negative messages commonly conveyed to sexual minorities from some faith-based affiliations, many gay men have dissociated themselves from anything having to do with religion, spirituality, or faith-based initiatives. As a result, traditional twelve-step meetings might be challenging for some gay men in recovery because many twelve-step supports ask members to recognize a power greater than oneself. Affirming counselors will explore clients' spiritual beliefs and clients' histories with faith-based organizations, if any. Counselors will work with clients to identity the most effective recovery supports available to clients. Affirming counselors will have knowledge of gay-only and gay-friendly recovery and/or faith-based supports within the community, as well as alternatives to traditional twelve-step models that will best meet the individual needs of clients.

Sexually-Transmitted Infections and Other Medical Issues

Because of the strong association between substance use and high-risk behaviors among gay men, affirming counselors will work with clients to seek out gay-affirming medical referrals at the start of treatment. Counselors will educate clients about risk factors and protective factors associated with substance use and STIs or other medical issues. If needed, providers will integrate risk reduction strategies or medication compliance plans into recovery plans. Gay-affirming substance abuse counselors will educate clients about the health benefits associated with being an abstinent gay man.

When providing gay-affirmative substance abuse counseling to gay male substance-abusing clients, we underscore the unique treatment needs and options for gay male youth because they are not typically discussed in treatment literature. As societal attitudes toward same-sex attracted individuals continues to improve, with great hope and optimism, the number of gay male adults and youth struggling with substance use disorders will decline. Service providers working with these individuals are encouraged to continue to develop, implement, and share with other professionals effective gay-affirmative treatment strategies and prevention efforts.

References

Adam, M., & Guttierrez, V. (2011). Working with gay men and lesbian women with addiction concerns. In G. W. Lawson and A. W. Lawson (Eds.) *Alcoholism and substance abuse in diverse populations* (pp. 213–225). Austin, TX: Pro-Ed.

Agrawal, A., & Lynskey, M. T. (2008). Are there genetic influences on addiction: evidence from family, adoption, and twin studies. *Addiction, 103,* 1069–1081. doi: 10.1111/j.1360-0443.2008.02213.x

Amadio, D. M. (2006). Internalized heterosexism, alcohol use, and alcohol-related problems among lesbians and gay men. *Addictive Behaviors, 31,* 1153–1162. doi: 10.1016/j.addbeh.2005.08.013

American Psychological Association. (2012). Guidelines for psychological practice with lesbian, gay, and bisexual clients. *American Psychologist, 67*(1), 10–42. doi: 10.1037/a0024659

Austin, A.M., Macgowan, M. J., & Wagner, E. F. (2005). Effective family-based interventions for adolescents with substance use problems: A systematic review. *Research on Social Work Practice, 15,* 67–83. doi: 10.1177/1049731504271606

Bandura, A. (1977). *Social learning theory.* Englewood Cliffs, NJ: Prentice-Hall.

Barrio, G., De La Fuente, L., Lew, C., Royuela, L., Bravo, M. J., & Torrens, M. (2001). Differences in severity of heroin dependence by route of administration: The importance of length of heroin use. *Drug and Alcohol Dependence, 63,* 169–177.

Berlin, M., & Lawson, A. W. (2011). A model for treating adolescent substance abuse. In G. W. Lawson and A. W. Lawson (Eds.), *Alcoholism and substance abuse in diverse populations* (pp. 243–273). Austin, TX: Pro-Ed.

Black, D., Gates, G., Sanders, S., & Taylor, L. (2000). Demographics of the gay and lesbian population in the United States: Evidence from available systematic data sources. *Demography, 37,* 139–154.

Blosnich, J. R., Jarrett, T., & Horn, K. (2011). Racial and ethnic differences in current use of cigarettes, cigars, and hookahs among lesbian, gay, and bisexual young adults. *Nicotine & Tobacco Research, 13*(6), 487–491.

Brannigan, R., Schackman, B. R., Falco, M., & Millman, R. B. (2004). The quality of highly regarded adolescent substance abuse treatment programs. *Archives of Pediatrics & Adolescent Medicine, 158,* 904–909. doi: 10.1001/archpedi.158.9.904

Brubaker, M. D., Garret, M., & Dew, B. (2009). Examining the relationship between internalized heterosexism and substance abuse among lesbian, gay, and bisexual individuals: A critical review. *Journal of LGBT Issues in Counseling, 3,* 62–89.

Cheng, Z. (2003). Issues and standards in counseling lesbians and gay men with substance abuse concerns. *Journal of Mental Health Counseling, 25,* 323–336.

Clatts, M. C., Goldsamt, L. A., & Yi, H. (2005). Club use among young men who have sex with men in NYC: A preliminary epidemiological profile. *Substance Use and Misuse, 40,* 1317–1330.

Cochran, S. D., Ackerman, D., Mays, V., & Ross, M. W. (2004). Prevalence of non-medical drug use and dependence among homosexually active men and women in the U.S. population. *Addiction, 99,* 989–998.

Cochran, B. N., & Cauce, A.M. (2006). Characteristics of lesbian, gay, bisexual, and transgender individuals entering substance abuse treatment. *Journal of Substance Abuse Treatment, 30,* 135–146.

Cochran, B. N., Peavy, K. M., & Robohm, J. S. (2007). Do specialized services exist for LGBT individuals seeking treatment for substance misuse? A study of available treatment programs. *Substance Use & Misuse, 42,* 161–176.

Cochran, S. D., Sullivan, J. G., & Mays, V. M. (2003). Prevalence of mental disorders, psychological distress, and mental health services use among lesbian, gay, and bisexual adults in the United States. *Journal of Consulting and Clinical Psychology, 71,* 53–61.

Cohen, S. (2005). Liberationists, clients, activists: Queer youth organizing, 1966–2003. *Journal of Gay & Lesbian Issues in Education, 2,* 67–86.

Colfax, G., Vittinghoff, E., Husnik, M. J., McKirnan, D., Buchbinder, S., Koblin, B., . . . Coates, T. J. (2004). Substance use and sexual risk: A participant and episode-level analysis among a cohort of men who have sex with men. *American Journal of Epidemiology, 159,* 1002–1012.

Copeland, A. L., & Sorenson, J. L. (2001). Differences between methamphetamine users and cocaine users in treatment. *Drug and Alcohol Dependence, 62,* 91–95.

Dahan, R., Feldman, R., & Hermoni, D. (2007). The importance of sexual orientation in the medical consultation. *Harefuah, 146*(8), 626–630.

Degenhardt, L. (2005). Drug use and risk behavior among regular ecstasy users: Does sexuality make a difference? *Culture, Health, & Sexuality, 7*(6), 599–614. doi: 10.1080/13691050500349875

Drumright, L. N., Little, S. J., Strathdee, S. A., Slymen, D. J., Araneta, M. R., Malcarne, V. L., . . . Gorbach, P.M. (2006). Unprotected anal intercourse and substance use among men who have sex with men with recent HIV infection. *Journal of Acquired Immune Deficiency Syndrome, 43*(3), 344–350. doi: 10.1097/01.qai.0000230530.02212.86

Fazio, A., Hunt, G., & Moloney, M. (2011). "It's one of the better drugs to use": Perceptions of cocaine use among gay and bisexual Asian American men. *Qualitative Health Research, 21*(5), 625–641. doi: 10.1177/1049732310385825

Ghaziani, A., & Cook, T. D. (2005). Reducing HIV infections at circuit parties: From description to explanation and principles of intervention design. *Journal of the International Association of Physicians in AIDS Care, 4*(2), 32–46. doi: 10.1177/1545109705277978

Goodenow, C., Szalacha, L., & Westheimer, K. (2006). School support groups, other school factors, and the safety of sexual minority adolescents. *Psychology in the Schools, 43,* 573–589.

Grossman, A. H., Haney, A. P., Edwards, P., Alessi, E. J., Ardon, M., & Howell, T. J. (2009). Lesbian, gay, bisexual and transgender youth talk about experiencing and coping with school violence: A qualitative study. *Journal of LGBT Youth, 6,* 24–46.

Gruskin, E. P., & Gordon, N. (2006). Gay/lesbian sexual orientation increases risk for cigarette smoking and heavy drinking among members of a large Northern California health plan. *BMC Public Health, 3*(6), 241.

Gruskin, E. P., Greenwood, G., Matevia, M., Pollack, L., & Bye, L. (2007). Disparities in smoking between the lesbian, gay, and bisexual population and the general public in California. *American Journal of Public Health, 97,* 1496–1502. doi: 10.2105/AJPH.2006.090258

Halkitis, P. N., & Palamar, J. J. (2006). Multivariate modeling of club drug use initiation among gay and bisexual men. *Substance Use & Misuse, 43,* 871–879. doi: 10.1080/10826080701801337

Halkitis, P. N., Palamar, J. J., & Mukherjee, P. P. (2007). Poly-drug use among gay and bisexual men: A longitudinal analysis. *Drug and Alcohol Dependence, 89,* 153–160. doi: 10.1016/j.drugalcdep.2006.12.028

Hatzenbuehler, M. L., Corbin, W. R., & Fromme, K. (2008). Trajectories and determinants of alcohol use among LGB young adults and their heterosexual peers: Results from a prospective study. *Developmental Psychology, 44,* 81–90.

Hegna, K., & Rossow, I. (2007). What's love got to do with it? Substance use and social integration for young people categorized by same-sex experience and attractions. *Journal of Drug Issues, 37,* 229–255.

Hirshfield, S., Remien, R. H., & Chiasson, M. A. (2006). Crystal methamphetamine use among men who have sex with men: Results from two national online studies. *Journal of Gay & Lesbian Psychotherapy, 10,* 85–93.

Holmes, S. E., & Cahill, S. (2004). School experiences of gay, lesbian, bisexual and transgender youth. *Journal of Gay & Lesbian Issues in Education, 1*(3), 53–66. doi: 10.1300/J367v01n03_06

Hughes, T. L. (2005). Alcohol use and alcohol-related problems among lesbian and gay men. *Annual review of Nursing Research, 23,* 283–325.

Hughes, T. L., & Eliason, M. (2002). Substance use and abuse in lesbian, gay, bisexual and transgender populations. *The Journal of Primary Prevention, 22,* 263–298.

Kalichman, S. C., & Cain, D. (2004). A prospective study of sensation seeking and alcohol use as predictors of sexual risk behaviors among men and women receiving sexually transmitted infection clinic services. *Psychology of Addictive Behaviors, 18,* 367–373.

Kaufman, M. (2006). *Smoking in U.S. declines sharply.* Retrieved from: www.washingtonpost.com/wp-dyn/content/article/2006/03/08/AR2006030802368.html (accessed January 12, 2014).

Kelly, B.C., Parsons, J. T., & Wells, B. E. (2006). Prevalence and predictors of club drug use among club-going young adults in New York City. *Journal of Urban Health, 83,* 884–895.

Kessler, R., Berglund, P., Demler, O., Jin, R., Merikangas, K., & Walters, E. (2005). Lifetime prevalence and age-of-onset distributions of DSM-IV disorders in the National Comorbidity Survey replication. *Archives of General Psychiatry, 62,* 593–602. doi: 10.1001/archpsyc.62.6.593

Klitzman, R. L., Greenberg, J. D., Pollack, L. M., & Dolezal, C. (2002). MDMA ("Ecstasy") use, and its association with high risk behaviors, mental health, and other factors among gay/bisexual men in New York City. *Drug and Alcohol Dependence, 66,* 115–125.

Kosciw, J. G., Greytak, E. A., Bartkiewicz, M. J., Boesen, M. J., & Palmer, N. A. (2012). The 2011 National School Climate Survey: *The experiences of lesbian, gay, bisexual and transgender youth in our nation's schools.* New York: GLSEN.

Kurtz, S. P. (2005). Post-circuit blues: Motivations and consequences of crystal meth use among gay men in Miami. *AIDS and Behavior, 9,* 63–72.

Lampinen, T. M., McGhee, D., & Martin, I. (2006). Increased risk of "club" drug use among gay and bisexual high school students in British Columbia. *Journal of Adolescent Health, 38,* 458–461. doi: 10.1016/j.jadohealth.2005.04.013

Lea, T., Reynolds, R., & de Wit, J. (2013). Alcohol and club drug use among same-sex attracted young people: Associations with frequenting the lesbian and gay scene and other bars and nightclubs. *Substance Use & Misuse, 48,* 129–136. doi: 10.3109/10826084.2012.733904

Lee, C. (2002). The impact of belonging to a high school gay/straight alliance. *The High School Journal, 85*(3), 13–26.

Lee, J. G. L., Griffin, G. K., & Melvin, C. L. (2009). Tobacco use among sexual minorities in the USA, 1987 to May 2007: A systematic review. *Tobacco Control, 18,* 275–282. doi: 10.1136/tc.2008.028241

Marshal, M. P., Friedman, M. S., Stall, R., King, K. M., Miles, J., Gold, M. A., & Morse, J. Q. (2008). Sexual orientation and adolescent substance use: A meta-analysis and methodological review. *Addiction, 103,* 546–556.

Matthews, C. R., Lorah, P., & Fenton, J. (2006). Treatment experiences of gays and lesbians in recovery from addiction: A qualitative inquiry. *Journal of Mental Health Counseling, 28,* 110–132.

Matthews, C. R., & Selvidge, M. M. D. (2005). Lesbian, gay, and bisexual clients' experiences in treatment for addiction. *Journal of Lesbian Studies, 9,* 79–90.

Matthews, C. R., Selvidge, M. M. D., & Fisher, K. (2005). Addictions counselors' attitudes and behaviors toward gay, lesbian, and bisexual clients. *Journal of Counseling & Development, 83,* 57–65.

McCabe, S., Hughes, T., Bostwick, W., & Boyd, C. (2005). Assessment of differences in dimensions of sexual orientation: Implications for substance use research in a college-age population. *Journal of Studies on Alcohol, 66,* 620–629.

McCabe, S., Hughes, T., Bostwick, W., West, B., & Boyd, C. (2009). Sexual orientation, substance use behaviors and substance dependence in the United States. *Addiction, 104,* 1333–1345. doi: 10.1111/j.1360-0443.2009.02596.x

McCabe, S. E., West, B. T., Hughes, T. L., & Boyd, C. J. (2013). Sexual orientation and substance abuse treatment utilization in the United States: Results from a national survey. *Journal of Substance Abuse Treatment, 44,* 4–12. doi: 10.1016/j.jsat.2012.01.007

Munafò, M. R., Hitsman, B., Rende, R., Metcalfe, C., & Niaura, R. (2007). Effects of progression to cigarette smoking on depressed mood in adolescents: Evidence from the National Longitudinal Study of Adolescent Health. *Addiction, 103,* 162–171.

Myer, I. H. (2003). Prejudice, social stress, and mental health in lesbian, gay, and bisexual populations: Conceptual issues and research evidence. *Psychological Beliefs, 129,* 674–697.

National Council on Alcoholism and Drug Dependence. (2013). *Learn about alcohol: FAQs/Facts.* Retrieved from: www.ncadd.org/index.php/learn-about-alcohol/faqsfacts (accessed January 12, 2014).

Operario, D., Choi, K-H., Chu, P. L., McFarland, W., Secura, G. M., Behel, S., . . . Valleroy, L. (2006). Prevalence and correlates of substance use among young Asian Pacific Islander men who have sex with men. *Prevention Science, 7*(1), 19–29. doi: 10.1007/s11121-005-0018-x

Parsons, J. T., Kelly, B.C., & Wesier, J. D. (2007). Initiation into methamphetamine use for young gay and bisexual men. *Drug and Alcohol Dependence, 90,* 135–144. doi: 10.1016/j.drugalcdep.2007.02.017

Ramchand, R., Fisher, M. P., Griffin, B. A., Becker, K., & Iguchi, M. Y. (2013). Drug use among gay and bisexual men at weekend dance parties: The role of intentions and perceptions of peers' behaviors. *AIDS Behavior, 17,* 1540–1549. doi: 10.1007/s10461-012-0382-z

Rosario, M., Schrimshaw, E. W., & Hunter, J. (2006). A model of sexual risk behaviors among young gay and bisexual men: Longitudinal associations of mental health, substance abuse, and the coming-out process. *AIDS Education and Prevention, 18,* 444–460.

Semple, S. J., Patterson, T. L., & Grant, I. (2002). Motivations associated with methamphetamine use among HIV+ men who have sex with men. *Journal of Substance Abuse Treatment, 22,* 149–156.

Senreich, E. (2009). A comparison of perceptions, reported abstinence, and completion rates of gay, lesbian, bisexual, and heterosexual clients in substance abuse treatment. *Journal of Gay & Lesbian Mental Health, 13,* 145–169. doi: 10.1080/19359700902870072

Shoptaw, S., Reback, C. J., Peck, J. A., Yang, X., Rotheram-Fuller, E., Larkins, S., . . . Hucks-Ortiz, C. (2005). Behavioral treatment approaches for methamphetamine dependence and HIV-related sexual risk behaviors among urban gay and bisexual men. *Drug and Alcohol Dependence, 78,* 125–134. doi: 10.1016/j.drugalcdep.2004.10.004

Smith, E. A., Offen, N., & Malone, R. E. (2005). What makes an ad a cigarette ad? Commercial tobacco imagery in the lesbian, gay, and bisexual press. *Journal of Epidemiology and Community Health, 59,* 1086–1091.

Stall, R. D., Greenwood, G. L., Acree, M., Paul, J. P., & Coates, T. J. (1999). Cigarette smoking among gay and bisexual men. *American Journal of Public Health, 89,* 1875–1878.

Stall, R., Paul, J., Greenwood, G., Pollack, L., Bein, E., Crosby, G., . . . Catania, J. A. (2001). Alcohol use, drug use, and alcohol-related problems among men who have sex with men: The urban men's health study. *Addiction, 96,* 1589–1601.

Stevens, P., & Smith, R. (2013). Substance abuse counseling: Theory and practice (5th ed.). Upper Saddle River, NJ: Pearson Education.

Thiede, H., Valleroy, L., MacKellar, D., Celentano, D., Ford, W., Hagan, H., . . . Torian, L. (2003). Regional patterns and correlates of substance use among young men who have sex with men in 7 U.S. urban areas. *American Journal of Public Health, 93,* 1915–1921.

Trocki, K. F., Drabble, L. A., & Midanik, L. T. (2005). Tobacco, marijuana, and sensation seeking: Comparisons across gay, lesbian, bisexual, and heterosexual groups. *Psychology of Addictive Behaviors, 23*(4), 620–631. doi: 10.1037/a0017334

Watson, L. B., Varjas, K., Meyers, J., & Graybill, E. C. (2010). Gay–straight alliance advisors: Negotiating multiple ecological systems when advocating for LGBTQ youth. *Journal of LGBT Youth, 7*(2), 100–128. doi: 10.1080/19361651003799700

Wong, C. F., Kipke, M. D., & Weiss, G. (2008). Risk factors for alcohol use, frequent use, and binge drinking among young men who have sex with men. *Addictive Behaviors, 33*(8), 1012–1020.

Woodford, M. S. (2012). *Men, addiction, & intimacy: Strengthening recovery by fostering the emotional development of boys and men.* New York: Routledge.

Wynn, R., & West-Olatunji, C. W. (2009). Use of culture-centered counseling theory with ethnically diverse LGBT clients. *Journal of LGBT Issues in Counseling, 3,* 198–214.

8 Recognizing the Needs of Sexual Minority Boys and Adolescents in Schools

Melissa M. Luke & Kristopher M. Goodrich

Professional school counselors have a professional and ethical responsibility to serve the academic, career, and personal/social developmental needs of all students (Campbell & Dahir, 1997; Green & Keys, 2001; Ratts, Ayers, & Bright, 2009). While other counselors working in a school setting may not be compelled in the same ways, surely any counselor working in a school context is concerned with meeting the needs of the overall student body. One population that has remained marginalized and underserved in schools consists of gay, bisexual, transgender, and questioning (GBTQ) students (Goodrich & Luke, 2009). Profound political, religious, and social stigma has influenced the perceptions of, and services provided to, this community. Research has shown that GBTQ students are at high risk for a number of negative academic, personal/social, and career outcomes, including verbal and physical harassment (Kosciw, Greytak, Bartiewicz, Boesen, & Palmer, 2012), academic drop-out (Kosciw et al., 2012), depression (Goldfried & Godfried, 2001; Grambling, Carr, & McCain, 2000), substance abuse (Goldfried & Goldfried, 2001), suicidal behaviors (Rutter, 2006), as well as a number of family-related concerns (Goodrich, 2009a; Saltzburg, 2004). In response to these factors, the American School Counseling Association (ASCA) has published ethical standards (ASCA, 2010) and a position statement (ASCA, 2007), reinforcing school counselors' responsibilities and commitment to effectively serve GBTQ students, regardless of one's beliefs or affiliations. It is clear that providing responsive services to GBTQ students and their allies is an essential responsibility of all school counselors (Goodrich & Luke, 2009; Luke & Goodrich, 2009).

Concurrently, recent scholarship has begun to inform us that counseling has been a gender bias profession, with training and services predominately oriented toward the needs of women and girls (Cassano, Perry-Parrish, & Zeman, 2007; Goodrich, 2009b; Robertson, Lin, Woodford, Danos, & Hurst, 2001; Wong & Rochlen, 2005). The above-cited authors have demonstrated through the exploration of how counselors view and address emotions with men (e.g., Robertson et al., 2001; Wong & Rochlen, 2005) has typically been much more expressive, and female oriented. This does not serve emotive, interactional, and relational patterns that many men have been socialized to take from boyhood (Cassano et al., 2007; Goodrich, 2009b) and thus may have a negative impact on the therapeutic relationship between counselor and client. As such, the goal of this chapter is to demonstrate how professional school counselors, or other counselors working in a school context, can address the needs of queer male youth, addressing the multiple identities relating to the child's gender and gender expression, as well as sexual/affectual orientation.

Discussion: Who are These Students?

Students who identify as GBTQ have disclosed publicly, privately, or personally their sexual/affectual orientation or gender identity. Gay (G) students are males who are emotionally, physically, and sexually attracted to other males. The term gay has also been utilized as an "umbrella" term by some to represent any person within the GBTQ community. Bisexual (B) students are individuals who are emotionally, physically, and sexually attracted to both males and females. Heterosexual, or straight, students are emotionally, physically, and sexually attracted to the opposite sex. Questioning (Q) students may be unsure of their sexual/affectual orientation, unwilling or unable to disclose, publicly or privately. Identifying as GBQ or straight is an expression of one's sexual/affectual orientation.

Transgender students are those who do not identify with the gender they have been assigned at birth (Carroll, Gilroy & Ryan, 2002; Ellis & Eriksen, 2002). These include a number of persons, such as those who identify as cross-dressers, drag kings or queens, transsexuals and intersex individuals, among others (Ellis & Eriksen, 2002). Intersex individuals are persons who were born with reproductive or sexual anatomy that does not fit the typical definitions of male or female, and occur in one of every 1500–2000 births (Intersex Society of America, 2008). Questioning (Q) students may be unsure of their gender identity, unwilling or unable to disclose, publicly or privately. Similarly, identifying as cisgender informs the world that the person identifies with the gender label they were assigned at birth; this can also be called gender normative. Labeling oneself as transgender, intersex, questioning, or cisgender is an expression of one's gender identity.

A Word on Inclusion

Although this chapter is focused upon "sexual minority boys and adolescents," we made the intentional decision to include transgender and intersex youth. Although these are gender identities, we believe the idea of allowing youth to self-define whom they are is critical, and as such we should be inclusive in our understanding of transboys and transmen, who have historically been omitted from the literature and training within the counseling and education fields (Luke, Goodrich, & Scarborough, 2011), and whose needs are not often addressed in schools (Scarborough, Goodrich, & Luke, manuscript submitted). Intersex persons may or may not define their gender identity as male, but for the purposes of this chapter, would present to professional school counselors as such. Therefore, we hope to bring a focus to this population so that all counselors may better serve their needs, now and in the future.

The Continuum of Sexual/Affectual and Gender Identities

When discussing GBTQ identity status, most people believe that everyone can hold just one identity within these categories. That assumption is inaccurate. In fact, although we are using the term sexual/affectual to describe relational affinity, it is possible for individuals to identify as relationally attracted to different genders across sexual and affectual processes. Further, sexual/affectual orientation and gender identity are separate concepts that can be, but are not necessarily, related to one another. People have both a sexual/affectual orientation and a gender identity. As such, a student can identify as transgender and straight, or transgender and gay. Similarly, a person can identify as male and straight, or female and bisexual. In considering the whole individual, a school counselor must be aware of both sexual/affectual and gender identity to appropriately work with their student population.

Research by Chung, Szymanski, and Amadio (2006) has suggested that approximately 6–10% of the student population identifies as gay, similar to the proportion of gay individuals in the general American population. It is currently unknown what percentage of either the general or student population identifies as bisexual, transgender, or questioning (Grossman & D'Augelli, 2006; Mallon, 2001). Nonetheless, it logically follows that the addition of BTQ students increases the proportion of GBTQ students that are present in schools (Goodrich & Luke, 2009).

Preparation of Professional School Counselors

Scholars, such as Singh and Burnes (2009) and Goodrich and Luke (2009) have discussed that professional school counselors are unprepared to address the needs of GBTQ youth. A follow-up study by Luke, Goodrich, and Scarborough (2011) found that, overall, school counselor education does little to address LGBTQ identity within school counseling training programs, and the majority of the training provided is focus on the adult LGBTQ community. As such, the developmental needs of GBTQ students appear to be unaddressed in most school counseling training programs. It is reasonable to speculate that this training gap may lead to a practice gap for many of these former school counseling students, wherein professional school counselors and other counselors working in schools have not been adequately trained in their preparation programs to work with the multiple and intersecting identities of GBTQ students.

In a recent study, Goodrich and Luke (2010) found that pre-service school counselors perceived that GBTQ students thought about, and engaged in, sexual behaviors more often than other students. Concurrently, the pre-service school counselors expressed the assumption that working with GBTQ students would require that they focus on sexuality in counseling in a different way from with other student populations. After the trainees interacted with GBTQ high school student groups, they realized that their original assumptions were inaccurate. Overall, GBTQ youth have similar needs when compared with other students (Windmeyer, 2009). The primary difference between GBTQ youth and their heterosexual, and cisgender peers, is the need to be accepted by others regardless of their sexual orientation and gender identity. This acceptance includes having a safe environment where GBTQ students can learn, interact, and grow with others (Windmeyer, 2009). Toward these ends, school counselors can effectively serve the GBTQ student population with the skills they currently possess, providing that they intentionally tailor their interventions in response to the unique needs of GBTQ students (Goodrich & Luke, 2009; Luke & Goodrich, 2009). As such, the following are offered as potential interventions across a comprehensive, developmental school counseling program (CDSCP), designed to facilitate students' success in the academic, personal/social, and career domains.

Academic Domain

Research has shown that GBTQ students academically achieve at much lower rates than their heterosexual and gender normative peers. Studies by the Gay, Lesbian, and Straight Education Network (GLSEN; Kosciw et al., 2012) and others have found that GBTQ students earned, on average, half a letter grade lower than their peers after controlling for socio-economic status. Researchers are trying to discern what accounts for the lower academic performance, but scholars suggest that the higher levels of harassment and lower levels of school relatedness may contribute. Accordingly, GBTQ students are two times more likely to miss school due to safety concerns, and students who reported having been frequently harassed were three times more likely to miss school. Finally, GBTQ students are twice as likely to report that they do not intend to go to college. It appears from this research that identifying as a GBTQ student can have long-lasting academic and career implications (D'Augelli, 2002).

There are many interventions that school counselors can utilize to assist their GBTQ student population academically. The first intervention that school counselors can implement would be to utilize a systematic and responsive system to identify and monitor students who are academically struggling in their schools (e.g., *School Counselor Accountability: A Measure of Student Success* [Stone & Dahir, 2007]). In meeting with these students, it is important for the school counselor to understand what symptoms or issues might be playing a role in the student's low achievement. As sexual/affectual orientation and gender identity have been connected to low achievement and failure to continue one's education (Kosciw et al., 2012), this is one of many potential issues that a school counselor should consider exploring and considering in the conceptualization of low achievement. If it discovered that a student's sexual/affectual orientation or gender identity is indirectly affecting academic achievement, it is imperative that the school counselor intervenes and assists the student with the related struggles. The focus of the intervention can be with the individual student (such as within the personal/social domain, discussed later in the chapter) or it can be more systemically oriented, such as in the events of mistreatment and school bullying (Berlan, Corliss, Field, Goodman, & Bryn Austin, 2010).

School counselors at the middle and high school levels can assist GBTQ students while creating their class schedules by considering issues of school climate and teachers' strengths (Ratts et al., 2009; Windmeyer, 2009). School counselors could endeavor to place students in classroom environments that promote safety, either based on classroom location and/or the teacher's likelihood to intervene if harassment is observed (Luke & Goodrich, 2008; Ratts et al., 2009). Harassment has been found to occur less frequently in classrooms that are centrally located, well lit, and/or frequently supervised. Additionally, it has been observed that some school stakeholders (i.e., administrators, teachers, paraprofessionals) are more likely than others to intervene if harassment occurs and that they do so, with differing levels of skill (Luke & Goodrich, 2009). Intentionally placing students in areas where they would be more closely supervised, comfortable, and safe, as well as with stakeholders that have the skills needed to appropriately respond to GBTQ student issues would be a responsive intervention that considered the unique needs of GBTQ students as compared with their peers.

Moreover, school counselors could also work with school stakeholders (i.e., teachers, administrators, paraprofessionals, peer leaders) to ensure that all school personnel are appropriately trained to supervise and effectively intervene when necessary (Luke & Goodrich, 2008). Examples of personnel that may encounter increased incidents of GBTQ students directed hostility and harassment include those supervising or associated with less structured activities such as on the school bus, in the hallways before and after school, study halls, locker rooms, cafeterias, and recesses or breaks, to name a few. School counselors can raise awareness with school staff about the different forms that harassment can take, where this tends to take place, and effective strategies to intervene. Further, professional school counselors can use their leadership and facilitation skills to conduct a training wherein they instruct and role-play different intervention techniques to combat harassment and show support to GBTQ students across the school curriculum.

School counselors also facilitate classroom guidance lessons about a host of academic and life issues as part of a comprehensive, developmental school counseling program. The topics of classroom guidance are largely dependent upon student and school need, but often include academic presentations, career presentations, and life skills training. School counselors can review their existent curriculum for the purposes of discovering how many of them are inadvertently biased and aimed at traditional students: heterosexual students who will engage in relationships with opposite sex partners, or students who will be unconcerned about certain types of discrimination at their workplace. School counselors can then adjust some of the language and topics addressed to make their curriculum more representative and inclusive to GBTQ students (Goodrich & Luke, 2009). For example, school counselors can include vignettes and information specific to GBTQ students and families in their already established school curriculum without a significant amount of revision.

Finally, school counselors can provide specific academic resources to students regarding their future academic goals. As it has been demonstrated that GBTQ students attend higher education at lower rates than their heterosexual and gender normative peers (Kosciw et al., 2012), school counselors can work with students to challenge misperceptions that LGBTQ students may not be safe or find comfort at a college or university. *The Advocate College Guide for LGBT Students* (Windmeyer, 2009) is one resource that provides students with information about the 100 "best campuses" for LGBT students, as ranked by LGBT and supportive college students. Additionally, college and university websites frequently have information about their GBTQ support centers, campus resources, and living-learning communities. A school counselor may assist students in locating this information and encourage students to further investigate them in person or electronically as part of their college search. Consulting with GBTQ alumni, providing mentoring networks, or referring students to local community resources (e.g., PFLAG) are all opportunities that might help to encourage and facilitate GBTQ students' post-graduate academic careers.

Persona/Social Arena

In a large-scale national study, Kosciw et al. (2012) found high rates of verbal and physical harassment of GBTQ students in schools across America. The survey found that 81.9% of GBTQ students reported verbal harassment and 38.3% reported physical harassment about their real or perceived sexual orientation, while 63.9% of students reported verbal harassment and 27.1% reported physical harassment about their gender expression. Concurrently, 84.9% public high school students reported hearing anti-gay remarks and epitaphs frequently or often at school, and 91.4% reported that they felt distressed because of this language. As most school counselors are involved in the implementation of some form of character education, school climate, or anti-bullying programming, these statistics about harassment in schools are particularly disturbing. School counselors should consider how an unwelcoming and hostile school environment can impact GBTQ students' ability to learn, socialize, and develop.

One intervention that school counselors can use to support GBTQ students is to assist school stakeholders to re-conceptualize verbal and physical harassment about sexual orientation and gender expression as bullying (Ratts et al., 2009). Bullying and mistreatment are familiar concepts in the school environment, and most school districts have clear policies and procedures about how to respond to these incidents. School counselors may want to frame GBTQ directed harassment within the existent policies and procedures. It has been suggested that doing so increases the likelihood that GBTQ students will be protected because the focus is shifted from the content and recipient of the harassment to the process and perpetrator. Many schools currently have guidance curricula about bullying, and sexual orientation and gender expression would be a simple yet critical addition into those lesson plans. Schools that host "No Name Calling Weeks" or other programming can also be utilized to address this issue as well (Ratts et al., 2009).

Additionally, school counselors can also think beyond the walls of their school when constructing interventions to assist GBTQ students. The field of school counseling has begun to recognize the successful student outcomes and the inordinate school and community benefits that have been demonstrated when partnerships are formed between schools, families, and communities (Bryan & Holcomb-McCoy, 2004). School–family–community partnerships have been linked to improved academic, social, and emotional outcomes for all students, but students of color, students living in poverty, and English language learners appear to particularly benefit (Luke, 2008a). Given the specialized education and training, school counselors are in the unique position to serve as a resource and educator for families and communities around critical issues, such as sexual orientation and gender identity. As such, school counselors need to be prepared to intervene with families and community partners to facilitate awareness of and communication about sexual/affectual orientation and gender identity issues, as well as to assist families and community members as they negotiate the related issues (Stone Fish & Harvey, 2005). Accordingly, school counselors need to familiarize themselves with national and local resources so that they can refer students, families, and school stakeholders to appropriate GBTQ literature, support networks, and community agencies.

Using their individual and group counseling skills, school counselors can facilitate sessions with students about issues they might be struggling with related to their sexual orientation. These might include depression (Goldfried & Godfried, 2001; Grambling, Carr, & McCain, 2000), substance abuse (Goldfried & Goldfried, 2001), increased familial conflict (Saltzburg, 2004), and suicidal behaviors (Rutter, 2006). Concurrently, school counselors could also introduce these topics into group counseling lessons to inform other students about the signs and symptoms that might suggest another classmate is having an issue and needs additional support or assistance. Although not all GBTQ students will struggle with such issues, school counselors need to be sensitive to the increased risks that can result from institutionalized bias and oppression related to GBTQ identity. Finally, as systemic change agents, school counselors address school climate through their support of Gay/Straight Alliances (GSA) or Acceptance Coalitions for LGBTQ students in schools (Lee, 2002; Goodrich & Luke, 2010). Lee found that the presence of a GSA within a school positively influenced various GBTQ student performance markers, even if the GBTQ students did not attend the actual GSA meetings. It was hypothesized that the mere presence of a GSA or Acceptance Coalition demonstrated GBTQ student support and, in turn, influenced a more accepting school climate.

It is important to reiterate that the presenting school counseling needs of most GBTQ students will parallel those of their heterosexual and gender normative peers. School counselors need to monitor the potential to misinterpret the salience or over-focus on issues related to sexual/affectual orientation or gender identity. As previously noted, Goodrich and Luke (2010) found that pre-service school counseling trainees had the tendency to over-conceptualize the importance of students' sexual orientation and gender identity when they first began working with the GBTQ population. GBTQ students face many of the same issues that their other peers face, and their sexual/affectual orientation or gender identity may not always be an influencing factor (Windmeyer, 2009). Although it is important to remember the unique needs that GBTQ students have, it is also important to remember that they are also students like any other. Sexual/affectual orientation and gender identity do not define the student.

Specific Male Interventions

As noted earlier, many individual counseling interventions have been created in response to the needs of gender-identified female clients (Cassano et al., 2007; Goodrich, 2009b; Robertson, Lin, Woodford, Danos, & Hurst, 2001; Wong & Rochlen, 2005). Although typical, emotive-based counseling interventions may be effective for some GBTQ-identified boys and adolescents, this may not be the case for all male youth. Rochlen (2005) addressed that the typical free-flowing and verbally expressive interview may not format well for traditionally socialized males, who struggle with identifying and expressing their emotions to others. As such, he, along with others, (e.g., Goodrich, 2009b) has argued for the need for more highly structured interviews when dealing with traditionally socialized boy and male clients, to meet their gender socialized needs. Similarly, counselors may wish to implement activity-based, expressive counseling interventions (e.g., Luke, 2008b, 2008c, 2008d), as these may better allow boys and men the opportunity to identify and explore their emotions, and provide better voice to the experiences that they may have trouble identifying with others. Luke (2010a,b) describes this type of expressive work as semi-structured individual and group interventions designed to facilitate an in-session experience that the counselor can then process with the client. It is important for counselors to recognize that talk-based communication is just one of many ways that GBTQ youth express themselves. Thus, activity interventions that incorporate visual, music, movement, and props as stimuli are recommended.

In addition, some child and adolescent clients might present with gender non-conforming behaviors and interests, which could lead to struggle with their peers and families. Students might face harassment, bullying, and other forms of mistreatment in schools due to this gender variant play. As such, professional school counselors might use psychoeducation with clients and their peers to find historical or current examples of gender variant play to normalize the GBTQ client's experience, and promote safety within the school. An example of this can be found in Goodrich's (2009b) review of the text *The Buffalo Soldier* (Bohjalian, 2002). Within that text, the story's main character, Alfred, is a 10-year-old African American boy living in a predominately White community in Vermont. As part of the story, he enjoys horseback riding and informs his peers of such. He later finds himself isolated and alone and, when exploring why other boys will not play with him in school, he finds out that most community members view horses as a hobby for girls. In reviewing this text through a counselor's eyes, Goodrich (2009b) recommended that counselors could teach youth the story about Buffalo Soldiers, African American soldiers who rode horses into battle and were seen as strong male leaders within the community. By reframing the experiences for his peers, Alfred was able to acquire cultural capital within the male community and was later adopted as a peer. Professional school counselors could similarly follow this example and adopt for other situations that may be viewed as gender non-conforming in schools. They might research and present about how male dancers have been recognized in numerous cultures for their strength and agility, how artists and musicians have been widely celebrated in countries throughout the world, and can even present how persons who cross gender lines within many indigenous cultures have been viewed as shamans and other religious and cultural leaders. By providing greater context, professional school counselors can normalize and validate the experience of being different, which might assist not only GBTQ students, but a host of other groups within schools.

Career Arena

As GBTQ students' identity has been shown to have an influence on their academic progress, it should not be surprising that LGBTQ identity also appears to have an influence on career aspirations, career preparation, and career achievement or success (D'Augelli, 2002). Thus, school counselors can explicitly address how academic decisions in the short term can impact their long-term career development as GBTQ students make course selections, as well as construct their academic program and career plans. It is advised that school counselors also consider how their own assumptions might influence their work with GBTQ students.

The first issue that school counselors should consider when working with an GBTQ student around their career development should be what values, biases, and assumptions that the school counselor has internalized about GBTQ individuals (Luke & Goodrich, 2008; Luke & Goodrich, 2009). There are many stereotypes about GBTQ individuals, including that they are more artistic, creative, original, and outgoing than their peers. For this reason, many GBTQ students might self-select or be influenced toward certain careers and away from others, based on this perception. In addition to "self-checking" themselves, school counselors need to address the potential of career foreclosure with their GBTQ students, to ensure students consider an array of careers in which they have aptitude, might enjoy, and have the potential to succeed. Just as school counselors challenge inaccurate societal gender and racial assumptions related to career, so too can they reduce the potential for GBTQ students being "tracked" into occupations or careers as a result of inaccurate stereotypes or assumptions.

Likewise, it is equally important for school counselors to assess GBTQ students' career development across traditional career and life-planning programs. This includes assessing the student's interests, aptitudes, achievements, values, and personality, as well as ecological factors that might influence or impact a student's career development (Hood & Johnson, 2007). School counselors can adapt conventional career interventions to meet the unique needs of GBTQ students. For example, while planning a school-wide "career fair," the school counselor can intentionally recruit the participation of GBTQ professionals, organize a panel of GBTQ speakers to discuss their respective career histories, or establish a mentoring networking for students who might otherwise struggle finding others like themselves in the occupational world.

As school counselors work individually or in smaller groups with students, they can assist GBTQ students in examining occupational and institutional environments when considering future careers. Counselors could encourage students to investigate professions that have historically been open to GBTQ employees, as well as look for certain signifiers to see if a potential employer is supportive of GBTQ identity. Examples of these signifiers could include employment non-discrimination statements that explicitly include sexual/affectual orientation and gender identity, values and missions statements consistent with inclusion, as well as other human resource policies such as same-sex partner benefits. The school counselor can also instruct the student in how to research if companies have a "critical mass" (or substantial number) of GBTQ employees, which might assist the student in feeling safe and comfortable in their future work environment. Additionally, counselors may wish to develop and access resources, such as the Human Rights Campaign (HRC) Corporate Equality Index (HRC, 2013), which is a rating of gay-friendly companies to assist in connecting students to historically GBTQ-affirming work environments. Further, it would be helpful for school counselors to support students in researching companies that have documented track records of institutional bias and discrimination toward GBTQ persons, so that a student can be informed and potentially more skillfully avoid problematic situations in the future. Not all students will need other GBTQ individuals at their place of employment, as some students might even enjoy being the first or one of a few "trail-blazing" employees at an organization. Others, however, might require a more inclusive and accepting atmosphere from the start. Although it is important for the school counselor to raise this discussion and students' awareness, students should not be dissuaded from pursuing careers that have historically not had visible GBTQ employees or from going into field that has, in the past, been less supportive of GBTQ identity.

GBTQ students face both similar and unique challenges in schools when compared with their heterosexual and cisgender counterparts. It is important for professional school counselors to know about the different developmental challenges GBTQ students face, as well as how they can intervene in a culturally appropriate way. In the pages that follow, a host of resources are provided for professional school counselors to add to their toolboxes. Although not an exhaustive list, it may help professional school counselors find other, more specific, resources that may prove useful for the specific students they work with in their schools.

Resources for Professional School Counselors

LGBTQ Youth Classroom Lesson Plans

Gay, Lesbian, and Straight Education Network (GLSEN) K-12 Curricula and Lesson Plans: www.glsen.org/educate/resources/curriculum

Safe Schools Coalition: Resources for K-12 Teachers and Curriculum Specialists: www.safeschoolscoalition.org/RG-teachers_k-12.html

Unheard Voices: Stories of LGBT History: www.adl.org/education/curriculum_connections/unheard-voices/

LGBTQ Safe School Kits/Manuals

GLSEN Safe Space: http://safespace.glsen.org/ (donation required for this resource)

Out for Equity: http://outforequity.spps.org/safe_schools_manual.html

Safe School Coalition: www.safeschoolscoalition.org/RG-teachers_k-12.html

LGBTQIAA Safe School Manuals

Out for Equity: http://outforequity.spps.org/safe_schools_manual.html

Georgia State Safe Schools Coalition: www.georgiasafeschoolscoalition.org

LGBTQIAA People of Color

The Task Force: www.thetaskforce.org/issues/racial_and_economic_justice

Human Rights Campaign: www.hrc.org/issues

Trans_Poc: A Community for Trans/GQueer/Questioning People of Color: http://trans-poc.livejournal.com/

LGBT Sports Issues

Changing the Game: http://sports.glsen.org/about-the-project/

Gay and Lesbian International Sports Association: www.glisa.org/

LGBTQIAA Families

GLSEN: www.glsen.org/jumpstart

Children of Lesbians and Gays Everywhere (COLAGE): www.colage.org/

Queerly Related Families:

Garner, A. (2005). *Families Like Mine: Children of Gay Parents Tell it Like It Is.* London: HarperCollins (book by Abigail Garner)

Family Religious Issues

Family Acceptance: www.familyacceptance.org
Gay Church: An Affirming Christian GLBT Site: www.gaychurch.org/

Religious Issues in Schools

Safe Schools on University (Religious) Campuses: www.nytimes.com/2011/04/19/us/19gays.html?_r=2
Religious Right versus Safe Schools: http://vimeo.com/15740584
Religion in Public Schools (Article in The School Administrator): www.aasa.org/SchoolAdministratorArticle.aspx?id=14762 (addresses successful and failed approaches)

Transgender Children and Adolescents

TransYouth Family Allies: Understanding Through Education: www.imatyfa.org/
Gender Spectrum: www.genderspectrum.org/resources

Other Resources

Students Seek Safe Schools (Article): www.resistinc.org/newsletters/articles/students-seek-safe-schools

Other Websites of Interest:

http://community.pflag.org/Page.aspx?pid=194&srcid=-2
www.glsen.org/cgi-bin/iowa/all/home/index.html
www.colage.org
www.familyequality.org
www.hrc.org
www.transparentcy.org
www.aclu.org/lgbt-rights
www.lambdalegal.org
www.casafeschools.org
www.glma.org
www.gsanetwork.org
http://nbjc.org
www.gaycenter.org/gip?gclid=CMrms6Te2JwCFeRL5QodWDEoIw
www.gender.org
www.isna.org

References

American School Counseling Association (ASCA). (2010). *Ethical standards for school counselors.* Retrieved from: www.schoolcounselor.org/files/EthicalStandards2010.pdf

American School Counseling Association (ASCA). (2007). *The professional school counselor and LGBTQ youth.* Retrieved online from: http://asca2.timberlakepublishing.com//files/PS_LGBTQ.pdf

Berlan, E. D., Corliss, H. L., Field, A. E., Goodman, E., & Bryn Austin, S. (2010). Sexual orientation and bullying among adolescents in the growing up today study. *Journal of Adolescent Health, 46*(4), 366–371.

Bohjalian, C. (2002). *The buffalo soldier.* New York: Vintage Books.

Bryan, J. A., & Holcomb-McCoy, C. H. (2004). School counselors' perceptions of their involvement in school-family-community partnerships. *Professional School Counseling, 7,* 162–171.

Campbell, C. A., & Dahir, C. A. (1997). *The name assigned to the document by the author. This field may also contain sub-titles, series names, and report numbers. Sharing the vision: The national standards for School Counseling Programs.* Alexandria, VA: American School Counselors Association.

Carroll, L., Gilroy, P. J., & Ryan, J. (2002). Counseling transgendered, transsexual, and gender-variant clients. *Journal of Counseling & Development, 80*(2), 131–139.

Cassano, M., Perry-Parrish, C., & Zeman, J. (2007). Influence of gender on parental socialization of children's sadness regulation. *Social Development, 16*(2), 210–231. Chung, Y. B., Szymanski, D. M., & Amadio, D. M. (2006). Empirical validation of a multidimensional model for assessing sexual orientation. *Journal of LGBT Issues in Counseling, 1*(3), 3–13.

D'Augelli, A. R. (2002). Mental health problems among lesbian, gay, and bisexual youth ages 14 to 21. *Clinical Child Psychology and Psychiatry, 7*(3), 439–462.

Ellis, K. M., & Eriksen, K. (2002). Transsexual and transgenderist experiences and treatment options. *The Family Journal, 10*(3), 289–299.

Goodrich, K. M. (2009a). Mom and Dad "come out": The process of identifying as a heterosexual parent with a lesbian, gay or bisexual child. *The Journal of LGBT Issues in Counseling, 3*(1), 37–61.

Goodrich, K. M. (2009b). Using race and gender as a counseling intervention in "The Buffalo Soldier". *The Journal of International Men's Health, 8*(3), 191–201.

Goodrich, K. M., & Luke, M. (2009). LGBTQ Responsive School Counseling. *Journal of LGBT Issues in Counseling, 3*(2), 113–127.

Goodrich, K. M., & Luke, M. (2010). Experiences of school counselors-in-training in group work with LGBTQ adolescents. *The Journal for Specialists in Group Work, 35*(2), 143–159.

Goldfried, M. R., & Goldfried, A. P. (2001). The importance of parental support in thelives of gay, lesbian, and bisexual individuals. *JCLP/In Session: Psychotherapy in Practice, 57*(5), 681–693.

Grambling, L. F., Carr, R. L., & McCain, N. L. (2000). Family responses to disclosure of self-as-lesbian. *Issues in Mental Health Nursing, 21*(7), 653–669.

Green, A., & Keys, S. G. (2001). Expanding the developmental school counseling paradigm: Meeting the needs of the 21st century student. *Professional School Counseling, 5,* 84–95.

Grossman, A. H., & D'Augelli, A. R. (2006). Transgender youth: Invisible and vulnerable. *Journal of Homosexuality, 51*(1), 111–128.

Hood, A. B., & Johnson, R. W. (2007). *Assessment in counseling: A guide to the use of psychological assessment procedures* (4th ed.). Alexandria, VA: American Counseling Association.

Human Rights Campaign (HRC). (2013). *Corporate Equality Index.* Retrieved online from: www.hrc.org/corporate-equality-index#.UiPIWuCVKLo (accessed January 14, 2014).

Intersex Society of America. (2008). *Frequently asked questions.* Retrieved online from: www.isna.org/faq (accessed January 14, 2014).

Kosciw, J. G., Greytak, E. A., Bartiewicz, M. J., Boesen, M. J., & Palmer, N. A. (2012). *The 2011 National School Climate Survey: Experiences of lesbian, gay, bisexual and transgender youth in our nation's schools.* New York: GLSEN.

Lee, C. (2002). The impact of belonging to a high school gay/straight alliance. *The High School Journal, 85*(3), 13–26.

Luke, M. (2008a). School-family-community partnerships: Implications for school counselors to bridge the gap in urban schools. *New York State School Counseling Journal, 5*(2), 13–22.

Luke, M. (2008b). Feeling 4-square. In L. L. Foss, J. Green, K. Wolfe-Stiltner, and J. L. DeLucia-Waack (Eds.), *School counselors share their favorite group activities: A guide to choosing, planning, conducting, and processing* (pp. 176–178). Alexandria, VA: Association for Specialists in Group Work.

Luke, M. (2008c). Termination capsule. In L. L. Foss, J. Green, K. Wolfe-Stiltner, and J. L. DeLucia-Waack (Eds.), *School counselors share their favorite group activities: A guide to choosing, planning, conducting, and processing.* (pp. 189–191). Alexandria, VA: Association for Specialists in Group Work.

Luke, M. (2008d). Props in a box. In L. L. Foss, J. Green, K. Wolfe-Stiltner, and J. L. DeLucia-Waack (Eds.), *School counselors share their favorite group activities: A guide to choosing, planning, conducting, and processing* (pp. 111–113). Alexandria, VA: Association for Specialists in Group Work.

Luke, M. (2010a). Person-centered therapy in expressive arts. In S. Degges-White and N. Davis (Eds.), *Bringing the arts to the science of counseling* (pp. 157–159). New York: Springer.

Luke, M. (2010b). Postcard poetry slam: A person-centered expressive arts intervention. In S. Degges-White and N. Davis (Eds.), *Bringing the arts to the science of counseling* (pp. 159–162). New York: Springer.

Luke, M., & Goodrich, K. M. (2008, June). The invisible 10: LGBTQ youth in schools. *American School Counselor Association Conference,* Atlanta, GA.

Luke, M., & Goodrich, K. M. (2009). School counseling for LGBTQ students: Expanding school counselors' knowledge, awareness, and skills. *New York School Counseling Journal, 6*(2), 44–47.

Luke, M., Goodrich, K. M., & Scarborough, J. L. (2011). Integration of the K-12 LGBTQ student population in school counselor education curricula: The current state of affairs. *Journal of LGBT Issues in Counseling, 5*(2), 80–101.

Mallon, G. P. (2001). *Lesbian and gay youth issues: A practical guide for youth workers.* Washington, DC: CWLA Press.

Ratts, M. J., Ayers, L., & Bright, M. (2009). Using programs such as no name calling week can help you address bullying and harassment issues in your school. *ASCA School Counselor, 47*(1), 21–25.

Robertson, J. M., Lin, C. W., Woodford, J., Danos, K. K., & Hurst, M. A. (2001). The (un)emotional male: Physiological, verbal, and written correlates of expressiveness. *The Journal of Men's Studies, 9*(3), 393–412.

Rochlen, A. B. (2005). Men in (and out) of therapy: Central concepts, emerging directions, and remaining challenges. *Journal of Clinical Psychology, 61*(6), 627–631.

Rutter, P. A. (2006). Youth adult suicide and sexual orientation: What should counselors know? *Journal of LGBT Issues in Education, 1*(3), 33–48.

Saltzburg, S. (2004). Learning that an adolescent child is gay or lesbian: The parent experience. *Social Work, 49,* 109–118.

Scarborough, J. L., Goodrich, K. M., & Luke, M. (manuscript submitted). Professional school counselors' education, needs, and experiences in working with LGBTQ-identified students.

Singh, A. A., & Burnes, T. R. (2009). Creating developmentally appropriate, safe counseling environments for transgender youth: The critical role of the school counselor. *Journal of LGBT Issues in Counseling, 3,* 215–234.

Stone, C. B., & Dahir, C. A. (2007). *School counselor accountability: A measure of student success* (2nd ed.). Boston, MA: Merrill.

Stone Fish, L., & Harvey, R. (2005). *Nurturing queer youth: Family therapy transformed.* New York: W.W. Norton & Co.

Windmeyer, S. L. (2006). *The advocate college guide for LGBT students.* New York: Alyson Publications Inc.

Windmeyer, S. L. (2009). Helping LGBTQ and ally students find the right college fit. *ASCA School Counselor, 7*(1), 24.

Wong, Y. J., & Rochlen, A. B. (2005). Demystifying men's emotional behavior: New directions and implications for counseling and research. *Psychology of Men & Masculinity, 6*(1), 62–72.

9 The Role of Career and Leisure Needs in the Lives of Gay Men, Adolescents, and Boys

Jane Goodman & Paul Battle

Introduction

Work plays a role in everyone's life. Work is the "systematic pursuit of an objective valued by oneself and desired by others" (Herr, Cramer, & Niles, 2004, p. 42). Work is not always a paid position; for example, students, stay at home dads, or volunteers in a variety of roles and settings are working. For most people, work is a paid activity that, when you include preparation, commuting, etc., consumes the majority of their waking hours. Work provides individuals with the resources to sustain life, that is, food and shelter, as well as the resources to enjoy a satisfying life, such as recreation, aesthetic pursuits, social activities, and so forth. From the perspective of Maslow's hierarchy of needs (1954), work can meet all of the eight needs he described (from most basic to most advanced):

1. Physiological needs;
2. Safety needs;
3. Needs for belongingness and love;
4. Needs for importance, self-esteem, respect, and independence;
5. Need for information;
6. Need for understanding;
7. Need for beauty;
8. Need for self-actualization.

Gay men, adolescents, and boys may experience additional challenges in meeting the advanced needs of the hierarchy. It is our intention in this chapter to demonstrate that career counseling can help gay men, adolescents, and boys explore their interests with the ultimate goal of finding work that meets more than their basic needs, that we hope meets their need for self-actualization. We recognize that most individuals during a lifetime engage in a series of work activities, changing jobs and often occupational areas as well as engaging in many leisure pursuits. We use the term career to define this sequence of occupational events, "The totality of work and leisure that one does in a lifetime" (Herr, Cramer, & Niles, p. 42). It is clearly beyond the scope of this chapter to describe all of career development theory and practice. There are many good career development texts (e.g., Capuzzi & Stauffer, 2012; Niles & Harris-Bowlsbey, 2005). What we will do here is describe the intersection of career planning and transitions with developmental and interpersonal issues particular to gay men, adolescents, and boys illustrated by several case examples. The importance of career development was eloquently stated by Friedman (2007) in the conclusion to *The World is Flat.* He stated that we need to be, "the generation of strategic optimists, the generation with more dreams than memories, the generation that wakes up each morning and not only imagines that things can be better but also acts on that imagination every day" (p. 635).

Case Study: Philip

Philip is a 21-year-old African American male. He is starting his third year in college. He has scheduled an appointment to see the academic counselor. For the past two years, Philip has taken general courses. He hasn't really devoted time to his coursework. He has spent his time coming to understand his sexual orientation. Since arriving at college he has become involved in a Gay/Straight alliance group. He dated and broke up with his first boyfriend. He has experienced the local gay nightclubs. Last year, he volunteered at the gay pride event booth handing out brochures for the community centers. He has built a strong support with other gay students at the university. However, every holiday his family asks what his major is, and what his career goals are after graduation. He often states he is studying to be a history teacher, as that is what the university paperwork states. Philip has not shared with his family his sexual orientation. He believes he may not be able to return to his hometown and be open about his sexual orientation. He has noticed that he really enjoys partaking in the gay pride events. He hopes his counselor can help him turn his involvement into some sort of career goal.

Interrelationship of Career and Personal Life

Philip provides us with an example of how career and personal lives are intertwined. As he plans for his life in the future, he is considering: his recently acknowledged sexual orientation; his educational activities; life issues such as where he will live; and, affecting and affected by all of these, his desired career life. Hansen (1997; 2002) proposed life-planning strategies under the overall heading, "weaving our lives into a meaningful whole," which included six tasks:

1. Finding work that needs doing;
2. Attending to our health;
3. Connecting family and work;
4. Valuing pluralism and diversity;
5. Managing transitions and organizational change;
6. Exploring spirituality and life purpose (Hansen, 2002, p. 61).

Super (1980) stated that work meets one's needs for recognition as a person, status, and opportunity for self-expression as well as providing financial support. He also emphasized the role of career as part of a complete life in his rainbow metaphor (1980). Others have described meaning and mattering as necessary components of a satisfying career. It seems clear that good career decision making includes all of these components. Dawis and Lofquist (1984) summarized this by saying that individuals in a job must meet the needs of the employer (be satisfactory) and themselves (be satisfied). Employees meet the needs of the employer by producing, creating, training, and managing to meet the requirements of the organization. A factory worker will work on the line. A teacher will teach students. A police offer will police a neighborhood. In each case employees also meet personal needs. They may feel successful and proactive as they are able to contribute to society. They also receive income to help manage their financial lives. Gay men may question if a workplace will allow them to be themselves and be honest about their sexual orientation.

When individuals are growing up, they explore interests through family activities, school, and recreational/leisure behavior. We will discuss gay boys' and adolescents' career exploration activities later in the chapter. Looking beyond young adults to middle-aged or older adults, we will also consider the special issues faced by those in career transition.

Case Study: Juan

Juan is a 40-year-old Mexican-American. He grew up in a traditional Mexican-American home, where he watched his father work two jobs to support the family; his mother take care of the large family. He was a good student and completed high school when he was still at home but did not pursue any further education. They are devout Catholics and believe that being gay is a sin. When Juan was 27, and came out as a gay man he became estranged from his family and went to live in a large city across the country. He became involved in a "gay friendly" interdenominational church and spent much of his leisure time in church-related activities. In the summer, he played in the city softball league on a team organized by the gay community center. Until recently Juan had a job in a factory that provided him with a comfortable living, but it was not particularly interesting or satisfying for him. He never disclosed his sexual orientation to co-workers because he feared they would make fun of him and thought he might get fired as the foreman made it clear he did not approve of gays. Recently, the factory relocated to a small town in another state. Juan had the opportunity to follow his job but chose to stay as he did not want to leave his circle of friends, social activities, and the gay community. It also gave him the opportunity to get away from the discriminatory people at the factory.

The Transition Model

Schlossberg (Anderson, Goodman, & Schlossberg, 2012) described four elements of transitions, called the 4S model for the first initial of each element, which we will discuss in the following in relation to Juan. The first element, *Situation,* is unique to each individual. Juan has made a good living with minimal education, and is living near friends—sometimes called a family of choice—but not near his family of origin. A family of choice is a non-biological family connection, yet provides the emotional support and commitment that is typically perceived from a traditional family, over a lifetime (Mitchell, 2008). The situation, losing his job, is not of his making and not under his control. He lives in a city with high unemployment as the factory that left was one of many to do so and was a large employer in itself. Let us presume that Juan has some savings and some severance pay to add to the unemployment that he will collect and that he has about a year to prepare for and secure another job before his money runs out.

The second element, the *Self,* describes Juan's internal resources. Juan has been independent since adolescence, and is used to relying on himself for emotional as well as financial support. He has a strong sense of self, and his self-concept is not closely tied to his occupational identity. He sees work as a means to an end and did not expect or receive much satisfaction from completing his assigned tasks. He did not build strong personal ties with co-workers. He often kept to himself. He felt most alive once the work day was over and he could participate in sports or attend church.

Juan's *Support* system includes his friends from church, the people in his softball league, and his faith. He does not have a partner though he dates now and again. He likes to read and generally describes himself as an introvert. He watches sports on TV but usually does so alone. He typically spends holidays at church functions, though occasionally he is invited to the home of one of his friends. He feels his estrangement from his family more acutely at holiday time and on his birthday. Juan belonged to his union, but was uninvolved and rarely even voted in union elections.

The fourth element of the Schlossberg system is *Strategies.* There are three types of strategies in this system: i) those that change the situation; ii) those that change the meaning of the situation, and iii) those that manage the stress of the transition. Juan has a year to find work, and this time he would like to find work that meets more than survival needs. He would like to find work that is satisfying in itself. One of the strategies he is considering is furthering his education. He always liked school and did well in his classes. Juan discovered some retraining opportunities in the area. In addition, he might consult a counselor at the unemployment office. He went there the first time to register for his unemployment benefits and noticed that they had employment counselors. Changing the meaning of the situation seems the easiest in all of this for Juan. He sees his layoff as a chance to change his career focus and pursue work that meets his intellectual and emotional needs. He has thought about several options in the past—dismissing them as unrealistic dreams—and would now like to at least find out if they are feasible. He plans to manage the stress of his transition by continuing his physical outlets.

Counseling Strategies

How should a career counselor help Philip and Juan with their career decisions? We propose a three part plan. (We presume here that the counselor has developed a relationship with the client and has confirmed that the goal for counseling is career decision making.) First, we suggest an educational component. Philip and Juan need to understand that what they are making is one decision in a series of decisions, one that will be repeated several times during their lives. We suggest using a theory like that of Gelatt (1991), which asserts that *positive uncertainty* is the cornerstone of creative problem solving. Helping clients understand that this decision is one of perhaps many decisions is usually a relief. Many have believed that this one decision will determine their entire career life. Clients may need to hear that changing majors or occupations is common as people learn more about themselves and their interests and as the world of work and opportunities changes. The educational component will also include teaching clients about decision-making strategies, life style implications of occupational decisions, and for those in transition or looking for a first job, job hunting strategies. The second stage will be to help clients evaluate interests, values, temperaments, skills and abilities, and the like. This should include looking at leisure activities as indicators of interests, with the understanding that it is hard to like something you have never tried. Many gay boys and adolescents have felt restricted in their choices of leisure activities, feeling unwelcome in team sports, for example. Or they may have joined high school clubs that did not accurately reflect real interests because they felt more accepted in those settings. Gay boys may experience leisure activities more negatively than heterosexual boys (Caldwell, Kivel, Smith, & Hays, 1998). Gay males may use their free time to do rebellious activities (Caldwell et al., 1998).

Finally, we suggest helping clients develop action plans that are appropriate for their developmental stage and life circumstances. (These would be quite different for Philip and Juan.) We recognize that there are many career counseling approaches. As mentioned above, we recommend the more detailed descriptions in the extant career literature. Let us look at gay boys, adolescents, and adults separately.

Case Study: Martin

Martin is a 10-year-old boy who is becoming aware that he has feelings for boys, unlike his classmates who constantly look at girls and are fascinated by their beginning development as they reach or approach puberty. Martin hears his older brother talk about girls he wants to date, and the concept is confusing and bewildering. Martin often hears his father mutter in a negative tone how something is gay and how someone he does not like may be queer. These cues that Martin picks up in his environment, at home and at school, make him believe that it may not be a good idea to talk about this awareness. Martin is good at sports like baseball and tennis, but does not like the rough and tumble of contact sports like football and basketball. He is an average student, preferring classes such as English and Social Studies to Math and Science. He enjoys music class, and had a solo in last year's choir performance. After the concert, Martin was teased by some older boys. Martin's family vacations usually involve visiting relatives and he really dislikes the contact with his cousins who consider roughhousing to be their preferred way of communicating. He frequently slips out of these encounters and finds a quiet place to read or play games on his iPod.

Young boys, like Martin, may find themselves in a confusing time of development where they may not understand the complex concept of a gay sexual orientation, but pick up on social cues of who is and who is not accepting. Boys may not know the complexity of sexuality, but they may feel that they are different. School counselors need to ensure an open and welcoming environment for boys that begin to question their sexuality. In her study, Fontaine (1998) found that 93% of school counselors worked with students regarding sexual orientation issues. She found that the counselors that had a negative belief of gay individuals did not have students see the counselor for identity issues, leaving one to question if students can sense when a counselor is not open minded and a safe person with whom to discuss sexual orientation concerns. Gay adolescents need school counselors who will promote their inclusion, be educated about their concerns, and provide visible cues of understanding such as a rainbow flag sticker (King, 2008).

School counselors providing career counseling assistance to boys questioning their sexual orientation need to foster exploration of a variety of interests. Fantasy plays a role in young childhood and should be encouraged. Perhaps the most important aspect of working with children is fostering a sense of self efficacy around making choices and of self-confidence and comfort with themselves in all of their complexity. The National Career Development Association considers the competencies necessary for career maturity to be identical for all ages, and lists them as follows:

Indicators and Learning Stages

Under each goal in the framework are indicators of mastery that highlight the knowledge and skills needed to achieve that goal. Each indicator is presented in *three learning stages* derived from *Bloom's Taxonomy:* knowledge acquisition, application, and reflection. The stages describe learning competency. They are not tied to an individual's age or level of education.

- *Knowledge Acquisition* (K). Youth and adults at the knowledge acquisition stage build comprehension. They can recall, recognize, describe, identify, clarify, discuss, explain, summarize, query, investigate, and compile new information about the knowledge.

- *Application* (A). Youth and adults at the application stage apply acquired knowledge to situations and to self. They seek out ways to use the knowledge. For example, they can demonstrate, employ, perform, illustrate, and solve problems related to the knowledge.
- *Reflection* (R). Youth and adults at the reflection stage analyze, synthesize, judge, assess, and evaluate knowledge in accord with their own goals, values, and beliefs.

(Retrieved from http://associationdatabase.com/aws/NCDA/asset_manager/get_file/3384/ncdguidelines2007.pdf; accessed May 5, 2012.)

We suggest that school counselors adapt these guidelines to the developmental level of their students. In Martin's case, it would be advisable for him to develop all of the skills described. The American School Counselor Association standards state that providing students with career development is one of the three cornerstones of a school counselor's job, along with academic and personal development (ASCA, 2004. ASCA identifies three standards with related competencies and indicators. The standards and competencies follow:

Standard A. Students will acquire the skills to investigate the world of work in relation to knowledge of self and to make informed career decisions.

C:A.1 Develop Career Awareness
C:A.2 Develop Employment Readiness

Standard B. Students will employ strategies to achieve future career goals with success and satisfaction.

C:B.1 Acquire Career Information
C:B.2 Identify Career Goals

Standard C. Students will understand the relationship between personal qualities, education, training, and the world of work.

C:C.1 Acquire Knowledge to Achieve Career Goals
C:C.2 Apply Skills to Achieve Career Goals

Martin is at the line between fantasy and exploration. Encouraging both aspects of career growth will help him become clearer about himself and how he fits into the world of work. Career counseling for gay boys also needs to include what is termed employment readiness by ASCA. For gay boys this means developing attitudes and skills such as perseverance, team work, oral and written communication, and delayed gratification, among others. For boys at the early stages of exploring their sexual orientation, these developmental skills need to be embedded in their psychosexual development and identity formation. In this confusing time for them, boys may choose to disengage in activities that have the appearance of being gay. Adolescents are at a point in their lives of crystallizing interests and trying them on for size, as it were. They can begin to learn about the world of work and its rapidly changing nature. This is a good time to help adolescents job shadow, find part time work, co-op or internship experiences and the like and to use these as an opportunity to check out work tasks and settings.

Adults need to develop a sequence of action steps that will lead toward desired work. An individual like Juan may need to look at short- and long-term goals. His short-term goal may be to earn enough to pursue his long-term goals. These steps will include job hunting skills, and should include the special issues that face gay men in the job search process such as being out in the workplace. Interviews are a particular area of concern for many, as they wonder how to respond to such questions as, "Are you married?", "Will your wife be willing to relocate?", or prejudicial and derogatory comments. These can be veiled. For example, a statement like, "We are all a close group of guys, do you think you will fit in?" can be meant to discourage a gay applicant.

Croteau, Bieschke, Fassinger, and Manning (2008a) found five career concerns for gay men in the workplace: i) identity development; ii) experiences of discrimination and the workplace climate; iii) managing sexual identity in the workplace (i.e., identity management); iv) influences of being gay on occupational interest choices; and v) appropriate career interventions. Most workplace research focuses on discrimination and identity management. More research on occupational interest and career interventions for gay men is needed.

When working with gay men, boys, and adolescents, career counselors should understand how sexual orientation may have an impact on career, career development, and job satisfaction. Pope, Prince, and Mitchell (2000) found that gay men have different career development challenges from heterosexuals, and may have few role models. They may also experience stereotyping about sexual orientations and careers that they could hold. As a result, Pope et al. (2000) found that gay men may prevent themselves from pursuing certain careers. They also stated that it is important for counselors to understand that there is a paucity of research literature examining the career development needs of gay men, adolescents, and boys.

Since the coming out process may begin at any age, the stress and the experience with the process can have different implications for men, teens, and boys. The process of addressing identity development and career development simultaneously is overwhelming (Pope et al., 2000). Some gay men may begin to process their sexual orientation in adolescence. Others will discover it in their early to mid-twenties, as late as 60, or even older. Boys and men will share some aspects of this experience, and may find some aspects different according to their age and the phase of their career, whether they are identifying interests, maintaining a career, or retiring from the workforce.

Gay men, boys, and adolescents experience the career exploration process similarly to their heterosexual counterparts. They search to find a career that interests them and provides them with the means to support themselves and their families. Career issues are often paralleled by the process of interplay of sexual identity formation. Some men may even believe that certain career options, such as those that are stereotyped by masculine men, are closed to them because of their sexual orientation. Since gay men may hide their identity in the workplace, this creates a lack of role models in careers for gay boys and adolescents (Herr, Cramer, & Niles, 2004).

Gay men, boys, and adolescents typically experience an identity development as described in Cass's (1979) identity development model. They conceptualize how others might feel about their being gay, and then they may decide to tell others. Gay men, boys, and adolescents usually experience a range of emotions before they accept themselves as a gay person (Cass, 1979). Others may never fully accept themselves as gay individuals. Although it is beyond this chapter to fully describe the identity development process, one must understand that gay men, boys, and adolescents may not easily accept their sexual orientation. Once an individual does accept himself as gay, others in his life may also experience a range of emotions and feelings before accepting or not accepting him. This continued process is carried into the work environment. Although a gay man may fully accept and be comfortable with a gay identity, each career transition may trigger the process again. Heterosexism is the "assumption that heterosexuality is the natural order of relational pairings" (Parnell, Lease, & Green, 2010, p. 249). Gedro (2009) stated:

> Although sexual orientation is generally invisible to most people, sexual orientation is also a workplace issue.... Sexual orientation manifests any time a worker places a picture of his or her spouse or children on a desk, wears a wedding ring, or brings a spouse to a company function. LGBT (lesbian, gay, bisexual and transgender) people do not have this privilege and must negotiate the heterosexism of their organizational settings through a variety of strategies.
>
> (p. 55)

Little research evaluates the emotional costs of keeping gay identity hidden in the workplace (Day & Schoenrade, 1997). Yet research has noted the emotional challenges of being out in the workplace. Gay men who are out in the workplace can experience emotional stress (Pope et al., 2004). Gay men who feared it would have a negative consequence if their sexual identity was known experienced less job satisfaction compared with those who were out (Ragins, Singh, & Cornwell, 2007). In addition, Sandfort, Bos, and Vet (2006) reported that 21% of gay men who were out in the workplace had their ideas rejected when presented to colleagues. Parnell et al. (2010) found that the top three career-related barriers for gay men are: dissatisfaction with career, difficulty networking, and discrimination based on their sexual orientation.

Identity Management

One area of research in the literature is the concept of identity management. Identity management refers to a gay man's "particular approach or strategy for presenting one's identity in the workplace" (Croteau, Anderson, & VanderWal, 2008b, p. 550). Identity management incorporates the decisions of gay men whether or not to disclose their sexual orientation to others in the workplace (Croteau et al., 2008b). To negotiate the heterosexism, heteroprejudice, and potential negative interactions in the workplace, gay men implement an identity management strategy.

Griffin (1992) and Woods (1993) studied gay men in the workplace and discovered that gay men adopt techniques to either reveal or hide their orientation. Both Griffin (1992) and Woods (1993) developed identity management models describing the techniques gay men use to manage their identities (Croteau et al., 2008a). Griffins' identity management model divided strategies into four categories: Passing, Covering, Implicitly Out, and Explicitly Out. Woods' identity management model divided gay men's strategies into three categories: Counterfeiting, Avoidance, and Integrating. Both Griffin (1992) and Woods (1993) found that most gay men purposefully manage their identities and their personal information in the workplace. The strategies range from those individuals that do everything to mask their sexual orientation to those that openly disclose and share everything. Identity management is a lifelong process because it involves the individual and the environment (Trau & Hartel, 2004). Therefore, if the work environment changes, the identity management strategy used may change.

Gay men decide how much personal information is shared about them in the workplace, which may have an impact on daily interactions. A gay man may decide not to disclose his sexual orientation and may avoid interactions where personal information is shared. He may avoid the "water cooler" conversation, eat lunch on his own, and skip office picnics or holiday parties. These missed interactions could affect the relationships he builds with others. Another man may disclose his sexual orientation in the workplace, however, depending on the workplace, he may encounter others that avoid him, a supervisor that does not promote him, or may find his salary lower than heterosexual co-workers (Badgett, Lau, Sears, & Ho, 2007). Gay men decide what to say about their sexual orientation; they decide who to say what to about their personal life; and who not to tell about their personal life. They then have to manage how the information is shared among co-workers and how others interpret that information.

For example, let us say a gay man participated in a gay baseball league on the weekends. On Monday he returns to work, and co-workers ask, "What did you do this weekend?" Depending on the identity management strategy, his answer could include several options. He could respond in any of the following ways:

1. It was a quiet weekend.
2. I played baseball with some friends.
3. I played on the gay baseball league.
4. Or he could simply not interact with his co-workers.

Each one of these statements would change the image his co-workers have of him. When career counselors work with a gay man, they need to explore the client's comfort level with sharing personal information in the workplace. They should explore how this decision and process affect the man's feelings. Time in sessions may be spent exploring his past experiences. There are many experiences, feelings, and thoughts that a gay man may consider when deciding whether or not to disclose his sexual orientation, and every gay man has different reasons for his decision. The identity management strategies are different, and no one strategy is better than the others; a client should decide what is comfortable for him within his work environment.

Case Study: Robert

Robert is a 16-year-old high school Junior. He has been playing on baseball, basketball, and football teams since he was 5 years old. He enjoyed the team sports. He spent most of his free time playing sports, and when not on a team, he played with the boys in the neighborhood. His parents have been strong supports. Like many young boys, Robert dreamed of being a pro-football player. When he entered high school, Robert joined the high school varsity football team. Robert has been informed by the coach he could attend college on a football scholarship. Robert believes that his family would only be able to provide minimum financial support for his college education, and an athletic scholarship would help his family. Recently Robert has begun to questioning his sexual orientation. He has kept the thoughts to himself. He worries how the teammates would treat him. Would they let him in the locker room? He has read about situations like his online and in blogs. Robert is feeling anxious from the pressure of his parents and coach to start looking at colleges and preparing for his senior year. He finds himself in the school counselor's office, looking for guidance.

Let us think of the case of Robert and other stereotypical masculine jobs, such as pro-football player, firefighter, or police officer. If a gay man had an interest in one of these careers, he may have to decide how his gay identity will affect his interaction with co-workers. If the gay man was open about his sexual attractions, how would the other team members and co-workers feel about sharing these spaces? In some cases men may decide not to pursue their interest to avoid these interactions. Others will pursue their interest, yet avoid disclosing their sexual orientation in order to avoid any uncomfortable jokes or discrimination.

These same emotions and personal beliefs are encountered by men who are accountants, lawyers, doctors, teachers, bankers, factory workers, store attendants, waiters, and so forth. Men must decide whether sharing their sexual orientation with others will affect their daily interactions and their career trajectory. In any career field, issues arise as to whether a gay man will experience discrimination such as anti-gay jokes, being denied a job offer, being unable to bring his partner to the office picnic, or being unable to cover his partner on the company's insurance policy.

Discrimination

Some counselors may question why gay men struggle with the decision of whether, when, and how to disclose their sexual orientation. Investigators have found that gay men experience job discrimination in a variety of ways, both overtly and subtly. Studies have shown that gay men typically earn less than heterosexual men (Black, Makar, Sanders, & Taylor, 2003). Gay men have been denied job opportunities, promotions, and have earned less pay because of their sexual orientation (Badgett et al., 2007). Gay men have thought that they have been denied job offers because of how the interviewers felt about gay individuals. Studies have shown that individuals believe gay men are less credible (Russ, Simonds, & Hunt, 2002). Even though a man may be a successful member of a workplace, he may fear that he could one of the first to be "downsized" because of his sexual orientation. Being gay in the workplace has many land-mines.

In addition to identifying income disparities, researchers have examined job burnout and satisfaction. Gay men who are "out" in the workplace can experience emotional stress (Pope et al., 2004). Day and Schoenrade (1997) wrote that research does not exist that evaluates the emotional costs of keeping gay identity a secret in the workplace. Ragins et al. (2007) noted that employees who feared a negative consequence if their sexual identity was known experienced less job satisfaction. College students have felt discrimination in internship placements (Messinger, 2004).

K-12 teachers in Griffin's (1992) study feared that being out would ruin their credibility among students, parents, and co-workers. Sandfort, Bos, and Vet (2006) reported that 21% of gay men who were out in the workplace had their ideas rejected when presented to colleagues, primarily because of their sexual orientation and who they were. Russ et al. (2002) reported that students believed a gay instructor was less credible than a heterosexual instructor, even though the presentation was identical except for the gender of the partner. When asked if they would hire this instructor, 93% of students who heard the heterosexual presentation said they would "unquestionably" hire the instructor; only 8% of the students who heard the gay instructor would "definitely" hire the instructor (Russ et al., 2002, p. 317). In the same study it was found that the students perceived they learned twice as much from heterosexual instructors.

Some researchers, for example, Schmidt and Nilsson (2006), have speculated that there is a bottleneck issue related to career development. Typically, gay men and adolescents tend to focus on their self-identity first. Due to this they may not fully attend to their career development. Philip's story is not uncommon (see earlier Case Study). He has focused his energy on exploring a gay identity and very little on his academic pursuits. He has arrived at a place where he is accepting himself as a gay man, and now he wishes to address his career development. Gay men represent a significant population on college campuses, yet are not always seen (Pope et al., 2000). College students may be directing time and focus toward developing their sexual identity development rather than their career development (Schmidt & Nilsson, 2006).

Case Study: Donald and John

Donald is a 47-year-old white male. He has been with his partner, John, for 17 years. They own a home together. They reside in a state that is accepting of gays. Two years ago they had a civil ceremony to recognize their union. They wanted to show others their commitment and devotion to each other. Donald is an accountant. He has recently been offered a position with another firm that would be a promotion and would provide him with a larger salary. In his current office, Donald's co-workers know he is gay. He has been able to bring John to office holiday parties. He also covers John on his current company's insurance policy as a domestic partner. John owns a flower shop. Donald learned that the new position would require him to move to a southern state to manage operations. The state recently passed a marriage protection act that stated that a marriage can only be between a man and a woman. Donald has not asked the new company about domestic partner benefits, but did not see any mention of them in human resources paperwork.

Workplace and Public Policy Considerations

Donald and John's situation demonstrates a multitude of issues for a family with dual careers. Career counselors working with heterosexual clients have many of the same issues. First, do they both want to move to another state and create a life together? Do they need the improved finances? Will John be able to sell his business or hire a manager and still be owner? Will they be able to make friends and a social support group in the new neighborhood? What sort of work will John do?

However there are, in addition, many issues that a gay couple may have to navigate that the heterosexual couple does not. Will the company provide health benefits for both individuals? By asking the human resources department, will Donald be outing himself to the new company? The state just passed an anti-gay marriage act. Are the individuals working in this new company open to a gay co-worker? How will the employees interact with a new gay supervisor? Will he be able to bring John to office social events?

In addition to knowing about dual career issues, career counselors should be aware of the legal issues experienced by gay men. Gay men may not feel the freedom to explore career options and relocation because of the differences in state legal protection or lack of protection for gay men in employment. Sexual orientation is not always included in a state's anti-discrimination laws, making it potentially legal to terminate employment for being gay. Sexual orientation may not be covered in the work place's anti-discrimination policies. In addition, depending on the state's legal definition of marriage, gay men may not be able to get insurance coverage or other benefit packages. Frequently, and unlike the situation with heterosexual couples, when a gay man includes his partner in his insurance, this may be viewed as income and he may be taxed on the benefit, decreasing his disposable income.

The ACA Advocacy Competencies (Ratts, Toporek, & Lewis, 2010) recommend that counselors advocate for their clients at the client/student level, the school/community level and in the public arena. Clearly career counselors need to be aware of the legal and social difficulties experienced by gay men and boys and be open to discussing and, when appropriate, advocating to change these circumstances.

Leisure

We have spent much of the chapter focusing on career and career counseling. As stated earlier, our definition of career is "The totality of work and *leisure* that one does in a lifetime" (Herr et al., p. 42). We often hear "find what you love to do, and make it into a career." But it is common not to be able to, or wish to, meet all personal and career needs in work. Many individuals receive fulfillment through leisure activities. One man may need to be creative, yet his work requires being analytic. This man may have a crafting hobby. Or another man may need to connect with the outdoors, and his employment finds him in a city high rise all day. This man may join a softball team or hike and camp outside of work hours. Leisure activities may aid in identity formation (Johnson, 1999).

It is in these leisure activities that teens and boys begin to explore their interests, and sometimes begin to reflect on understanding their own identity. In their study about adolescents' leisure activities, Kivel and Kleiber (2000) found that gay or questioning boys may use leisure activities to explore their sexual orientation. The authors found four main themes in their study. Gay youth often turn to reading. In books gay people are able to explore other worlds and also begin to find characters who may also be questioning their sexuality. Media consumption, such as watching television and movies, also is a place where youth can explore a different society and study the character who challenges the norms of sexual orientation. Music, whether in a band or choir, is a place that many gay youth find a place to enjoy. The other theme the researchers found was sports; although in their small sample size, there were no adolescents that played high school sports. We do know that some gay men partake in gay sports, as evidenced by those that partake in the Gay Games (Symons, 2010).

Johnson (1999) found that gay adolescents select leisure activities in order to avoid homophobia experiences, belong to a group of like individuals, or negate discomfort. Gay adolescents may select activities where they can be comfortable with being themselves and open about their sexual orientation. They may experience homophobia in their schools and communities and, therefore, choose to avoid participation that could lead to additional exposure to bias. Gay adolescents tend to choose to participate in groups where they can be with other individuals that identify as gay. Being involved in a leisure group with other gay adolescents can provide social support as well as promoting positive self-esteem.

In many urban areas, there are a wealth of activities that are designed for gay men and boys. These activities allow men to partake in their interest and be themselves. In some urban and suburban areas, men can find a variety of organized gay sports. They may find leagues in baseball, basketball, bowling, golf, tennis, swimming, and so forth. For those that are not sports talented, there may be crafting clubs, like scrapbooking or sewing, or gay book clubs. In some areas, there may be clubs where men play card games or board games, or perhaps electronic games. Leisure groups may allow kinship or community feeling. Men may not have to worry about managing what others may find out about them. They provide social outlets for men who may not enjoy night clubs or bars.

Young boys may explore leisure activities that may not be stereotypically boys'. Boys are often raised with a lot of roughhousing. They may tend to play sports or pretend to be soldiers, or get involved with mechanical things. However some boys may drift toward leisure activities that may not be viewed as masculine, like sewing, designing clothing, cooking or baking, or playing dress up or house. Career counselors may struggle with balancing the gender norms of young boys with allowing them to pursue their interests. Parents may bring boys into treatment with the goal of attempting to make them subscribe to more traditionally masculine activities. It is important to find something in our lives to do outside of work. A person's career is the total of work and leisure activities throughout one's life. It is our belief that career counseling can help gay men, boys, and adolescents have more satisfying lives.

References

American School Counselor Association (ASCA). (2004). *ASCA national standards for students.* Alexandria, VA: Author.

Anderson, M. L., Goodman, J., & Schlossberg, N. K. (2012). *Counseling adults in transition: Linking Schlossberg's theory with practice in a diverse world.* New York: Springer.

Badgett, M. V. L. (1995). The wage effects of sexual orientation discrimination. *Industrial and Labor Relations Review, 48*(4), 726–739.

Badgett, M. V. L., Lau, H. Sears, B., & Ho, D. (2007). *Bias in the workplace: Consistent evidence of sexual orientation and gender identity discrimination.* Los Angeles, CA: The Williams Institutes.

Black, D. A., Makar H., R., Sanders, S. G., & Taylor, L. J. (2003). The earnings effects of sexual orientation. *Industrial and Labor Relations Review, 56*(3), 449–469.

Caldwell, L. L., Kivel, B. D., Smith, E. A., & Hayes, D. (1998). The leisure context of adolescents who are lesbian, gay male, bisexual and questioning their sexual identities: An exploratory study. *Journal of Leisure Research, 30*(3), 341–355.

Capuzzi, D., & Stauffer, M. D. (2012). *Career counseling: Foundations, perspectives and applications* (2nd ed.). New York: Routledge.

Cass, V. C. (1979). Homosexuality identity formation: A theoretical model. *Journal of Homosexuality, 4,* 219–235.

Croteau, J. M., Bieschke, K., Fassinger, R., & Manning, J. L. (2008a). Counseling psychology and sexual orientations: History, selective trends, and future directions. In S. Brown and R. Lent (Eds.), *Handbook of counseling psychology* (4th ed.) (pp. 194–211). New York: John Wiley and Sons.

Croteau, J. M., Anderson, M. Z., & VanderWal, B. (2008b). Models of workplace identity disclosure and management: Reviewing and extending concepts. *Group and Organization Management,* 33, 532–565.

Dawis, R. V., & Lofquist, L. H. (1984). *A psychological theory of work adjustment: An individual differences model and its applications.* Minneapolis, MN: University of Minnesota Press.

Day, N., & Schoenrade, P. (1997). Staying in the closet versus coming out: Relationships between communication about sexual orientation and work attitudes. *Personnel Psychology, 50,* 147–163.

Fontaine, J. H. (1998). Evidencing a need: School counselors' experiences with gay and lesbian students. *Professional School Counseling, 1*(3), 8.

Friedman, T. L. (2007). *The world is flat: A brief history of the twenty-first century.* New York: Picador.

Gedro, J. (2009, February). LGBT career development. *Advances in Developing Human Resources, 11.* Online publication: doi: 10.1177/1523422308328396.

Gelatt, H. B. (1991). *Creative decision making: Using positive uncertainty.* Los Altos, CA: Crisp.

Griffin, P. (1992). From hiding out to coming out: Empowering lesbians and gay educators. In K. M. Harbeck (Ed.), *Coming out of the classroom closet* (pp. 167–196). Binghamton, NY: Harrington Park Press.

Hansen, L. S. (1997). *Integrative life planning: Critical tasks for career development and changing life patterns.* San Francisco, CA: Jossey Bass.

Hansen, L. S. (2002). Integrative life planning (ILP): A holistic theory for career counseling with adults. In S. Niles (Ed.), *Adult career development: Concepts, issues, and practices* (pp. 59–76). Tulsa, OK: National Career Development Association.

Herr, E. L., Cramer, S. H., & Niles, S. G. (2004). *Career guidance and counseling through the lifespan: Systematic approaches* (6th ed.). Boston, MA: Pearson.

Johnson, C. W. (1999). Living the game of hide and seek: Leisure in the lives of gay and Lesbian young adults. *Leisure/Loisir, 24*(3–4), 255–278.

King, S. (2008). Exploring the role of counselor support: Gay, lesbian, bisexual, and questioning adolescents struggling with acceptance and disclosure. *Journal of GLBT Family Studies, 4*(3), 361–384.

Kivel, B. D., & Kleiber, D. A. (2000). Leisure in the identity formation of lesbian/gay youth: Personal, but not social. *Leisure Sciences, 22,* 215–232.

Maslow, A. (1954). *Motivations and personality.* New York: Harper & Row.

Messinger, L. (2004). Out in the field: Gay and lesbian social work students' experiences in field placement. *Journal of Social Work Education, 40*(2), 187–204.

Mitchell, V. (2008). Choosing family: Meaning and membership in the lesbian family of choice. *Journal of Lesbian Studies, 23*(2–3), 301–313.

Niles, S. G., & Harris-Bowlsbey, J. (2005). *Career development interventions in the 21st century* (2nd ed.). Upper Saddle River, NJ: Pearson.

Parnell, M. K., Lease, S. H., & Green, M. L. (2010). Perceived career barriers for gay, lesbian and bisexual individuals. *Journal of Career Development, 39*(3), 248–268.

Pope, M. S., Prince, J. P., & Mitchell, K. (2000). Responsible career counseling with lesbian and gay students. In D. A. Luzzo (Ed.), *Career counseling of college students* (pp. 267–281). Washington, DC: American Psychological Association.

Pope, M., Barret, B., Szymanski, D. M., Chung, Y. B., Singaravelu, H., McLean, H., & Sanabria, S. (2004). Culturally appropriate career counseling with gay and lesbian clients. *Career Development Quarterly, 53,* 158–176.

Ragins, B. R., Singh, R., & Cornwell, J. M. (2007). Making the invisible visible: Fear and disclosure of sexual orientations at work. *Journal of Applied Psychology, 92,* 1103–1118.

Ratts, M. J., Toporek, R. L., & Lewis, J. A. (2010). *ACA advocacy competencies: A social justice framework for counselors.* Alexandria, VA: American Counseling Association.

Russ, T. L., Simonds, C. J., & Hunt, S. K. (2002). Coming out in the classroom . . . an occupational hazard: The influence of sexual orientation on teacher credibility and perceived student learning. *Communication Education, 51*(3), 311–324.

Sandfort, T. G. M., Bos, H., & Vet, R. (2006). Lesbians and gay men at work: Consequences of being out. In A. Omoto & H. Kurtzman (Eds.), *Sexual orientation and mental health* (pp. 225–244). Washington, DC: American Psychological Association.

Schmidt, C. K., & Nilsson, J. (2006). The effects of simultaneous developmental processes: Factors relating to the career development of lesbian, gay, and bisexual youth. *Career Development Quarterly, 55,* 22–37.

Super, D. E. (1980). A life-span, life-space approach to career development. *Journal of Vocational behavior, 16,* 282–298.

Symons, C. (2010). *The gay games.* New York: Routledge.

Trau, R. N. C., & Hartel, C. E. J. (2004). One career, two identities: An assessment of gay men's career trajectory. *Career Development International, 9,* 627–637.

Woods, J. D. (1993). *The corporate closet: The professional lives of gay men in America.* New York: The Free Press.

Part IV

Counseling Special Populations: Sexual and Gender Minority Boys, Adolescents, and Men

10 Non-Gay Men and Boys

Working With Men, Teens, and Boys Who Identify as Bisexual

Jason Patton, Jeff Lubsen, & Stacee Reicherzer

Bisexuality and Terminology

Bisexuality, which James (1996) defined as "the sexual or intensely emotional, although not necessarily concurrent or equal, attraction of an individual to members of more than one gender" (p. 218), is often misunderstood and, therefore, maligned by both the lesbian and gay, and heterosexual communities in twenty-first century Western culture. Many in the gay male community have conceptualized male bisexual identity as a choice to retain some semblance of heterosexual privilege, or as a state of confusion that occurs in the process of coming out as gay, but that is ultimately transitory (Anderlini-D'Onofrio & Alexander, 2009). Heterosexuals have often regarded bisexuality as being morally inferior to opposite-sex attraction (Fox, 1996). It bears noting, though, that bisexuals have a number of personal and relational resources from which they can draw to be resilient, despite the likely presence of multiple marginalizing, stigmatizing, and oppressing forces (Rostosky, Riggle, Pascale-Hague, & McCants, 2010).

The salience of sexuality, both personally and societally, is undeniable, and mental health professionals are charged with competently meeting the biopsychosocial and advocacy-related needs of sexual minority clients; examples of this call to action include those from the American Counseling Association (ACA, 2005), American Psychological Association (APA, 2002), and the National Association of Social Workers (NASW, 1996). The ultimate challenge for mental health practitioners who work with clients who are attracted to, or have sexual intercourse with, both sexes is that there is a lack of solid, research-grounded information from which to draw. Though there is a growing body of knowledge that helps these professionals meet the needs of lesbian and gay clientele, there exists a dramatic scarcity of information that directly relates to bisexuality (Israel & Mohr, 2004). Researchers and authors often assume bisexual experiences are equivalent enough with gay and lesbian experiences to tack them in name onto research—the outcomes of these studies should be met with some level of skepticism, as bisexual persons have unique circumstances, needs, and clinical presentations (Mohr, Weiner, Chopp, & Wong, 2009; Ross, 2009). A working knowledge of the many factors impacting the lives of bisexual clients necessitates a continuously evolving understanding of myriad societal, contextual, cultural, and developmental influences (Yuk Sim Chun & Singh, 2010).

In order to meet professional organizations' dicta to serve these sexual minority members, and to begin to develop conceptual and functional knowledge of bisexual clients' specific experiences, mental health, health, and helping practitioners must adopt a working definition of pertinent concepts. Sexuality and attraction are nuanced, so much so that they are necessarily complex and difficult to encapsulate.

Brewster and Moradi (2010) adopted a series of definitions in order to facilitate such a discussion of this level of complexity, as these discussions warrant the further delineation of related terms (Moradi, Mohr, Worthington & Fassinger, 2009; Worthington, Savoy, Dillon, & Vernaglia, 2002): *Sexual identity* is made up of a personally defined set of sexually-related beliefs, wants, needs, and information that comprise one's sexuality; *sexual orientation* is part of this, and contains information about affection, relational desires and patterns, and sexually-related personal needs and wants. *Sexual orientation identity* is a further extension that includes internal and external messages and portrayals of these subjective definitions and content.

Sexual orientation identity presents an added level of complexity, as the language that describes it is socially constructed, personally defined, and potentially variant over time. It is of import to note that one who names herself or himself *bisexual* may or may not engage in sexual activity with persons of the same sex or those of the opposite sex. Furthermore, many may experience some level of same-sex and opposite-sex attraction or engage in sexual activity with members of both sexes but not call herself or himself bisexual. In particular, there appears to be a trend among youth with attraction to, or sexual experiences with, members of both sexes to eschew labels altogether, or to develop more inclusive language (Entrup & Firestein, 2007; Russell, Clark, & Clary, 2009). For the purposes of this chapter, men who experience some level of sexual attraction to both men and women, or who have sexual intercourse with members of both sexes, will be referred to as bisexual. Other contemporary language incorporates the use of terms such as *men who have sex with men* (MSM) to be inclusive of both gay and bisexual males (Young & Meyer, 2005). These groupings are often employed in research, as a concession to the fact that simple classifications of *gay* and *bisexual* would not necessarily capture all men who have had, or have, sex with other men. Popular media plays a role in the adoption of commonly understood language about sexuality as well. An example of this is the adoption of the term *down low* (DL), which is primarily used to describe African American men who engage in sexual activity with other men while living ostensibly heterosexual lives; it can be assumed that these men would not generally identify as bisexual (Heath & Goggin, 2009).

Inherent in some interpretations of the social implications of both MSM, who do not hold sexual orientation identities of *gay* or *bisexual* (Young & Meyer, 2005), and men who keep their attractions or sexual encounters with other men on the DL (Boykin, 2004) is some level of *biphobia,* be it internalized, experienced, or inferred. Biphobia can be thought of as an extension of homophobia, whereas it is a fear of, or negativity toward, same-sex attraction and intercourse (Eliason, 1997). According to Gooβ (2008), however, biphobia may have compounded negative affect on bisexual persons. This notion seems to suggest that marginalization along these bounds may come from heterosexual, as well as gay and lesbian, sources (Sue & Hunt, 2001). In other words, bisexual men's experiences are even further removed from heterosexual, hegemonic society and are distinct from, and treated as less-than by, sexual minority subcultures.

Conceptualizing Attraction

As experiences of sexual identity are inherently complex, and clients are best served by self-identifying and self-defining the many layered elements of their inner lives, it may be useful for helping professionals to employ more concrete representations in their work with these clients. A number of these models have been developed that can serve as practical tools in this process. Perhaps the most influential of these, to date, was created by Dr. Alfred Kinsey and a teams of researchers, who developed a rating scale for sexual orientation (Kinsey, Pomeroy, & Martin, 1948) that ranged from 0 for exclusively heterosexual to 6 for exclusively homosexual. Kinsey regarded anyone as bisexual in the range of 2–4 (2 = "predominantly heterosexual; more than incidentally homosexual," 3 = "equally heterosexual and homosexual," 4 = "predominantly homosexual; more than incidentally heterosexual") (The Kinsey Institute, 2011), with 11.6% of males, ages 20–35, averaging a score of 4 on the scale. In essence, the scientific community found that men, at least according to Kinsey's extensive research, had experiences that we would today often classify as bisexual.

Kinsey's work revolutionized our ability to conceptualize sexuality, and did so in an era that was particularly hostile to the United States' burgeoning awareness of experiences outside of heteronormativity (Reicherzer, 2005). This research, however, has since been heavily scrutinized, primarily for samples that were not representative or were evaluated in a statistically unsound manner (Cochran, Mostellar, & Tukey, 1953). More recent data representing the prevalence of non-heterosexual identities suggest that Kinsey's data either over-estimated these numbers or is not indicative of modern sexual practices and identities; for instance, a 2002 National Center for Health Statistics survey found that 1.8% of men identified as bisexual (Mosher, Chandra, & Jones, 2005). It should be noted, though, that 3.9% defined themselves as "something else," which may contain some who would fall under the umbrella of bisexuality in Kinsey's original format. A more recent study, the National Survey of Sexual Health and Behavior, found that 6% of men in their sample identified as bisexual (Herbernick et al., 2010).

An example of how someone, who for the purposes of this chapter we will call bisexual, might plot himself on Kinsey's original scale might be helpful.

Case Study: Tom

Tom, a 33-year-old biracial man of African American and Caucasian descent, presents for counseling with a primary concern of wanting to reason through whether he should "come out" to his family. He indicates that he has not really thought much about his sexuality, but wants to discuss it with someone who will appreciate him, despite whatever he says or decides. During the first few counseling sessions, Tom indicates that he has had sexual experience with both men and women throughout his life. He says that, in fact, his level of attraction to men and women really matches up with how often he has had sexual intercourse with both. He relates that most of the time he has had sex with other men, but that a little less than half of the times have been with women. Likewise, he finds himself more often attracted to men than women, but "not by a great deal." Tom and his counselor consider the usefulness of plotting him on this scale, given his recent interest in thinking about himself, his sexual identity, and his sexual orientation identity. Tom decides that a "4" describes him perfectly. After discussing it, he chooses to call himself "predominantly male-attracted and bisexual."

While emerging data suggest that Kinsey's original numbers may not apply to the twenty-first century American population, it is important to note that more recent conceptions of sexuality take into account complexities that might further impact interpretation of those numbers. For Tom, considering Kinsey's original scale made sense, as he thought of his attraction and encounters of sexual engagement as basically commensurate. He was looking to focus in on this aspect of his experience and come up with a self-definition as part of the process of deciding whether or not to "come out." The process of counseling would likely have continued with him considering the relative importance of this information, as well as that of sexual orientation, the responses he wanted, feared, or might expect, and so forth.

For many people, such a narrow focus in conceptualizing sexuality would present a challenge; there might be instances in which the outcome (at least at the point of arriving at a score on the scale) could feel out-of-synch with the person's self-definition. Consider the fact that same-sex contact at some point during individuals' lives occurs more often than does sexual orientation identification as *homosexual* or *bisexual* (Reece et al., 2010). In other words, men may be more likely to have same-sex experiences than they ever would to name themselves gay or bisexual. What might be the impact of scoring someone something other than a "0" in this instance? Could scoring oneself or seeing one's score that implied something other than fully heterosexuality result in a level of shock or even harm? Additionally, continuingly emergent cultural competence dictates responsiveness to the needs of those who fall into categories like MSM, on the DL, and so forth. An even further level of complexity is necessary, when one considers that gender and sex are not, based on current scientific and emerging cultural trends, truly dichotomous. Also, some clients may be fully, perhaps exclusively, sexually aroused by images, thoughts, and contact with one sex, but feel compelled to create a love-based, emotionally monogamous relationship with the other sex. To this end, Moe, Reicherzer, and Dupuy (2011) conceptualized a model that examined sexuality not as a single phenomenon, but as multiple continua of sexuality and romantic relationships.

Within this model, five dimensions are considered in describing sexual and relational orientation more fully: i) Desire of Sex Characteristics; ii) Desire of Gender Expression; iii) Sexual and Relational Interest; iv) Relational Orientation; and v) Community Identification.

Relational Orientation refers to one's desire for emotional connection, often in the form of romantic partner bonding between two or more people; these people may or may not be sexually attracted to, or involved with, each other. The Desire of Sex Characteristics consists of two continua—one that reflects the desire of genitalia; the other is focused on the desire of secondary sex characteristics. The distinction between these two refers to the fact that someone who is transsexual may have genitalia of one sex, as she or he did not go through full sexual reassignment surgery, but does choose to augment her or his body with procedures and hormones to attain secondary sex characteristics like breast or buttocks. An example could be a transsexual man (born female) who has taken hormones, has facial hair, has had his breasts removed, but still has a vagina. Also, a person may be at the midpoint in each of these continua, with equal desire between sexes, which may occur simultaneously, opposing across time, or by degree at different points.

The Desire of Gender Expression describes an attraction to traits that the individual (client) has identified as feminine or masculine. These messages are informed by one's culture and dominant and submissive images available at any given time (Reicherzer, 2005). Both genders may be, by degree, desirable, or there may be a strong attraction to one or the other. Used with the Desire of Sex Characteristics continuum, the Desire of Gender Expression continuum may allow expression of one's attractions to masculinity, femininity, or both in women, men, or to body-blended transgender persons and those who identify as neither male nor female.

In Moe et al.'s (2011) model, the degree of sexual and relational interest, itself, is seen as a variable of consideration. For some persons, low sexual interest may preclude sexual activity that is based on the other scales, and low relational interest may lead the person to not choose romantic partner bonding. Relational Orientation, a developing concept that we have identified in our clinical work, describes a relative interest in preferences for relationship patterns. For instance, a man may be relationally attracted only to women, in that he sees himself only ever having a romantic partnership with one or more women; simultaneously, he may have a high degree of sexual attraction to men.

Finally, the concept of Community Identification, the last continuum, allows one to specify herself or himself according to sexuality as bisexual, lesbian, gay, heterosexual, or any other salient identity. This is a significant consideration that should not be overlooked by counselors and other helping professionals, as the socio-political culture in which we live is a central consideration for each person's identity.

Consider the possibility that Tom's younger cousin, Jameson, comes to a community-counseling clinic after learning from Tom about his process of defining his bisexuality. Tom had felt dramatically better after this process and this knowledge facilitated Jameson's decision to do something similar.

Case Study: Jameson

Jameson is a 27-year-old Caucasian man who has a "pretty short list of sexual experiences." He knows that he has some level of attraction to both men and women, but he feels confused by the meaning of words he has heard like pansexual *and* asexual. *Do they apply to him in any way? He wants to figure these aspects of himself out by engaging the counseling process. Jameson asks if there is any "formal or tangible process for delineating (his) sexuality." Jameson's counselor refers to the multiple continua model of sexual and relational orientations (Moe et al., 2011) as a tool that might be useful. Jameson plots himself as slightly to the left of both the desire for genitalia and sex characteristics continua, indicating that he feels most attracted to these elements (maleness).*

Furthermore, he plots himself somewhat further to the left of the gender expression orientation, noting that he likes "manly men" and, when he feels attraction to women, he does not really like "girly girls." None of this information is surprising to Jameson, but as he thinks about the next few components he finds himself increasingly excited by what he sees as an emergence of "a new way of thinking about (himself)." He plots himself about one third of the way from the right on the level of sexual and relational interest, indicating that he has a fairly high degree of interest; furthermore, he plots himself fully to the left in terms of gender relational orientation, indicating that he sees himself "falling in love with men." To him, the clarity brought by engaging in this process "feels affirming." Jameson had always thought of himself as gay, but still attracted to women, but he had no way of clearly describing all that this meant. After thinking about these elements at this level of complexity and interaction, he has decided to name himself as "bisexual, but relationally attracted to men." Finally, he states that his current level of community identification has been low, but that he feels validated in this process and can see movement happening in this respect.

One can see the potential power of such an exercise when terms like *gay* and *bisexual* hold socially conscribed connotations.

Considering the innumerable permutations of sexual attractedness, relational attractedness, and community identification, mental health and other helping practitioners have a rich wealth of information to integrate. Beyond consideration of where one falls along either of these models' continua, as well as how one chooses to define one's sexual orientation identity, counselors should take into account the contextual factors that impact a client's unique presentation and understanding. For a client who is a bisexual man, this warrants an understanding of historical forces that may have lasting, limiting, and perhaps unacknowledged bearing on how he is perceived by others and how he perceives himself.

Marginalization

General negativity toward bisexual men, in particular, should be considered in the context of hegemonic ideals of masculinity, whereas all men experience impact of expectations about what it means to be a man—heterosexual, bisexual, gay, or of any other sexual orientation identity. Several authors have noted that, in most Westernized countries, men currently experience limited acceptable forms and range of expression of emotionality; furthermore, men are generally conditioned not to be intimate (even emotionally) with other men (Burleson, 2005; Parent & Moradi, 2009). Automatic assumptions extend from these proscriptions of intimacy; whether a man holds a sexual orientation identity of *straight* or *bisexual* but transgressed the male-intimacy prohibition, he is assumed to be secretly gay.

Perhaps one of the most significant factors related to marginalization is that bisexual social ecologies are often not easily conceptualized within a binary framework of sexual orientation. Sue and Hunt (2011) pointed out that bisexual identities often fall into the wide gap between the polarized identities of either gay or straight, when in reality the very definition of bisexuality is problematic due to the connotation that sexual expression can only be framed between two opposing genders.

According to Sue's and Hunt's (2011) analysis, this binary, *yin/yang* framework further results in greatly reduced ability to comprehend and accept the distinct experiences of those who may express their sexuality without gender-specificity. Lesbian and gay (LG) populations may actively or unintentionally marginalize persons with bisexual identities, reducing them into an either-or scenario, in which bisexuals are considered in denial of a truer underlying polarized identity. One potential result of this overlooking or ignoring of the idea that sexual and gender identity might simply be framed in a different manner for bisexual individuals by LG cultures, is marginalization and alienation of those identifying as bisexual. In the same way, dominant, heteronormative culture may also view those with bisexual identities as illegitimate, either ascribing them as sexual deviants who fail to repress their gay natures, or as individuals in subterfuge of truer underlying identities.

Hequembourg and Brallier (2009) supported the idea that bisexual marginalization is based in heterosexist gender role constructs. Both heterosexual and LG individuals reported viewing bisexuality as inauthentic and even potentially deceptive. Interestingly, Yost and Thomas (2012) found that bisexual men and women were viewed oppositely by heterosexual peers. Bisexual men were assumed by respondents to be surreptitiously gay, whereas bisexual women were thought to be "really heterosexual." This paradox should be further considered in light of the fact that women who are bisexual or "performative(ly) bisexual" experience largely positive responses from heterosexual men (Fahs, 2011). One might consider this relative acceptance and functional encouragement of women having sex with other women for the sake of men's desire to be a form of delegitimization and objectification. The belief that these women would really, deep-down, be heterosexual serves to complete the fantasy. Bisexual men do not appear to suffer this form objectification, but they also do not enjoy the relative level of freedom of sexual expression that it unlocks, socially.

This denial of legitimacy and authenticity of bisexuals' experience is further illuminated by a common phenomenon within sexual minority culture, particularly by gay men, which suggests that male bisexuality is only a function of men who are attracted to other men but are too afraid, homophobic, or socially conditioned to fully admit it. Burleson's (2005) explanation of this minimization and disbelief experienced by bisexual men by others, particularly gay men, is encapsulated in the words "bi now, gay later." The myth follows that essentially all men who identify as bisexual are, in fact, gay. They are assumed to be cowardly, lying to themselves and others, and likely to be happiest if they fully came out as gay. Furthermore, this falsity assumes the belief that as a man develops in courage and experience, he will fully embrace being gay.

Negativity from LG communities toward bisexuals goes beyond disbelief and delegitimization. Sue and Hunt (2011) suggested that bisexuality is viewed as a threat to gay and lesbian rights based on the concept of choice. One basic tenet of lesbian and gay human rights challenges has been the concept that there is no choice to sexual identity—this is behind the oft-repeated statement "people are born gay." Bisexuality presents a challenge to this, in that a bisexual framework reconsiders sexuality and gender in terms of preference or taste, the very notion that gay and lesbian activists have fought to dispel. In this case, civil liberties could be defined in terms of preference and choice providing a broader level of protection than what is currently socially defined as normal. The very notion of a bisexual identity is potentially placed at odds with conventional ideas of what is considered natural or normal sexual expression. Furthermore, there may be a fear from within advocacy and activist efforts that increased visibility of bisexuality could compromise social change and social justice efforts targeted at securing rights and protections for members of the LG community.

Internalized biphobia, as well as shame, extending from internalized negativity about being bisexual, may enforce suppression of one's true inner desires or hiding these desires from others, which has been shown to have negative health effects including, but not limited to, unhealthy or unsafe sexual practices, depression, and substance abuse (Coleman, 1985). How does one combat shame? Would it uniformly be appropriate for a practitioner to advocate for a client fully acknowledging and coming out as bisexual if that were her or his true inner self-identification? The answer may not be so simple. Certainly, authenticity is a commonly shared goal across theoretical orientations and perspectives. For an adolescent at risk or currently experiencing bullying because of her or his perceived sexual orientation, for instance, uniformly coming out would need to be well considered, with heavy emphasis placed on weighing the risks against the benefits. She or he could be hurt in the process and deserves to be well-informed.

Counselors and other mental health practitioners have been similarly complicit in the marginalization and subjugation of bisexual men. For instance, two research studies, by Mohr, Weiner, Chopp, and Wong (2009) and Ross (2009), confirmed that some counselors who think of themselves as affirming of differences of sexual orientation would be more likely to name bisexual clients "confused" or "conflicted" than either gay or heterosexual ones. Considering the mental healthcare field's history with these concepts and clients of sexual diversity, this continuing trend is beyond disconcerting—in violation of multicultural and sexual orientation competencies described by the ACA (2005), the APA (2002), and the NASW (1996). These social and institutionalized negative forces are not without impact or import. Eady, Dobinson, and Ross (2011) pointed out that bisexual individuals may be at an increased risk for minority stress as a result of the marginalization by both dominant and sexual minority cultures. This rejection can also be translated through mental healthcare providers' lack of cultural awareness and sensitivity. A professional's microaggressions against bisexual individuals can include: expressing judgment about the invalidity of bisexual identities (perhaps by implicitly naming the client "conflicted"); pathologizing bisexual behaviors; or over-identifying with bisexual clients through overly intrusive questioning or improper assumptions of commonality between her or his and the client's experience. Bisexuals may avoid the healthcare system in self-preservation, resulting in missed screenings and poorer health outcomes.

The culmination of these forces creates a virtual vacuum in which people with bisexual identities find themselves to be pariahs, separated from mainstream culture, LG subculture, other elements of social connection and resilience, and their own truest selves. The invisibility of this identity is compounded by the fact that many of those who may at some point behave in a manner consistent with being identified as bisexual actually shun their own identity to adopt a discrete and binary identity of either heterosexual or gay, due to the complications that could ensue (Moore & Norris, 2005). In other words, a bisexual person may deny this part of his or her identity or lead a less-than-fulfilling sexual life in an effort to self-protect and maintain a sense of community.

Impact and Development

The effects of marginalization, stigmatization, and oppression on bisexual boys and men can be ascertained across all levels of at least pubescent and post-pubescent development (Brewster & Moradi, 2010; Kennedy & Fisher, 2010). In fact, it is possible that there is impact even before full realization of attraction occurs; however, research on this phenomenon would be very difficult, costly, and time consuming to conduct. An examination of the gravity of these influences, and a model to incorporate and conceptualize all elements of one's identity into a holistic assessment of development is an important step in counselors' and other helping professionals' preparations to meet the needs of this population.

Puberty and adolescence are periods of dramatic flux in the realms of identity, self in relation to others, and relational structures. Sexual identity is one of the emergent themes during these times, as well; for those who will later identify as sexual minority members, stress and fear often coincide with this evolving awareness (Savin-Williams & Diamond, 1995). Persons of sexual minority status may experience an even greater degree of angst during these stages. As has been identified, those who are sexual minority members often feel intensely isolated from social support systems. This disproportionately results in a number of mental health problems that may begin to emerge in adolescence through adulthood, such as post-traumatic stress disorder (Roberts, Austin, Corliss, Vendermorris, & Koenen, 2010), substance-use disorders (McCabe, Bostwick, Hughes, West, & Boyd, 2010), as well as major depression and panic disorder (Meyer, 2003). Furthermore, bisexual persons are also at an increased risk for both suicidality and self-harm (Pallotta-Chiarolli & Martin, 2009; Oswalt, 2009). It should be noted again, though, that most of the research that has indicated these mental health detriments for bisexual persons does so by combining either gay and bisexual men or lesbian, gay, and bisexual persons in general. Given the additional levels of isolation from social support systems, bisexual men may even experience greater degrees of these disparities from the general population than do either lesbian women or gay men.

Bisexual adolescents have distinct identity development-related needs from other sexual minority youth. As we have established, they are isolated from both heterosexual and LG social support groups. These support networks based on difference (in this case, minority status) could, if present, serve as important vehicles for ameliorating the negative effects of the resultant minority stress through cohesion and a unified voice (Meyer, 2003). Many secondary schools across the U.S. have instituted, or have allowed students and allies to create, *Gay–Straight Alliances,* also known as ally organizations, in order to foster the communities of resistance against the forces of social opprobrium (Kennedy & Fisher, 2010). These alliance projects create a space of safety; environments in which supportive relationships with like-minded or sexual and gender diversity-friendly peers naturally develop. However, the overwhelming majority of these kinds of alliances are not bi-specific, nor do their titles even directly address bisexual student members (Kennedy & Fisher, 2010). This is a notable recreation of the kind of invisibility, furthered marginalization, and functional discounting of experience that bisexual persons often face throughout life.

It seems to be the case that one's multiple minority status (here, being bisexual and having an ethnic minority heritage, for example), as it relates to a bisexual orientation identity, is multiply complicating—it may create an increasingly worsening scenario in terms of the accessibility of the support that a group of similarly marginalized persons may encourage (Yuk Sim Chun & Singh, 2010). In order to best conceptualize the culmination of all of the life-circumstance and identity-components present for bisexual persons who are multiple-minority members, an encompassing, holistic approach offers the broadest and clearest portrayal. Yuk Sim Chun and Singh (2010) created the bisexual youth of color intersecting identities development model. It stands to reason, though, that the model shows broad applicability to bisexual people in general, in that it takes into account any ethnicity, bisexual identity, and a number of salient identity markers. These characteristics are present for all bisexual persons, be they of ethnic minority or hegemonic ethnicity status, and they may be sources of concern or detriment by degree.

The bisexual youth of color intersecting identities development model is a graphical representation from the most over-arching context (an examination of the socio-political climate) to a series of intersecting identities, including elements of the following: being a youth who is a sexual and gender minority member; having a bisexual sexual orientation identity; gender identification; ability considerations; socio-economic status; religious and spiritual aspects; and one's race and ethnicity. All of these sources of identity-related information intersect each other and co-create an individual's life circumstance. Considerations of all of these personal elements create a picture of one's identity development that takes place in the context of the broader culture, including all of the potentially oppressive and resilience-fostering elements.

A brief example of these elements in a hypothetical counseling client's life may assist in concretizing these constructs. Consider the following:

Case Study: Frederico

Frederico, who goes by Fred, is a 16-year-old student at the local high school in Uvalde, Texas. He attends a counseling session (initially with his mother), in which he discloses that he experiences crushes on both male and female classmates; however, he has not acted upon these urges, but he has shared them with some close friends and his mother—his best friend and mom were "not at all surprised" and "not about to hit the fan based on (him) being bi, *anyway." Several other friends with whom he shared his sexual orientation identity told him that he is "confused" or "probably just a* fag.*" He tells his counselor that he essentially just wants a safe place to talk about his concerns and "deal with the hate" with which some people have seemed to respond.*

Fred's counselor knows that an ecological perspective would offer a rounded assessment of the forces impacting him; as such, she employs the bisexual youth of color development model. She explores with him his ethnic heritage, which he describes as "Latino," and that both of his parents were first-generation

U.S. Americans; all of his grandparents were from central Mexico. He currently identifies as bi*. Gender identification is explored in language with which Fred is familiar, through discussions about feeling "like most guys," including talk about his interest in sports, preference for tee shirts and basketball shorts, etc. As a result, he considers himself "masculine," "manly," and "rough and tumbly." Fred further identifies that he is in accelerated courses and has been told that he is exceptionally bright; however, he does not know his intelligence quotient. From her intake process, she knows that his parents make about $125,000 per year, which is almost $100,000 more than the median family income in Uvalde. Both of Fred's parents have some post-secondary education. Though Fred still occasionally attends Mass with his mother and he is "technically Catholic," he says that he and his father are "not really all that religious," but he "suppose(s) (he) still believes in God and all that." Finally, Fred explains that he is not aware of any ally organizations at his school, or in the surrounding area for that matter, though he intends to look into it further. He concludes by saying, "Maybe I'm supposed to be the one to make that happen. I wonder what that would take. <pause> I don't know if I'm ready for a fight yet."*

Fred and his counselor are now able to explore how each of these elements fits into the broader context of his life and relationships. They have a wealth of information to discuss how he functions in the broader environments of school, Uvalde, southern Texas, Texas, the U.S., America, and the world, along with all of the politics, assumptions, and systems of power those entail. Counseling support can then follow the usual process of bolstering his resources, removing barriers, fostering healthy connections, and so forth.

As Fred has multiple identity markers, these put him at risk for marginalization and, potentially, discrimination and hate. In fact, his presentation suggests that these forces are already at play, as evidenced by the rejection he has experienced in coming out to peers. Though Fred seems fairly well adjusted, the negative power of words like *fag* cannot be overlooked. Furthermore, Fred's closing words from this discussion suggest that he is already experiencing a degree of isolation related to his sexual orientation identity. A culturally and contextually responsive professional would help Fred think of ways to access a growth and resilience-fostering network. Now that all of the elements in the bisexual youth of color intersecting identities development model have been explored, the process of working to support continued, healthy development and resilience in the face of the destructive forces of biphobia, racism, and the like must continue to be foci of the counseling process.

Yuk Sim Chun and Singh's (2010) model offers mental health and other helping professionals a bird's-eye view of the subjectivity and richness inherent in a bisexual client's life. Indeed, just as people of all ethnicities are impacted by the elements that can be elucidated in the process of considering these characteristics and forces, so are bisexual clients of all ages. Helpers' efforts to support resilience, fulfilling relationships, health, and wellness in bisexual clients are best served by intentional response to all that is identified in this process. We suggest holding fast to these principles when working with adults across all stages of development, as well.

Brewster and Moradi (2010) examined developmental considerations for bisexual adults across emerging, early, and middle stages. Emerging adulthood, in this case, is the period of increasing independence from one's childhood and adolescent lives, which occurs between the ages of 18 and 25. This period can be tumultuous in a number of ways, including identity development and self-exploration (Levinson, 1986). Brewster and Moradi (2010) point out that normative development during this time results in a firming of one's sexual identity, including a strengthening of ties between romantic and sexual interests. One might say that sex becomes less of a *game* for those who move through this period; it is no longer just for fun (Arnett, 2000). It should be noted, though, that those who have disparate self-scorings along Moe et al.'s (2011) scales related to sexual and relational interest and relational orientation may not share this experience. It is important, in any case, that bisexual persons in emerging adulthood find validation and support for their own unique experiences. Furthermore, should a person have a high degree of sexual interest but little interest in a relationship, he or she should not experience judgment in relation to her or his needs and wants. Indeed, there is no reason to think highly sexually active persons with several partners are morally corrupt or unethical. This, too, holds true for those whose relational structures involve multiple love interests or negotiated sexual engagement with those who are not primary members of a romantic relationship (Easton & Hardy, 2009). A misuse of information related to what has been thought of as normative by a professional, who is necessarily in a position of power, could result in psychological distress to the point of harm.

Those in early adulthood (from one's middle 20s to early 40s) generally experience a concretization of a sense of self and more stable relationships; however, there is also potential for stress at this time related to relational strain, as well (Levinson, 1986). Brewster and Moradi (2010) found that, for their participants, men in early adulthood differed only from middle adulthood (extending from the mid-40s through the early 60s) in terms of same-sex emotional attraction, whereas they were more likely to express this desire. Another consideration for bisexuals in early adulthood comes from research by Weinberg, Williams, and Pryor (2001), who found that, for their middle-aged participants who were bisexuals out during the AIDS crisis, bisexual identities were stable from earlier periods in their lives and, in general, they held positive perceptions about their lives.

Middle adulthood (from one's mid-40s to early 60s) is often considered to be a time of diminished physical capacities and increased sense of responsibility to others for the future (Levinson, 1986). Those in this later stage may be at a distinct bisexual identity developmental disadvantage in some ways, though. As there have been increasingly complex, accurate, and affirmative media portrayals of sexual minority members of late (Keppel, 2006; Meyer, 2009), it stands to reason that, without this influence during their formative years, it is less likely that older adults have witnessed messages of strength and positivity of bisexuals. For participants in Brewster and Moradi's (2010) research, bisexual participants in middle adulthood, as well as those in early adulthood, were more likely to be in a marriage or partnership than those in emerging adulthood, who were more likely to be single or dating casually. These findings suggest relational progression toward commitment that is generally established after one's mid-20s. This finding is consistent with Levinson's (1986) model of adult development in general, in which desire for a relationship emerges at younger ages, but stable relationships tend to be established in early adulthood and hold importance through middle age. It is important for those in helping professions to be aware of the fact that across any stage of development, sexual identity may not necessarily dictate sexual engagement.

As bisexual men appear to be as likely to be out at any stage, considerations for the coming out process and continued bisexual identity development should be made for these clients of all ages. One aspect of this becomes clear as consideration is given to the fact that those in the early and middle stages of adulthood are likely to be married or partnered is that a decision to come out to one's opposite-sex spouse can create relational trauma for both parties. Yet, undisclosed and non-negotiated sexual engagement with people other than one's partner in order to fulfill a sexual need can have extremely damaging consequences. For some bisexual clients, indeed for people of all sexualities, negotiated non-monogamy or a polyamorous relationship may create a path to fulfillment (Mint, 2004). However, as there exist commonly held controlling images of bisexual persons that they are cheaters, promiscuous, and any number of unsavory, value-laden, sexually-related stereotypes, helpers should keep their assumptions in check. When a helper's personal system of values is triggered by the experience of a client, then she or he must act according to the given standards and expectations of her or his field. As counselors, for instance, do not place these values off on their clients (ACA, 2005), nor do they hold clients to their own expectations and ideals, a general sense of openness and respect for essential human experience and need are key.

A helper would be best served to make developmental considerations for and with her or his clients in light of the many cultural and contextual needs that are present in their lives. Each circumstance and characteristic exists in relation to myriad other elements. Tailored responses to needs presented in the process of exploring these issues can, in turn, be constructed.

Supporting Resilience

Though there are quite possibly a number of marginalizing and oppressing forces present in the lives of bisexual clients, there are, undoubtedly, a number of sources of strength and resilience that practitioners can help them identify, bolster, and engage. Also, emerging evidence suggests some general positive qualities that bisexuals share. For instance, Fox (1996) identified that bisexual persons are generally well adjusted. In particular, they tend to have relatively high levels of self-esteem and they are assertive. One could interpret this information in light of those previously explored negative forces to be evidence of an ability to not only persevere, but to excel in some important ways. This perseverance is reflected in positive thoughts about themselves and a willingness to rise to an occasion and seek to make change when needed.

Rostosky et al. (2010) found a number of other strengths in their review of responses from 157 bisexual adults. Perhaps one of the more striking and powerful tendencies in responses was a sense of wholeness and authenticity. In fact, the authors wrote, "For these participants, despite experiences of rejection, claiming a bisexual identity felt real, right, and true" (p. 136). This is, assuredly, a clear indication of resilience, in that it confirms that not only were they able to survive oppressive forces, they *rose above.*

As those who suffer minority-stress can be helped through strengths-based and positive-identity focused approaches (Firestein, 2007), helping professionals can support this transformational process by working to break down internalized negative messages and their concomitant controlling images. They can work with these clients to create a different, positively focused understanding of the circumstances, explicit, and implicit forces at play, as well as the transformation that can occur by weathering them.

Such a strengths-based reconceptualization of one's experience can support the development of a growth-fostering environment for bisexual clients. Bisexual men may be at particular risk, given the controlling images modern, Western society holds for what it means to be a man and how immoral it is for men to act upon urges of any level of same-sex attraction. Mental health, healthcare, and helping professionals are called upon to act to protect and promote health and wellness for these persons.

The first step in assisting bisexual clients may be to call attention and bring surcease to discrimination and pain. Supporting a client's ability to self-advocate may be part of this, but a broader level of advocacy is in order, as well. Social change and justice efforts to bring awareness to the presence and worth of bisexual people can translate into individual benefit. Helping professionals can organize or support these initiatives in any number of ways, including coalition building, establishing ally and support groups, and lobbying for non-discrimination and harassment policies that protect bisexual people from institutionally supported oppression. Bisexual men often describe feeling ostracized from GL resources and support because of misconceptions and negativity, so social change efforts must also hold emphasis on the potential for inclusiveness and understanding from other members of sexual and gender diversity. As a result, a more powerful community of resistance and resilience for all LGBT people can continue to emerge.

The isolation experienced by bisexual clients can be profound, so mental health, health, and helping professionals should be prepared to assist in efforts to access resources and community. Part of this responsibility is to be aware of local, regional, state, and national resources for bisexual people. For bisexual students, as well as educators, law makers, and parents, the Gay, Lesbian, and Straight Education Network has compiled recommendations, helpful statistics, and resources. For more general bisexuality-related material and assistance, one also might consider accessing the American Institute of Bisexuality, *The Journal of Bisexuality,* and bimagazine.org. An additional kind of resource and support, especially for those early in the stages of sexuality exploration and bisexual identity development, is media with diverse, complex, and healthy images of bisexual people. Though there is still only limited positive representation, a few examples are the film *Bi The Way,* the television show *BiCities,* and a number of presentations available through GLBT television networks like LOGO and HERE. A word of caution about providing these kinds of resources is necessary, though, as helping professionals should never advise a resource that they have not vetted to be applicable and positive.

Though the needs of bisexual male clients are many and diverse, the effort entailed in providing and assisting with the access of resources may be time-consuming and challenging, and the forces of biphobia and negativity are strong, the potential for growth and transformation abounds. The truest guiding principle for how to best help bisexual people comes directly from their messages about themselves: difference is a good thing. If one holds fast to principles of essential human goodness, people's natural drives to rise above, and that another's cultural and contextual experiences are necessarily her or his own—perhaps different, but no less valuable, then the extended positive regard, warmth, and acceptance can have lasting, powerful, growth-fostering impact.

References

American Counseling Association (ACA). (2005). *ACA code of ethics.* Alexandria, VA: Author.

American Psychological Association (APA). (2002). Ethical principles of psychologists and code of conduct. *American Psychologist, 57,* 1060–1073.

Anderlini-D'Onofrio, S. & Alexander, J. (2009) Introduction to the special issue: Bisexuality and queer theory: Intersections, diversions, and connections. *Journal of Bisexuality, 9*(3/4), 197–212. doi: 10.1080/15299710903316489

Arnett, J. (2000). Emerging adulthood: A theory of development from the late teens through the twenties. *American Psychologist, 55,* 469–490.

Boykin, K. (2004). *Beyond the down low: Sex, lies, and denial in Black America.* Carroll and Graf: New York.

Brewster, M., & Moradi, B. (2010). Personal, relational and community aspects of bisexual identity in emerging, early and middle adult cohorts. *Journal of Bisexuality, 10,* 404–428. doi: 10.10808/15299716.2010.521056

Burleson, W. (2005). *Bi America: Myths, truths, and struggles of an invisible community.* New York: Harrington Park Press.

Cochran, W., Mostellar, F., & Tukey, J. (1953). Statistical problems of the Kinsey Report. *Journal of the American Statistical Association, 48*(264), 673–716.

Coleman, E. (1985). Integration of male bisexuality and marriage. In F. Klein and T. Wolf (Eds.), *Two lives to lead: Bisexuality in men and women* (pp. 189–207). New York: Haworth Press.

De Bruin, K., & Arndt, M. (2010). Attitudes toward bisexual men and women in a university context: Relations with race, gender, knowing a bisexual man or woman and sexual orientation. *Journal of Bisexuality, 10*(3), 233–252. doi: 10.1080/15299716.2010.500955

Dodge, B., & Sandfort, T. (2007). A review of mental health research on bisexual individuals when compared to homosexual and heterosexual individiduals. In B.A. Firestein (Ed.), *Becoming visible: Counseling bisexuals across the lifespan* (pp. 28–51). New York: Columbia University Press.

Eady, A., Dobinson, C., & Ross, L. E. (2011). Bisexual people's experiences with mental health services: A qualitative investigation. *Community Mental Health Journal, 47,* 378–389. doi: 10.1007/s10597-010-9329-x

Easton, D., & Hardy, J. (2009). *The ethical slut: A practical guide to polyamory, open relationships & other adventures.* Berkeley, CA: Celestial Arts.

Eliason, M. (1997). The prevalence and nature of biphobia in heterosexual undergraduate students. *Archives of Sexual Behavior, 26*(3), 317–26. doi: 10.1023/A:1024527032040

Entrup, L., & Firestein, B. A. (2007). Developmental and spiritual issues of young people and bisexuals of the next generation. In B. A. Firestein (Ed.), *Becoming visible: Counseling bisexuals across the lifespan* (pp. 89–107). New York: Columbia University Press.

Fahs, B. (2011). *Performing sex: The making and unmaking of women's erotic lives.* Albany, New York: The State University of New York Press.

Firestein, B. (2007). Cultural and relational contexts of bisexual women: Implications for therapy. In K. Bieschke, R. Perez, and K. Debord (Eds.), *Handbook of counseling and psychotherapy with lesbian, gay, bisexual, and transgender client* (pp. 28–51). New York: Columbia University Press.

Fox, R. (1996). Bisexuality in perspective: A review of theory and research. In B. A. Firestein (Ed.), *Bisexuality: The psychology and politics of an invisible minority* (pp. 3–52). Thousand Oaks, CA: Sage.

Gooβ, U. (2008). "Concepts of Bisexuality." *Journal of Bisexuality,* 8, 9–23. doi: 10.108015299710802142127

Heath, J., & Goggin, K. (2009). Attitudes towards male homosexuality, bisexuality, and the down low lifestyle: Demographic differences and HIV implications. *Journal of Bisexuality, 9*(1), 17–31. doi: 10.1080/15299710802659997

Hequembourg, A., & Brallier, S. (2009). An exploration of sexual minority stress across the lines of gender and sexual identity. *Journal of Homosexuality, 56,* 273–298. doi: 10.1080/00918360902728517

Herbernick, D., Reece, M., Schick, V., Sanders, S., Dodge, B., & Fortenberry, J. D. (2010). Sexual behavior in the United States: Results from a national probability sample of men and women ages 14–94. *The Journal of Sexual Medicine, 7*(5), 277–290. doi: 10.1111/j.1743-6109.2010.02012.x

Israel, T., & Mohr, J. (2004). Attitudes toward bisexual women and men: Current research, future directions. *Journal of Bisexuality, 4,* 117–134.

James, C. (1996). Denying complexity: The dismissal and appropriation of bisexuality in queer, lesbian, and gay theory. *Queer studies: A lesbian, gay, bisexual, and transgender anthology,* 217–240.

Kennedy, K., & Fisher, E. (2010). Bisexual students in secondary schools: Understanding unique experiences and developing responsive practices. *Journal of Bisexuality, 10,* 472–485.

Keppel, B. (2006). Affirmative psychotherapy with older bisexual women and men. *Journal of Bisexuality, 6,* 85–104.

The Kinsey Institute (2011). *Kinsey's heterosexual-homosexual rating scale.* Available from: www.kinseyinstitute.org/research/ak-hhscale.html (accessed January 17, 2014).

Kinsey, A. C., Pomeroy, W. B., & Martin, C. E. (1948). *Sexual behavior in the human male.* Philadelphia, PA: Saunders.

Levinson, D. (1986). A conception of adult development. *American Psychologist, 41,* 3–13.

McCabe, S., Bostwick, W., Hughes, T., West, B., & Boyd, C. (2010). The relationship between discrimination and substance use disorders among lesbian, gay, and bisexual adults in the United States. *American Journal of Public Health, 100*(10), 1946–1952.

Meyer, I. (2003). Prejudice, social stress, and mental health in lesbian, gay, and bisexual populations: Conceptual issues and research evidence. *Psychological Bulletin, 129,* 674–697.

Meyer, D. (2009). "I'm just trying to find my way like most kids": Bisexuality, adolescence and the drama of *One Tree Hill. Sexuality and Culture, 13,* 237–251.

Miller, M. (2002). "Ethically questionable?": Popular media reports on bisexual men and AIDS. In B. Beemyn and E. Steinman (Eds.), *Bisexual men in culture and society* (pp. 93–112). New York: Harrington Park Press.

Mint, P. (2004). The power dynamics of cheating: Effects on polyamory and bisexuality. *Journal of Bisexuality, 4*(3–4), 55–76. doi: 10.1300/J159v04n03_04

Moe, J., Reicherzer, S. L., & Dupuy, P. J. (2011). Models of sexual and relational orientation: A critical review and synthesis. *Journal of Counseling & Development, 89*(2), 227–233.

Mohr, J., Weiner, J., Chopp, R., & Wong S. (2009). Effects of client bisexuality on clinical judgment: When is bias most likely to occur? *Journal of Counseling Psychology, 56,* 164–175.

Moore, D. L., & Norris, F. H. (2005). Empirical investigation of the conflict and flexibility models of bisexuality. *Journal of Bisexuality, 5,* 5–25. doi: 10.1300/J159v05n01_02

Moradi, B., Mohr, J. J., Worthington, R. L., & Fassinger, R. E. (2009). Counseling psychology research on sexual (orientation) minority issues: Conceptual and methodological challenges and opportunities. *Journal of Counseling Psychology,* 56, 5–22.

Morris, R. (1992). *Oceanic homosexualities.* Garland Press: New York.

Mosher, W., Chandra, A., & Jones, J. (2005). *Sexual behavior and selected health measures: Men and women 15–44 years of age, United States, 2002. Advance data from vital and health statistics No. 362.* Hyattsville, MD: National Center for Health Statistics.

National Association of Social Workers (NASW). (1996). *Code of ethics of the National Association of Social Workers.* Washington, DC: Author.

Oswalt, S. (2009). Don't forget the "B": Considering bisexual students and their specific health needs. *Journal of American College health, 57*(5), 557–560.

Pallotta-Chiarolli, M., & Martin, E. (2009). "Which sexuality? Which service?": Bisexual young people's experiences with youth, queer, and mental health services in Australia. *Journal of LGBT Youth, 6,* 199–222.

Parent, M., & Moradi, B. (2009). Confirmatory factor analysis of Conformity to Masculine Norms Inventory and development of the CMNI-46. *Psychology of Men and Masculinity, 10,* 175–189.

Reece, M., Herbenick, V., Schick, D., Sanders, A., Dodge, B., & Fortenberry, J. D. (2010). Sexual behaviors, relationships, and perceived health among adult men in the United States: Results from a national probability sample. *The Journal of Sexual Medicine, 7*(5), 291–304. doi: 10.1111/j.1743-6109.2010.02009.x

Reicherzer, S. L. (2005). Coming out and living out across the lifespan. In D. Comstock (Ed.), *Diversity in development: Critical contexts that shape our lives and relationships* (pp. 161–184). Belmont, CA: Thompson/Brooks-Cole.

Roberts, A., Austin, S., Corliss, H., Vendermorris, A., & Koenen, K. (2010). Pervasive trauma exposure among US sexual orientation minority adults and risk of posttraumatic stress disorder. *American Journal of Public Health, 100*(12), 2433–2441.

Ross, L. (2009). *Understanding the context of bisexual mental health in Ontario.* Presented to the American Psychological Association, Toronto, ON, Canada.

Rostosky, S., Riggle, E., Pascale-Hague, D., & McCants, L. (2010). The positive aspects of a bisexual self identification. *Psychology & Sexuality, 1*(2), 131–144.

Russell, S. T., Clarke, T. J., & Clary, J. (2009). Are teens "post-gay"? Contemporary adolescents' sexual identity labels. *Journal of Youth Adolescence, 38,* 884–890.

Savin-Williams, R., & Diamond, L. (2000). Sexual identity trajectories among sexual-minority youth: Gender comparisons. *Archives of Sexual Behavior, 29,* 607–627.

Sue, H., & Hunt, R. (2011). Bisexuality and identity: The double-edged sword: Stonewall research into bisexual experience. *Journal of Bisexuality, 11,* 290–299. doi: 10.1080/15299716.2011.571995

Yost, M., & Thomas, G. (2012). Gender and binegativity: Men's and women's attitudes toward male and female bisexuals. *Archives of Sexual Behavior, 41,* 691–702.

Young, R., & Meyer I. (July 2005). The trouble with "MSM" and "WSW": Erasure of the sexual-minority person in public health discourse. *American Journal of Public Health, 95*(7), 1144–1149. doi: 10.2105/AJPH.2004.046714

Yuk Sim Chun, K., & Singh, A. (2010). The bisexual youth of color intersecting identities development model: A contextual approach to understanding multiple marginalization experiences. *Journal of Bisexuality, 10,* 429–451. doi: 10.1080/15299716.2010.521059

Walker, M. (2005). Critical thinking: Challenging developmental myths, stigmas, and stereotypes. In D. Comstock (Ed.), *Diversity and development: Critical contexts that shape our lives and relationships* (pp. 47–66). Belmont, CA: Brooks/Cole.

Weinberg, M., Williams, C., & Pryor, D. (1994). *Dual attraction: Understanding bisexuality.* New York: Oxford University Press.

Worthington, R. L., Savoy, H. B., Dillon, F. R., & Vernaglia, E. R. (2002). Heterosexual identity development: A multidimensional model of individual and group identity. *Counseling Psychologist,* 30, 496–531.

11 Counseling in the Periphery of Queer Discourse

Transgender Children, Adolescents, Women, and Men

Stacee Reicherzer, Andrew S. Garland-Forshee, & Jason Patton

Human rights initiatives for lesbian women and gay men have made significant advances in recent years, both in the U.S. and globally. The spectrum of needs for Queer youth concerning bullying (Faye, Newman, Daley, & Solomon, 2009), coming out experiences (D'Augelli, Grossman, Starks, & Sinclair, 2010), and general risk factors (Heck, Flentje, & Cochran, 2011; Travers et al., 2010) are gaining traction in counseling and social services literature, as are concerns for Queer adult populations such as historical silencing and oppression (Craft, Serovich, McKenry, & Lim, 2008), partner bonding (Chan & Cavacuiti, 2008; Gottman et al., 2003; Reicherzer, 2011), substance abuse (Talley, Sher, & Littlefield, 2010), and aging (Landers, Mimiaga, & Krinsky, 2010). In spite of these broad gains and the common inclusion of bisexual- and transgender-identified persons in the LGBT/GLBT acronym, the majority of research and clinical emphasis is given to lesbian- and gay-identified adolescents and adults.

Mental health and social service professionals' oversight of the specific needs of transgender persons occurs alongside emerging evidence that indicates that transgender boys and men (natal females) who are masculine- or male-identified, as well as transgender girls and women (natal males) who are femme- or female-identified and who may or may not have had gender-affirming hormonal regimens or surgeries, may be particularly vulnerable populations. In a study of sexual risk taking by transgender girls, Wilson, Garofalo, Harris, Belzer, the Transgender Advisory Committee, and the Adolescent Medicine Trials Network for HIV/AIDS Intervention (2011) identified that participants were highly unlikely to use condoms during receptive anal sex, particularly when under the influence of drugs. In a correlational study that examined HIV prevalence, sexual risk behaviors, and substance use among adult Latino gay and bisexual men and transgender women, Ramirez-Valles, Garcia, Campbell, Diaz, and Heckathorn (2008) estimated that as much as 40% of the population sampled had abused drugs in the 6 months prior to the study, and that 25% had engaged in unprotected sex within the prior 12 months. No studies were found that specifically identified risk factors for transgender boys and men.

The social problems reflected in studies such as those described above indicate significant failings that begin in school and community systems and that perpetuate in both the generalized social mistreatment as well as the specific lack of services that occur for populations of transgender adults. In addition, the erasure of transgender lived experiences in counseling and social service literature, even that specifically identified as addressing an LGBT topic, indicates the limits not only on efforts to identify and address service gaps for these communities, but an apparent ignorance by clinicians and researchers that their use of "LGBT" or "GLBT" does not, in fact, address transgender concerns so much as it does lesbian and gay issues.

This chapter will demonstrate practical and evidence-based skills for addressing the needs of transgender individuals. We will draw from both the body of literature as well as our own clinical experiences in serving these communities in mental health and family counseling settings. In the interest of affirming the rights of transgender individuals to name their genders and the fact that being transgender indicates at least some degree of dissonance with birth-assigned gender, we specifically reference all natal male and transgender- or female- identifying people as "transgender girls" (for children and adolescents) or "transgender women" (for adults) and use the female pronouns "she" and "her." In referencing natal female and transgender- or male-identifying people, we use "transgender boys" and "transgender men," respectively. We recommend that readers who are unacquainted with this reference system will become so for ease in conceptualizing the experiences of your transgender clients.

In the matter of pronouns, we recognize that many counselors are new to work with the transgender community, and thus will struggle to think of and reference a client's gender according to this individual's identity, rather than what is necessarily biological (natal). We too have stumbled on pronoun use at times as counselors when we receive a referral from a male client whose intake paperwork indicates a man's name such as "Robert," and who initially appears to be what is societally constructed as masculine, only to learn that the client wants to live as a woman and be called "Susan." Similarly, in our work with youth, we have struggled to help parents recognize when a child does not identify with the name and gender that were assigned at birth, but identifies with a different gender.

As counselors and advocates for the rights of gender self-determination, however, and understanding that our role is to support client efficacy and mental health, we play a critical role in perhaps being the first relationship where a client's identified gender is acknowledged. Given the statistics described previously on risk factors for the population, we own a significant role in providing acceptance and support of the gender identity that our client identifies as correct for her, him, or hir.

Examining Sex and Gender

Whereas experiences for transsexual women and men only came to be discussed in the medical community with the advent of what we now identify as gender-affirming surgery (surgical procedures that correct the genitalia so that it is female or male in appearance and function), transgender persons have existed across human history through a variety of cultural expressions (Meyerowitz, 2002). These include, but are not limited to, the *hijra* of India (Nanda, 1990), the *kathoey* of Thailand (Totman, 2003), the *vestidas* of urban areas in Mexico (Prieur, 1996), and the *tobeija* of the Balkans (Grémaux, 1996). In addition, many North American Native communities including the Navajo, Hopi, Lakota, Zuni, Illinois, Arapaho, and other tribes have often revered people who were called *two-spirit* (Williams, 1992) or *berdache* (Roscoe, 1996), and seen as possessing the strengths of both males and females. Yet, in spite of the long history that differing gender expressions have occupied across humanity's saga, transgender individuals in the U.S. and other seemingly socio-culturally advanced nations face extreme marginalization at the hands of trans-ignorant and transphobic people in the societies that they occupy.

For this section, it is important to understand the very diverse community of individuals who identify, or have identified, as transgender. It is also important to state that the term *transgender* is an umbrella term that describes many individuals whose gender identities and expressions exist in a continuum that is either partially or fully experienced as female/feminine or male/masculine.

Sex refers to a both a person's primary (genitalia) and secondary (breasts, facial hair) sex characteristics. Each individual is born with either male or female genitalia, or in cases in which a person is born intersex, a combination of both sets of features (in which case, the person's sex can exist anywhere on the continuum in relation to categorically male or female sex features). A number of intersex experiences exist, and we encourage readers to visit the Intersex Society of North America (ISNA, 2011) to learn more.

It is important to consider that probably most transgender women are not medically classified as intersexed (American Psychiatric Association, 2000) but rather, are born anatomically male. Some, but not all of these women, will, through the use of estrogen and sex-affirming surgeries, migrate their bodies along the sex continuum from male to female (Meyer et al., 2006). The availability of surgical procedures to migrate sex features from male to female, which began in the 1920s, led to the development of the term "transsexual" (Feinberg, 1996) for describing the women who undergo this procedure. Today, this term may still be assumed by women who use or have used hormones and/or surgeries to migrate from male to female, although some will use the more inclusive term "transgender." Others will simply refer to themselves as "women" without designating themselves as transgender or transsexual.

Comparatively, many natal born females who identify as men may also choose to undergo transition from female to male through the use of testosterone, chest surgery, hysterectomy, and other medical procedures (Rubin, 2003; Vanderburgh, 2011). Although several sex-affirming interventions have been available for transgender men since the mid-twentieth century (Kotula, 2002; Meyerowitz, 2002), most of these options are costly and often reported to be inconsistent in appearance and function (Rubin, 2003; Yerke & Mitchell, 2011). As a result, many transgender men choose to use a combination of hormones, surgeries, and their innate masculinity to integrate into larger social contexts (Green, 2006) and often refer to themselves as FTM (Female-to-Male), trans, transguy, transman, guy, male, or men (Forshee, 2008).

Simply stated, the noun "sex," (as opposed to the verbal form, which refers to sex acts) may be best understood as the features of the body. A person's sex may or may not align with her or his gender identity, which is the felt sense of being male, female, or in a space that is located somewhere between the two. Many transgender persons do not identify as women or men, and do not wish to be described as such. Some prefer the use of non-gender specific pronouns, such as sie or ze, rather than "she" or "he," and "hir," rather than "her" or "him" (Feinberg, 1996). Others, however, do possess a strong desire to align their sex features with their female gender identities, and choose to migrate their sex features accordingly.

Importantly, many transgender women elect to use hormone replacement therapies, breast implants, and other surgeries to migrate many or most of their secondary sex features from male to female, but do not elect to undergo genital surgeries (Meyer et al., 2006). Whereas their identities may be partially or totally female, these women do not identify a need for genital surgery. This can be for a number of reasons (often in combination) that we have seen in our clinical and research practices, as well as personal knowledge gained as members of this community: i) the surgery is financially inaccessible; ii) the medical procedures are believed to be too invasive or painful; iii) retaining male genitalia along with breasts, buttocks, and other female features is physically, psychologically, and/or emotionally satisfying and feels appropriate; iv) they exist in romantic relationships in which partners do not wish for them to change their genitalia; v) their identities as pre-operative or non-operative transsexuals are a distinction that is financially more lucrative (this is particularly true for transgender women who work in the drag industry, much of which requires participants to be anatomically male, as well as those who work in sex industries in which their pre-operative or non-operative status is seen as desirable).

As noted above, many transgender men also choose to affirm their gender in the form of testosterone therapies, "top surgery" including breast reduction or removal (mastectomy), and "bottom surgery" to reconstruct genitalia (metoidioplasty or phalloplasty). Despite the medical advances in these areas, it is worth noting that although recent studies suggest "top surgery" as an important gender-affirming procedure for transgender men (Yerke & Mitchell, 2011), many elect to avoid "bottom surgery" altogether (Forshee, 2008; Rubin, 2003). There are many reasons (similar to those of transgender women) for this decision, including the high cost of surgery, aesthetic satisfaction of surgical results, lack of potential functionality of the phallus/penis, and extensive recovery time and risk of infection. Furthermore, many younger transgender men feel bottom surgery is unnecessary for them to live fully integrated males lives, thus challenging societal notions of what constitutes maleness and masculinity, noting "Yes, I am man enough" (Yerke & Mitchell, 2011, p. 73) without the presence of a penis.

The third continuum, gender expression, refers to external characteristics and behaviors that are societally constructed as masculine or feminine. These include such culturally variable elements as clothing, appearance, speech patterns, and demeanor. Expectations for what is masculine or feminine tend to evolve over time. Consider, for example, the impact the women's movement and feminism have had on our society's gender roles over the last century. Women and men are now more able to pursue educational and professional opportunities, socio-political movement, and a style and manner of dress than were never conceivable in the early twentieth century. Some transgender girls and women express themselves on the feminine end of the gender expression continuum, while others may prefer a more gender-neutral identity that is centered in the continuum between masculinity and femininity. Likewise, some transgender boys and men are comfortable expressing themselves on the masculine side of the spectrum, while many are comfortable balancing their gender expression and employing various qualities of masculinity and femininity given the respective social situation, context, and queer-friendly space (Halberstam, 2005).

Transgender femininity, when represented with high heels, short dresses, and bold make-up, has at times been misunderstood and misrepresented as presenting a retrogressive image of women. The feminist scholar Janice Raymond (1980) was particularly critical of transgender women, whom she saw as medically anomalous creations by male doctors who were supplanting natal females to create their own perfected images of womanhood. From our experience with particularly feminine-expressed transgender women, make-up, clothing, and hairstyles represent liberation and self-expression. In a qualitative case study (Reicherzer & Spillman, 2012) conducted to examine three transsexual entertainers, participant "Amanda" (alias), as a symbol of her strength as a transsexual woman, created a colorful collage that included pictures of a Barbie along with ads for fashionable women's clothing, make-up, and perfumes. Written in bold letters with hearts dotting lowercase "I's" was this self-affirmation:

> These articles on this page symbolize my strength and resilience as an individual. No matter how hard people try to bring me down or hurt me emotionally, I know who I really am and as long as I am true to myself, no one can break my wall of strength! I am finally me! I have found myself! I love the new me! Welcome to true living!
>
> (p. 34)

As Amanda's self-affirmation illustrates, transgender women must find the symbols of their own strength and resilience in a culture that has often taught them little of how to develop a life of gender authenticity. As is true for many transgender girls and women, Amanda struggled to find acceptance for her femininity as a boy, when she was shamed by her family for playing with her sister's dolls, or dressing-up in her mother's clothes.

Given that most transgender men are socialized as females, their experiences of masculinity differ from natal born men. This kind of "trans masculinity" provides transgender men a bird's-eye view of living in a binary gender system (Devor, 1997). Although some men connect with the overt forms of stereotypical and essentialist masculinity (i.e., facial hair, muscles, hyper-masculine expressions and gestures), other men are comfortable with more nuanced and subdued forms of male identity, accessing a "conscious masculinity," an approach to picking and choosing (for better or worse) a more personalized form of masculine gender expression.

In a phenomenological study on the perceptions of masculinity among transgender men (Forshee, 2006), one of the participants, "Bruce," suggested that his conscious choice of how to express his own masculinity was one of the major assets of being transgender. When asked how he thinks other people perceive his gender expression, Bruce stated:

> I like to think they perceive it as a softer, gentler version of your average non-trans male. That's one of the gifts that I get in transitioning is [sic] I get to decide what kind of a man I want to be. I don't have the baggage of having been socialized as male from infancy.
>
> (p. 98)

As this comment suggests, transgender men are not bound by binary conventions of masculinity, rather, they consciously choose along a continuum of expressions and behaviors afforded, perhaps not realized, to all men. At birth most natal born men are absorbed into male culture unconsciously, setting into motion a lifetime of gendered identities, expectations, and roles. In choosing a conscious masculinity perspective, transgender men deconstruct the status quo of masculinity, developing new possibilities for all men and boys.

The next section will discuss these experiences more fully, describing both the lived realities that transgender children and adolescents face, as well as the roles of counselors in work with this community.

Growing up Transgender

The genesis of transgender identity has yet to be clearly defined. Emerging evidence points to genetic (Hare et al., 2009) and neurological (Green, 2002) differences as well as cognitive, developmental, and socio-cultural variations (Fausto-Sterling, 2012) among natal males and females who are transgender and those who are not; however, additional studies are needed to lead to formally conclude the origins of transgender experiences. What is known and observable is the fact that some natal males begin demonstrating significantly feminine traits at very early ages, just as some natal females begin demonstrating marked masculine traits. In a mixed-method survey to examine identity development among 121 transgender participants, Kennedy and Hellen (2010) demonstrated that the largest percentage of participants identified age five as the period when they realized their gender distinction. Even as toddlers, many transgender children begin displaying gender non-conforming behaviors.

Transgender Children and Adolescents

As we have discussed earlier, gender identity is a developmental process stretching across a wide continuum of expressions, identities, and roles. As such, not all expressively masculine females or feminine males will identify as transgender, yet as children make-meaning from the myriad social and cultural "gendering" influences, some natal females will and do express a male-affirming identity while some natal males do so of a female-affirming identity. In addition to providing specific counseling interventions for children and families, this section will briefly examine identity development for transgender girls and boys, emphasizing developmental concepts, nuances, and concepts.

Awareness of gender and gender identity tends to emerge between the ages of two and three (Brill & Pepper, 2008), with some researchers positing a potential awareness of gender before birth (Fausto-Sterling, 2012). At the earliest stages of development, children have a *pre-symbolic* understanding of gender, associating faces, voices, and gestures with specific gendered people (i.e., parents and siblings); this soon moves to *symbolic* understanding of gender though images, toys, music, clothing, etc., between four and five years (Fausto-Sterling, 2012; Kennedy & Hellen, 2010). A recent study suggests that most transgender adults have an understanding of their gender variance before the age of five (Kennedy & Hellen, 2010), and at this critical moment transgender boys and girls may begin to display gender non-traditional behaviors. More specifically, transgender boys may refuse to wear "girl" clothing and may show a preference for stereotypical "boy" playthings (Brill & Pepper, 2008). In the case of transgender girls, this may include playing with dolls or dress-up, as illustrated in Reicherzer and Spillman's (2012) case of Amanda, presented above.

Moving into elementary school, transgender children tend to conceal their gender identities to a greater or lesser degree. According to Ehrensaft (2011), children tend to exhibit an authentic "true gender self" (p. 101) in surroundings that are familiar, affirming, and comfortable such as trans-positive therapy groups, loving homes, and supportive communities. Conversely, when confronted with social contexts that require adaptation to essentialist gendered expectations (i.e., a disapproving parents or schools), children tend to accommodate these circumstances by embodying a "false gender self," or an external presentation based on social conventions of traditional gender expressions rather than on an authentic sense of self. The latter response is based in survival and can become increasingly difficult and potentially detrimental to self-concept as children grow, develop, and enter puberty (Vanderburgh, 2011; Ehrensaft, 2011).

Adolescence is a time of tremendous biological, psychological, and social transformation. Predominant characteristics typically associated with puberty tend to be the most dramatic of these changes. Whereas many youth welcome the emerging physical characteristics that separate and demarcate the end of childhood, for transgender boys, puberty is often one of the most feared and confusing times in their development (Brill & Pepper, 2008). As transgender girls move into adolescence, they often face ridicule and taunting from other school children that becomes more pronounced as they age. As the child develops cognitive abilities to recognize her transgender identity, or even that she is simply different from other children, it often has a deleterious effect on her self-worth (Ehrensaft, 2011; Kennedy & Hellen, 2010; Reicherzer & Anderson, 2006; Vanderburgh, 2009).

Due to the incongruence experienced between identity and the onset of puberty as well as the cultural, medical, familial, and social misunderstanding of transgender youth, adolescents are at a higher risk for depression, low self-image substance abuse, homelessness, HIV/AIDS, and suicide attempt than their non-transgender identified peers (Durso & Gates, 2012; Kenagy & Hsieh, 2005). Thus, transgender youth who come from non-affirming environments are at a higher risk of lower self-esteem and personal harm.

Although physical (i.e., surgical and hormonal) transition is not recommended in early childhood (Vanderburgh, 2011), many transgender children begin to transition socially before the onset of puberty. The World Professional Association of Transgender Health (WPATH)'s Standards of Health for Transgender, Transsexual, and Gender Nonconforming Persons (Coleman et al., 2011) for use by therapists, physicians, human service practitioners, and other helping professionals to aid in the guidance of culturally responsive care for transsexual, transgender, and gender non-conforming people. As such, using the *Standards of Care* (SOC) as a tool for engagement, counselors can proactively engage families in dialogue regarding the benefits and challenges of social transition.

According to the SOC, transgender adolescent boys who feel strongly identified as male, and transgender adolescent girls who feel strongly identified as female may consider partially reversible hormone interventions (i.e., testosterone for boys, estrogen for girls) after the age of 16. Chest surgery for both males and females may be carried out earlier than 18 years (the age of majority) if the client has been living in her or his gender for an extended period and after one year of testosterone or estrogen treatment (Coleman et al., 2011, p. 178), although breast implants may not be recommended for transgender girls until they have been on estrogen for a period of time in order to allow normal breast development. Counselors who are interested in working with transgender adolescents should use the *Standards of Care* (2011) as a framework for developing culturally relevant and responsive care for this population.

Vanderburgh (2009) identified that severe parental overreaction through punishment of the child or other efforts to alter the child's gender behavior tend to be not only ineffective in changing the gender expression, but also traumatizing for the child. Corroborating this, we as the authors of this chapter have worked with many transgender women and men whose memories of severe parental punishment have served as legacies of shame and trauma. Familial reaction plays a significant component in the child's self-worth as she or he develops gender identity, and even a single supportive caregiver in a family that is otherwise cruel or indifferent may be a source of resiliency throughout the child's development. To illustrate this, we will use the example from "Valerie," a participant in Reicherzer and Spillman's (2012) study of transsexual women of Mexican origin. Valerie, as a transgender girl, described herself as feeling alone and isolated as a child. She was targeted by sexual abuse predators from a very young age, and was unable to trust her abusive mother or siblings, who attempted to exorcise what they believed to be a demon from her when she reported abuse. Valerie's grandmother served as Valerie's protector, and in her adulthood Valerie attributed much her of strength to her grandmother's love.

Based in her clinical practice, Ehrensaft (2011) conceptualized that three types of familial situations exist when presented with gender non-conforming children: transforming, transphobic, or transporting. Each of these styles is seen as either supporting or impeding the child in her or his lifespan development. Ehrensaft theorized that transforming parents, because they are comfortable in their own gender roles, are able to support their transgender child through the complexity and struggle of her or his own identity development. These parents are not seen as being without their own challenges, as reconciliation and grief are identified as natural elements of the parents' development. Transphobic parents ultimately see their children as an extension of themselves and, being insecure in their own genders, are unable to reconcile themselves to their child's gender non-conforming behavior. These parents often become abusive of the child as their rejection of her or his identity fails to elicit change. Transporter parents, like the transphobic parents, punish the child when she or he begins to present a transgender identity, but swiftly rush into trying to force themselves to accept the gender. Ehrensaft identified that parents who do this without ever exploring their own ambiguities and emotions are deceiving themselves and their transgender children.

As counselors and researchers, we have found that families can present a blended style of engaging their children, with some family members transforming and adapting through their own struggles, while others transported and foreclosed on self-reflection. Perhaps most challenging are stories of transphobic parents, highlighted in cases like that of "Kate" (alias) (Patton & Reicherzer, 2010) whose mother physically assaulted her for years before throwing her own out of the home when Kate was an adolescent. Kate became involved in sex-work because of the limited means she had for financial sustenance, and led an enormously complicated life that we identified as rooted in her disrupted childhood bonds.

Perhaps the most challenging component of transgender adolescent development is the lack of identifiable resources. Teens who remain with their parents are often forced to live with abuse and degradation surrounding their gender identities, while those who run away or are placed in foster care may face even greater challenges (Turner, 2009).

Resiliency in Transgender Womanhood

Our discussion of transgender girls and women has, to this point, highlighted some of the challenges that are faced by this community in a culture of misunderstanding. Whereas many of the problems such as drug abuse and sexual risks (Ramirez-Valles, Garcia, Campbell, Diaz, & Heckathorn, 2008), interpersonal violence and familial rejection (Patton & Reicherzer, 2010), and chronic depression that are experienced by transgender girls are often present for transgender women, we have also observed significant resiliency in this adult population. Transgender women are survivors of extraordinary challenges that are often mitigated by poverty (Reicherzer, Patton, & Glowiak, 2011), discrimination on the basis of their race or ethnicity (Kenagy, 2005), and religious excommunication followed by identifying new and affirming faiths (Kidd & Witten, 2008). In our clinical work with transgender women, however, we have found that there is also joy and personal satisfaction in being able to live experiences that require such deeply honest and authentic personal examinations.

Importantly, we wish to point out that many transgender women do not come out and begin living as transgender until middle or even later adulthood due to factors that can include denial or inability to recognize a transgender identity; or the inability to articulate and live in a transgender identity due to external social pressures (family, job, etc.). Many clients with whom we have worked are newly transitioning from male to female in their 40s, 50s, or even 60s. There are unique challenges that we have found for this population in that many wish to pass as women but are physically unable to do so due to the delayed use of hormonal and surgical interventions. Some of these clients had successfully integrated as heterosexual men throughout their lives, often including marriages to natal females, and parenting. We have found a particular challenge in supporting our midlife transitioning clients as they experience the loss of male privilege (walking alone at night, being less conspicuous in public settings, etc.) and often hostile reactions to their presentations as transgender women. For those who have never experienced being publicly humiliated, job discrimination, and familial rejection, there is often surprise and dismay in encountering these experiences.

The first authors counseled a client who had worked as a school librarian for most her of life as a male. When she transitioned to female in her mid-40s, she expected to use her experiences as opportunities to educate the students and faculty at the school. When she instead encountered snickering and other cruel behaviors, she developed extreme rejection sensitivity, perceiving that she was constantly being watched and targeted. In spite of our best efforts, the client was unable to cope with the challenges her new identity brought, and she committed suicide three years after what was supposed to have been a gender-affirming surgery.

Having learned lessons through both painful work such as the case described above, as well as rewarding cases that affirmed clients in their gender journeys, we have identified that emphasis in client strength and resiliency is a significant focus for counseling with this community. As clients reveal their stories to us, listening for themes that represent examples of personal wisdom, abilities to find caring others, or pragmatism in finding gainful employment provides a context that we find useful in helping clients identify how to use these resources to resolve current problems in living. Being feminist scholars and practitioners, we authors emphasize empowerment as centrally thematic in our work with clients. We often find ourselves connecting clients and their families (particularly if the clients are transgender girls or adolescents) with community resources that include support groups, medical referrals, and legal services. We believe that our work is in supporting transgender clients to have a voice in the services provided for them, and seek to support clients in self-determining social justice needs of those around them.

Transgender Men: Navigating Manhood

As noted above, much of the literature on transgender people lacks a direct focus on the lives, experiences, and specific needs of transgender men, specifically in the fields of public health (Feinberg, 2001), HIV/AIDS research (Namaste, 2001), and human services (Forshee, 2007). Transgender men are also underrepresented when it comes to understanding how they experience their lives as men (Forshee, 2006; Green, 2005). Having been socialized as female, transgender men have a unique perspective on navigating the social codes of masculinity as a strategy of cultural resilience. Yet, because the lived experiences between transgender women and men differ, these issues must be approached separately (Forshee, 2008).

Forshee's (2006) phenomenological study of transgender men's experiences identified specific themes focused on the participants' construction of masculinity, the dynamic social nuances and rules of being a man, the physical embodiment of masculinity, and the developmental nature of identity construction in the process of transitioning from female to male. The participants were self-identified transgender men, regardless of current or past surgical or hormone intervention, or being "out" to others as transgender. Furthermore, the men in this study came from a wide range of life experiences. Some men were previously part of lesbian feminist communities, while others were in current heterosexual relationships. Two men identified situations and experiences unique to being men-of-color, and each person represented different socio-economic backgrounds, academic achievements, and occupations. Based on the findings, the men in this study held similar thoughts on the social construction of masculinity, yet numerous factors influenced their experiences.

Age, for instance, provides diverse developmental insight. For the men in this study, age-related perspectives include: length of time lived as female; typical developmental influences such as psychological, cognitive, and biological maturation; socio-cultural contributions, including peer relationships; and choice of self-identifying terminology (three identified as *transguy,* two as *transmen,* one as *FTM,* and another as *male*). When it comes to the experience of living as men, the interior lives of transmen should be taken seriously (Rubin, 2003). Similar to Rubin's findings, this study found that transgender men are consistently in search of their authentic selves, in that meaning is constructed from everyday interactions between the self and the environment (Kegan, 1982). Whereas the men were not challenged to place their experiences into meaningful contexts, they did struggle when describing masculinity as a social and cultural construct. This may be due to the fact that it is often difficult to intellectually describe one's lived experience. Masculinity, for these men, was much more experiential than scholastic, fundamentally rooted in an ongoing tension between what it *means* to be a man, and the actual practice of *living* as a man.

A singular consolidated definition of masculinity (or manhood) does not exist (Halberstam, 2005), yet in their search of self-knowledge, the participants in Forshee's (2006) study challenged their essentialist views of masculinity in order to find a comfortable "fit" within the culture of manhood. Numerous factors influenced their experiences, including unspoken codes by which many men are socialized. Although the researcher originally thought that the issue of toileting and using men's restrooms might be a source of discomfort for the participants, the results did not support this idea. Nonetheless, socially acceptable "male" restroom etiquette (e.g., no eye contact and the absence of casual conversation) was stringently followed.

Another insightful outcome of this study was that most of the men reported vast differences in their post-transition interactions with women. These encounters were surprising, and disappointing to the men, particularly if their previous communities consisted primarily of women (i.e., lesbian feminist communities). This desire for connection is also echoed in Kupers' (1993) work on men, intimacy, and power. The data suggest that the men in this study possessed unique perspectives on the male/female gender divide often unavailable to a singular sex or gendered perspective. Participant "Dan" stated that not being male for the first 40 years of his life colored his perception of the world and what it means to be a man. Comparatively, participant "Leon" described the benefits of having lived so much of his life as female:

> It was really useful to walk around in the female body for 42 years. I would recommend it to any guy, to tell you the truth. I think it was a real eye opener, and it wasn't because I experienced things as a female myself, but I had access to women's experiences, because women share things with each other. I know how women are really treated; I know what women's experiences are like because I have had hundreds of women tell me their deepest darkest realist thoughts about that, because they trust other women. I had an "in" to that, that other guys don't usually have, and there is no way in hell I would abuse women. . . . Seeing that power differential from this side, it's mind boggling . . . I highly recommend men spend 42 years in a female body before they do anything about being a real guy. Because it was a real eye-opener—it's a real eye opener.
>
> (Forshee, 2006, p. 98)

A final insight was the participants' perspectives on having, or lacking, a functional penis. Although not all of the men shared the same opinion, most of the men felt that either having or not having a penis was not reflective of one's masculinity or manhood. In essence, these men did not feel that the presence of a penis made someone more of a man, or was a necessary component of masculinity. Notably, a majority of the men were using testosterone and only one participant had completed bottom surgery, with the remaining men citing cost as well as inadequate aesthetic and functional outcomes or barriers for reasons to avoid surgery. As mentioned above, genital surgeries for transgender men are not only costly but also lack the medical and technological savvy needed to construct a fully functioning and sexually pleasurable penis (Kotula, 2002; Rubin, 2003). These findings correspond with Green's (2005) anecdotal interactions with trans and biological men, and Rubin's (2003) phenomenological study on identity and embodiment among transgender men.

Our clinical work with transgender men has led us to conclusions that corroborate Forshee's findings. To illustrate this, we present the case of "Brett" (alias), a client who worked with Stacee for two years.

Case Study: Brett

Brett presented for counseling in his mid-30s, identifying that he had lived in a masculine identity for some time, and wished to "make the process complete." In this, he was seeking through counseling to identify steps and procedures for transitioning his body from female to male. As Brett described, he had come out as a lesbian in high school and identified as such for several years. In his late 20s, he noticed that being a masculine woman was not congruent, and began binding his breasts and asking people to call him "Brett" instead of his given name, "Brenda." As Brett described, this created challenges for him in the lesbian community because his circle of friends could not, as he explained "relate to me as a man." Further, Brett identified that his lesbian friends accused him of "colluding with patriarchy" in his male identification. As such, Brett was fairly isolated in his experience.

A major focus of our counseling work, in addition to identifying the most salient masculine symbols that attracted Brett, was connecting him to community resources. Locating a transgender support group for both women and men was particularly constructive to Brett, as he was able to meet other men like him. Over our time together, I referred Brett to a doctor to prescribe hormones and, later, to a surgeon who performed his double mastectomy and chest reconstruction. As Brett transitioned his body, he gained confidence. He began dating a woman, and after several months, they were living together.

Brett integrated easily into society as a man, growing a full beard and with a voice deepened by his testosterone regimen. One challenge that remained, however, was in integrating with non-transgender men. Brett relayed a story to me of meeting a male buddy at the gym. Brett expressed that he had enjoyed talking to the guy and appreciated having a friend who was a familiar face at the gym every day. One day, the man used the word "fag" in talking about another man who was gay, which was particularly stressing to Brett, given that Brett had been socialized in the Queer community. Exploring this further with him, we determined that because the man at the gym encountered Brett as another man, he presumptuously assumed that use of "fag" would be normative shared language that was commonly acceptable to both him and Brett.

Counselor Considerations

As we have illustrated through our discussion, transgender individuals seek counseling services to address experiences that may or may not be related to societally-based oppression and mistreatment. Social problems, for both of these communities, however, often become salient at very young ages and thus shape identity development across the lifespan. Whereas acknowledgment and addressing these forces cannot be underestimated, we sincerely advocate for strengths-based, resiliency-oriented counseling and psychotherapeutic practices. For transgender populations we have found that positive relational templates provide the mechanisms by which efficacious growth and wellness are possible; also, they serve as foundations for future growth, fostering relationships that honor the essential human diversity.

We also recognize that each person, regardless of sexual or gender identity, is infinitely complex—and that additional experiences of race and ethnicity, physical ability, socio-economic status, and other cultural components need to be considered in supporting the development and articulation of client phenomena. To this end, we recommend that counselors and psychotherapists consider this chapter a beginning point for lifelong continuing education efforts toward service for this community.

Counselors who work in school settings and with youth play a critical role in advocating for and, at times, protecting the child. It is important that counselors support and encourage a child's gender identity development as a normative individual experience that is defined not by social strictures, but by what the child determines to be a correct expression of gender for her or him. In many cases, this means that school counselors are tasked with educating parents, teachers, and other adults on the needs of the child for safety in gender exploration.

Counselors working with adults may encounter transgender individuals in any variety of clinical settings, as transgender people can have the same problems with violence, drug abuse, etc. that anyone in society may experience. Whereas the individual's transgender experience may not be the area of counseling focus, we strongly recommend that counselors who work with transgenders in these diverse settings consult the WPATH Standards to support their understanding of how to tailor interventions used.

Work with transgender clients is extremely varied, given the numerous contexts in which people can encounter a need for counseling services. It is our hope that this chapter has helped clarify the experience of gender in a way that will support efficacious and strength-based approaches in work with the population.

References

American Psychiatric Association. (2000). *Diagnostic and statistical manual of mental disorders* (4th ed., Text Revision). Washington, DC: Author.

Chan, E., & Cavacuiti, C. (2008). Gay abuse screening protocol (GASP): Screening for abuse in gay male relationships. *Journal of Homosexuality, 54*(4), 423–439. doi: 10.1080/00918360801991455

Coleman, E., Bockting, W., Botzer, M., et al. (2011). Standards of care for the health of transsexual, transgender, and gender-nonconforming people, version 7. *International Journal of Transgenderism, 13,* 165–232.

Craft, S. M., Serovich, J. M, McKenry, P. C., & Lim, J. (2008). Stress, attachment style, and attachment style among same-sex couples. *Journal of GLBT Family Studies, 4*(1), 57–63. doi: 10.1080/15504280802084456

D'Augelli, A. R., Grossman, A. H., Starks, M. T., & Sinclair, K. O. (2010). Factors associated with parents' knowledge of gay, lesbian, and bisexual youths' sexual orientation. *Journal of GLBT Family Studies, 6*(2),178–198. doi: 10.1080/15504281003705410

Devor, H. (1997). *FTM: Female-to-male transsexuals in society.* Bloomington, IN: Indiana University Press.

Durso, L. E., & Gates, G. J. (2012). *Serving our youth: Findings from a national survey of service providers working with lesbian, gay, bisexual, and transgender youth who are homeless or at risk of becoming homeless.* Los Angeles, CA: The Williams Institute with True Colors Fund and the Palette Fund.

Ehrensaft, D. (2011). Boys will be girls, girls will be boys: Children affect parents as parents affect children in gender nonconformity. *Psychoanalytic Psychology: June 13, 2011.* doi: 10.1037/a0023828

Fausto-Sterling, A. (2012). The dynamic development of gender variability. *Journal of Homosexuality, 59,* 398–421.

Faye, M., Newman, P.A., Daley, A., & Solomon, S. (2009). Bullying of lesbian and gay youth. *British Journal of Social Work, 39*(8), 1598–1614. doi: 10.1093/bjsw/bcm148

Feinberg, L. (1996). *Transgender warriors: Making history from Joan of Arc to RuPaul.* Boston, MA: Beacon Press.

Feinberg, L. (2001). Trans health crisis: For us it's life or death. *American Journal of Public Health, 91*(6), 289–299.

Forshee, A. S. (2006). *Perceptions of masculinity among transgender men* (Doctoral dissertation). Retrieved from ProQuest database (3204046).

Forshee, A. S. (2007). Turning off the gender autopilot: Meeting the human service needs of transgender men. *Journal of Human Services, 27*(1), 25–38.

Forshee, A. S. (2008). Transgender men: A demographic snapshot. *Journal of Gay and Lesbian Social Services, 20*(3), 221–234.

Gottman, J. M., Levenson, R. W., Gross, J., Frederickson, B. L., McCoy, K., Rosenthal, L., . . . Yoshimoto, D. (2003). Correlates of gay and lesbian couples' relationship satisfaction and relationship dissolution. *Journal of Homosexuality, 45*(1), 23–43. doi: 10.1300/J082v45n01_02

Green, J. (2005). Part of the package: Ideas of masculinity among male-identified transpeople. *Men and Masculinities, 7*(3), 291–299.

Green, J. (2006). Look! No, don't! The visibility dilemma for transsexual men. In S. Stryker & S. Whittle (Eds.), *The transgender studies reader* (pp. 499–508). New York: Routledge.

Green, R. (2002). Family co-occurrence of "gender dysphoria": Ten sibling or parent-child pairs. *Archives of Sexual Behavior, 29*(5), 499–508.

Grémaux, R. (1996). Woman becomes man in the Balkans. In G. Herdt (Ed.), *Third sex third gender: Beyond sexual dimorphism in culture and history* (pp. 241–281). New York: Zone Books.

Halberstam, J. (2005). *In a queer time & place: Transgender bodies, subcultural lives.* New York: New York University Press.

Hare, L., Bernard, P., Sanchez, F. J., Baird, P. N., Vilain, E., Kennedy, T., & Haley, V. R. (2009). Androgen receptor repeat polymorphism associated with male-to-female transsexualism. *Biological Psychiatry, 65*(1), 93–96. doi: 10.1016/j.biopsych.2008.08.033

Heck, N., Flentje, A., & Cochran, B. N. (2011). Offsetting risks: High school gay-straight alliances and lesbian, gay, bisexual, and transgender youth. *School Psychology Quarterly, 26*(2), 161–174. doi: 10.1037/a0023226

Intersex Society of North America (2011). Available from www.isna.org (accessed January 18, 2014).

Kegan, R. (1982). *The evolving self: Problem and process in human development.* Cambridge, MA: Harvard University Press.

Kenagy, G. P. (2005, February 1). Transgender health: Findings from two needs assessment studies in Philadelphia. *Health & Social Work, 30*(1), 19–26.

Kenagy, G. P., & Hsieh, C. -M. (2005). The risk less known: Female-to-male transgender persons' vulnerability to HIV infection. *AIDS Care, 17* (2), 195–207.

Kennedy, N., & Hellen, M. (2010). Transgender children: More than a theoretical challenge. *Graduate Journal of Social Science, 7*(2), 25–43.

Kidd, J., & Witten, T. (2008). Understanding spirituality and religiosity in the transgender community: implications for aging. *Journal of Religion, Spirituality, & Aging, 20*(1/2), 29–62.

Kotula, D. (2002). *The phallus palace.* Los Angeles, CA: Alyson.

Kupers, T. A. (1993). *Revisioning men's lives: Gender, intimacy, power.* New York: The Guilford Press.

Landers, S., Mimiaga, M.J., & Krinsky, L. (2010). The open door project task force: A qualitative study on LGBT aging. *Journal of Gay and Lesbian Social Services, 22*(3), 316–336. doi: 10.1080/10538720903426438

Meyerowitz, J. (2002). *How sex changed: A history of transsexuality in the United States.* Cambridge, MA: Harvard University Press.

Namaste, V. K. (2001). HIV/AIDS and female-to-male transsexuals and transvestites: Results from a needs assessment in Quebec. In W. Bockting and S. Kirk (Eds.), *Transgender and HIV: Risks, prevention, and care.* New York: The Haworth Press.

Nanda, S. (1990). *Neither man nor woman: The Hijras of India.* Belmont, CA: Wadsworth.

Patton, J., & Reicherzer, S. (2010). Inviting "Kate's" authenticity: Relational-cultural theory applied in work with a transsexual sex-worker of color using the ACA Transgender Competencies. *Journal of LGBT Issues in Counseling, 4*(3&4), 214–227. doi: 10.1080/15538605.2010.524856

Prieur, A. (1996). *Mema's house: Mexico City.* Chicago, IL: University of Chicago Press.

Ramirez-Valles, J., Garcia, D., Campbell, R. T., Diaz, R. M., & Heckathorn, D. D. (2008). HIV infection, sexual risk behavior, and substance use among Latino gay and bisexual men and transgender persons. *American Journal of Public Health, 98*(6), 1036–1042.

Raymond, J. (1980). *The transsexual empire.* London: The Women's Press.

Reicherzer, S. L. (2011). Eye movement desensitization and reprocessing in counseling a male couple. *Journal of EMDR Research and Practice, 5*(3), 111–120. doi: 10.1891/1933-3196.5.3.111

Reicherzer, S. L. Patton, J. L., & Glowiak, M. (2011). *Counseling transgender trauma survivors.* Retrieved from http://counselingoutfitters.com/vistas/vistas11/Article_97.pdf

Reicherzer, S. L., & Spillman, J. A. (2012). A multiple case study examination of resiliency factors for Mexican and Mexican-American transsexual women. *International Journal of Transgenderism, 13*(3), 147–164. doi: 10.1080/15532739.2011.679245

Roscoe, W. (1996). How to become a Berdache: Toward a unified analysis of gender diversity. In G. Herdt (Ed.), *Third sex third gender: Beyond sexual dimorphism in culture and history* (pp. 329–372). New York: Zone Books.

Rubin, H. (2003). *Self-made men: Identity and embodiment among transsexual men.* Nashville, TN: Vanderbilt University Press.

Singh, A., Hayes, D. G., & Watson, L. S. (2011). Strength in the face of adversity: Resilience strategies for transgender individuals. *Journal of Counseling and Development, 89*(4), 20–27.

Talley, A. E., Sher, K. J., & Littlefield, A. K. (2010). Sexual orientation and substance abuse trajectories in emerging adulthood. *Addiction, 105*(7), 1235–1245. doi: 10.1111/j.1360-0443.2010.02953.x

Totman, R. (2003). *The third sex. Kathoey: Thailand's ladyboys.* London: Souvenir Press.

Travers, R., Guta, A., Flicker, S., Larkin, J., Lo, C., McCardell, S., . . . the Toronto Teen Survey Team (2010). Service provider views on issues and needs for lesbian, gay, bisexual, and transgender youth. *Canadian Journal of Human Sexuality, 19*(4), 191–198.

Turner, J. L.(2009). From the inside out: Calling on states to provide medically necessary care to transgender youth in foster care. *Family Court Review, 47*(3), 552 doi: 569. doi: 10.1111/j.1744-1617.2009.01273.x

Vanderburgh, R. (2009). Appropriate therapeutic care for families with pre-pubescent transgender/gender dissonant children. *Child & Adolescent Social Work, 26*(2), 135–154. doi: 10.1007/s10560-008-0158-5

Vanderburgh, R. (2011). *Transition and beyond: Observations on gender identity* (2nd ed.). Portland, OR: Author.

Williams, W. (1992). *The spirit and the flesh: Sexual diversity in American Indian culture.* Boston, MA: Beacon Press.

Wilson, E. C., Garofalo, R., Harris, R., Belzer, M., the Transgender Advisory Committee, & the Adolescent Medicine Trials Network for HIV/AIDS Intervention (2011). Sexual risk-taking with transgender male-to-female youths with different partner types. *American Journal of Public Health, 100*(8), 1501–1505.

World Professional Assocation of Transgender Health (2011). *Standards of care for transgender, transsexual, and gender-nonconforming persons.* Retrieved from: www.wpath.org/documents/Standards%20of%20Care%20V7%20-%202011%20WPATH.pdf

Yerke, A. F., & Mitchell, V. (2011). Am I man enough yet? A comparison of the body transition, self-labeling, and sexual orientation of two cohorts of female-to-male transsexuals. *International Journal of Transgenderism, 13*, 64–76.

Index